The Arc of Ambition

The Arc of Ambition

Defining the
Leadership Journey

~

James Champy

Nitin Nohria

PERSEUS BOOKS

Cambridge, Massachusetts

Many of the designations used by manufacturers and sellers
to distinguish their products are claimed as trademarks.
Where those designations appear in this book and Perseus
Books was aware of a trademark claim, the designations have
been printed in initial capital letters.

A CIP catalog record for this book is available from the
Library of Congress.

ISBN 0-7382-0103-0
Copyright © 2000 by James Champy and Nitin Nohria

Perseus Books is a member of the Perseus Books Group.

Text design by Heather Hutchison
Set in 12-point Fairfield Light by the Perseus Books Group

1 2 3 4 5 6 7 8 9 10—03 02 01 00 99
First printing, November 1999

Perseus Books are available at special discounts for bulk pur-
chases in the U.S. by corporations, institutions, and other organizations. For more information, please contact the Special
Markets Department at HarperCollins Publishers, 10 East
53rd Street, New York, NY 10022, or call 1-212-207-7528.

Find us on the World Wide Web at
http://www.perseusbooks.com

To my son Adam and his generation
—James Champy

To my father, Kewal Krishan Nohria,
who epitomizes the arc of ambition
—Nitin Nohria

Contents

Acknowledgments xi

1 Without ambition, no conquests are made, no lands discovered, no businesses created.

    Ambition is the root of all achievement. 1

2 Talent hits a target no one else can hit; genius hits a target no one else can see.

    See what others don't. 23

3 It takes a strong character and a lot of willpower to hold onto a dream under adverse circumstances.

    Follow a steadfast path. 51

4 Opportunity knocks with all the temerity of a brown trout hiding in an overfished stream.

    Seize the moment. 71

5 History is a long list of warnings about the folly of overreaching.

    Temper ambition. 97

6 Greatness must be driven by a purpose beyond money.

    Inspire with a greater purpose. 115

7   Compromise is bad for ambition.
     Never violate values.   141

8   Power comes from other people.
     Keep control by giving it up.   163

9   Reinvention is the key to longevity.
     Change or die.   183

10 The dead can't lead the living.
     Leave gracefully.   207

     Epilogue   235

Sources and Recommended Reading   241
Index   257

Acknowledgments

No book is written without the help and inspiration of others. We are grateful to all those people of great and good ambition who are our subjects. We particularly thank those who shared with us their time, wisdom, and experiences. Not only have they given us the insights necessary to write this book, but their stories are rich in inspiration.

We also thank those who conspired with us in the book's creation. Donna Sammons Carpenter and the other talented writers, editors, and researchers at Wordworks, Inc., have assisted in the preparation of this book. Among them are Maurice Coyle, Ruth Hlavacek, Richard Laurie, Martha Lawler, Toni Porcelli, Cindy Sammons, John Sammons, Robert W. Stock, Robert Shnayerson, and Jozefa Stuart.

Helen Rees, our agent, did her job well, as did the dedicated people at Perseus Books. We especially want to thank our editor, Nick Philipson, who spurred us on through the two years we worked on this book. We also want to acknowledge those who work with us at our "day jobs"—for Nitin, the people at the Harvard Business School, and for Jim, the people at Perot Systems. Their ideas and criticism along the way have been invaluable.

And finally we must thank the individuals who allowed us to write this book, our families. Jim thanks Lois and Adam for always being there to talk about the book's ideas and for giving him evenings and weekends to work on endless drafts. Nitin thanks Monica, Reva, Ambika, and Suzie for their encouragement and humor throughout the time spent working on this project. The good news is that it is now done.

Without Ambition, No Conquests Are Made, No Lands Discovered, No Businesses Created

Ambition Is the Root of All Achievement

~

People have always felt somewhat ambivalent about ambition. We see it as dangerous yet essential. We disapprove of those who abuse it, but we dismiss those who lack it. We see too little of it as a failing, too much of it as a sin. We sense that ambition is combustible, a form of energy that can bring us immortal glory but also destroy us forever, depending on how we use it. Simply put, ambition is what makes us *go*. Ambition is the spirit of success, of striving for something worth achieving.

THIS BOOK IS AIMED at all those who dream of achieving greatness in any field. We offer it as a handbook of lessons derived from the lives of great achievers past and present. The first lesson is that achievers in all fields—art, business, politics, science—and of all ages face similar challenges in accomplishing something great. What changes is the context within which the challenges occur.

The principles of this book come not from conventional psychology (clinical or theoretical) but from life experiences. They are derived from our own long observation of ambitious people, both past and present, in all walks of life.

Our ideas apply equally to those who pursue their particular ambition acting on their own and to those who act as members of large organizations. Indeed, this book is for anyone who sets out to accomplish anything truly excellent, no matter where or how.

We have found that the careers of ambitious people typically follow a predictable path—the *arc of ambition*. Hence the title of this book.

The curve of the arc isn't necessarily the same for every individual. For some, the rise of the curve is slow. The first dreams are just that, dreams. They are personal, secret, not even divulged to family or friends. Then, as the curve rises, these dreams provide a springboard for action.

Samuel Moore Walton comes to mind. His dreams began while he was still a schoolboy, selling milk from the cows on his family's Depression-poor farm. But Walton did not open his first Wal-Mart store until he was forty-four years old.

For others, the curve rises quickly. Ambition thrusts the dreamers into the limelight, sometimes right onto the world stage, at an amazingly early age.

Michael S. Dell, founder of Dell Computer Corporation is a prodigious example. In the early 1980s, while only a college student, Dell began building computers tailored to the specific needs of his customers. When his customer base grew, he quit college. The company he founded in 1984 to build computers to fit demand quickly became successful. It went public in 1988. Michael Dell became a billionaire when he was thirty-one years old.

Most of us dream of greatness at an early age. We envision growing up to emulate our favorite role models, whether they be parents, teachers, or athletes. Schoolbooks introduce us to national heroes, from Abe Lincoln to Rosa Parks and Sally Ride. All this nurtures the seedling of ambition that is planted at birth.

Your goal may be expansive—to become a twenty-something Internet millionaire, to run for the United States Senate, to win an Olympic gold medal, to write a novel. Or it may be more modest—to become mayor of your hometown, to run a local business, or to teach a subject you love. Whatever the size of your goal, it is ineluctably driven by ambition, the unique human energy that primes our efforts and shapes our achievements. Understanding how the arc of ambition works in your own life will almost certainly make those efforts more effective.

Our book maps the arc's three principal segments. The first segment covers the rise of ambition: the initial dream of an individual and the perseverance and courage he or she must exercise in pursuit of that dream.

The second section of the arc covers the apex of ambition. It usually is demonstrated by those who seek to build some organization larger than themselves. It could be a business, a university, even an army.

The third section confronts the decline of ambition—the time when every achiever must cope with his or her hardest challenges.

In the pages ahead, we explore the mysterious process whereby great men and women emerge, often from obscurity, to trace their own arcs of ambition. Is it their doing, the luck of the draw, or some supernatural talent scout at work? Do achievers make history, or does history make achievers?

Some nineteenth-century thinkers, among them the Scottish essayist and historian Thomas Carlyle and the German philosopher Georg Wilhelm Friedrich Hegel, argued that "heroes" shape events. Others, such as Russian novelist and moral philosopher Leo Tolstoy, countered that great men and women are pretty much the products of their times.

The facts, we believe, support both theories, weakening each. Had Madame Curie and her husband not "discovered" radium, for example, might not someone else have accomplished the feat soon thereafter? Without Abraham Lincoln at the helm, would the United States have ceased to exist? If William H. Gates III were not the unique person he is, would Microsoft Corporation have been founded by another? Without the vision and drive of Akio Morita, would Sony Corporation still have become the global powerhouse it is today?

We can surmise that achievers arise from a rich ragout of unpredictable *ifs*. If people have the talent and the training, if they are in the right place at the right time, and if they have the inner drive we call ambition, they may succeed and hold onto their success.

Quite often, great achievers spring from obscurity. And, just as often, their very obscurity galvanizes their ambitions.

John Keats, the major sonneteer of nineteenth-century English Romantic poetry, was the tubercular son of a London stable-keeper. He was completely disconnected from the perks and playing fields of Eton and the political benches of Westminster. Yet, long before the sons of upper-class families were sent out across the world to rule an empire, he toiled at poetry so effectively that today he remains among the two or three masters of melodic verse in the English language.

Howard Schultz, who built Starbucks Corporation from a single store on the Seattle, Washington, waterfront into a worldwide chain with more than 2,400 retail locations, traces the roots of his ambition to the poverty of an apartment in Brooklyn, New York. "From my personal experience," he says today, "the more uninspiring your origins, the more likely you are to use your imagination and invent worlds where everything seems possible. That's certainly true for me."

Relentless hard work in the service of an ardent ambition often prevails. Consider Leonardo da Vinci, the polymathic Renaissance painter, sculptor, engineer, musician, and scientist. We tend to think of Leonardo as a unique marvel placed on earth to teach the rest of us a little humility, and perhaps that was so. "Leonardo," says Roger A. Enrico, chairman and chief executive officer of PepsiCo, Inc., and a student of da Vinci, "mastered the sweet things of life, like the Mona Lisa, and the not-so-sweet, like war machines. Artist, engineer, scientist, mathematician—if he did it, he excelled."

But Leonardo made good not so much by divine guidance as by constant hustle and a prodigious output of ideas supported by incessant labor. For him, living and leveraging were one.

Consider the sales pitch he sent the war-worried Duke of Milan in 1482. Most of the letter offers various ingenious solutions to the duke's urgent problems with military defense and enemy bombardments. But then Leonardo gets around to what he really wants, an art grant, a meal ticket allowing him to paint and tinker on the duke's money. "In time of peace," he finally mentions, as if in passing, "I can perform sculptures in marble, in bronze or in terra cotta. In painting, I am able to do what another may."

What is this drive, this compelling hunger to achieve, this *ambition?* Ambition started out as a pedestrian notion derived from the Latin word *ambitionem,* meaning to walk around soliciting votes. But its reality can be fierce and its results momentous.

Listen to the Roman historian Suetonius on the subject of Julius Caesar's ambition. "At Gades, Caesar saw a statue of Alexander the Great in the Temple of Hercules and was overheard to sigh impatiently: vexed, it seems, that at an age when Alexander had already conquered the whole world, he himself had done nothing epoch-making." In time, Caesar made up for that slow start.

Or hear Napoléon Bonaparte, that avatar of ambition, describe himself under its spell: "I feel myself driven toward an end that I do not know. As soon as I shall have reached it, as soon as I shall become unnecessary, an atom will suffice to shatter me. Till then, not all the forces of mankind can do anything against me." Nor, in fact, could they—for a time.

In modern usage, ambition is both goal and goad—a compulsion to strive for something worth achieving. No action—and certainly no great enterprise—is thinkable without it. Ambition can transform anything. It has tamed continents and launched civilizations, built cathedrals and toppled despots, cured diseases and put men on the moon. Ambition can change a simple idea into a global business. It can inspire a gifted teacher to redeem wasted minds. It can turn a family of immigrants into a financial dynasty. It can lift a political prodigy from the obscurity of a trailer childhood to election as the president of the United States.

Ambition keeps altering the human condition, not always for the best, yet on the whole, for good rather than ill. In the table of human elements, ambition is the catalyst that ignites daring achievers and converts the ordinary to the extraordinary. In every field, those who make things happen are propelled by some powerful desire to change their worlds and their own destinies in the process.

Ambition drives those intrepid individuals who see what no one else has seen and achieve what no one else thought could be achieved—forever changing the context of their art or science or industry, opening the way for hundreds of other innovations. By flying the Atlantic Ocean for the first time, Charles Lindbergh triggered the rise of global airlines and foreshadowed space exploration. By charting the human subconscious for the first time, Sigmund Freud invented psychoanalysis and undoubtedly changed the role of religion. By organizing an assembly line for the first time, Henry Ford launched worldwide auto-mobility and its profound economic consequences.

We believe these achievers, and others like them, have much to teach us. Their challenges were, in principle, not so different from those that anyone aspiring to greatness faces today. Yet, the quest for greatness has lately encountered something new and acutely important. Both ambition and achievement now rise and fall with unprecedented speed.

This new condition grows out of a sea change in our technological context, a kind of seismic wave that sweeps over the world every half-century or so and reinvents our lives. Each new context brings forth its own versions of the three archetypal figures of achievement.

First come those we call the *Creators*. They are the true innovators, who pioneer a new technology to the point of making an old field technically obsolete. In the arts, dancers like Isadora Duncan and Martha Graham shook off the constraints of classical ballet and introduced the modern age to dancers everywhere. Cubism in painting showed us another way of looking at the objects around us and led the way to the twentieth century explosion of abstract expressionism. And Ernest Hemingway's terse style broke the florid tone of Victorian writing. In the sciences, pioneers from Albert Einstein to Norbert Wiener to Jonas Salk gave the human species unprecedented control over nature.

Next come the *Capitalizers,* who market the innovative technology so energetically that a whole new infrastructure is required to accommodate its distribution. The nation's electronic subsystem, for example, has been rebuilt at least three times in the past seventy years or so, from telegraph to telephone, from radio to television, from cable to Internet. In the arts and sciences, the followers and imitators of the Creators have capitalized on the freedom to experiment and try out new ideas and approaches. One of the great Capitalizers was Albert H. Barr, who made the most of the modernist ferment in New York City in the early twentieth century to create the Museum of Modern Art. In the same era Lincoln Kirstein helped galvanize and organize the modern dance movement.

Finally come the *Consolidators,* the professional managers in business and the museum curators and the theater producers in the arts. In business, it is the ambitious Consolidators who make new technologies work consistently and profitably in corporate settings. Eventually, however, Consolidators tend to look inward to their own corporate cultures rather than outward to changing customer needs, thereby losing the creative and subversive impulses that had brought forth the new technology in the first place. Thus the opportunity is opened for the cycle of creative destruction to begin anew.

The first technological sea change in the United States, born during and after the Civil War, was the fifty-year explosion of late-nineteenth-century industrial and railroad expansion that tamed the continent and turned the United States into a world power. The biggest winners were eight or nine of the most ambitious opportunists ever to soar straight up from poverty to plutocracy, among them Jay Gould, Jim Fisk, Jay Cooke, Andrew Carnegie, Philip Armour, James Hill, and John D. Rockefeller. In a few short years of cutting corners and dodging convention, they focused on turning the superabundant resources of the United States into personal wealth beyond the wildest dreams of even their own fervent imaginations.

The Scottish immigrant Andrew Carnegie, for example, was a seventeen-year-old telegraph clerk in 1852 when he began formulating the huge aspirations that eventually made him the country's top steel tycoon. His goal, the boy clerk wrote, was "to become independent and then enjoy the luxuries which wealth can (and should) procure." Within two years, Carnegie was turning stock market tips into a fortune, all on borrowed money.

The second technological revolution arose in the early 1900s from the mass-production techniques of Henry Ford, a classic Creator. His Model-T spawned the automobile industry that soon challenged the railroad industry, created a booming oil industry, and enabled Americans to become suburban car commuters after World War II.

Detroit's automakers changed the world's business and cultural contexts, with immense consequences for everything from air quality to the fate of big cities and small towns. And not surprisingly, in a pattern familiar to business historians, those automakers eventually became inward-turned Consolidators, slow to understand their customers' sudden switch to Japan's far more efficient cars during the oil crunch of the 1970s and 1980s.

The third technological turning point, now in full sway, has basically derived from the convergence of information and communications technology. These technologies have together created an entirely new context, the information economy, which the Internet supports in a now instantly connected world. Like the printing press, the steam engine, and the automobile, the computer has transformed the very nature of work, introduced extraordinary efficiencies in advanced countries, and instilled others with a consuming ambition to catch up.

But all this progress has a double edge: While triggering great high-technology breakthroughs and enormous opportunities, it also has vastly increased the pace of business and the intensity of competitive pressure. Growth is at such a breakneck pace that whole industries seem to coalesce one year and obsolesce the next. The average life cycle of the strongest companies has reportedly shrunk to less than fifteen years, half of what it was in the 1950s. The driver is, of course, the avalanche of innovations that keep streaming out of start-up companies that, last year, may have been mere garage shop operations.

Not only business but all other aspects of our society have been profoundly altered. In one generation, medicine has changed radically. Diagnosis now relies on an array of tests.

We have CAT scans, PET scans, ultrasound sonograms, MRIs, and many other sophisticated tools. Artists today use computer imaging in their work. Mixed media in entertainment—be it serious plays, pop performances, or movie special effects—have become almost old hat. Professional athletes train by observing themselves and their rivals on the computer screen, as do golfing hopefuls watching their idols execute the perfect swing. There is little in the realm of human endeavor that has not been touched by continuing advances in technology. Just as cyberspace has pushed the boundaries of the earth, so technology is a tool that can help achievers ascend the arc of ambition.

These new tools not only force us to alter our present but also leave us with a largely unusable past and unknowable future. Often, we seem to be caught between two choices: Hunker down (and fail) or bravely improvise (and hope). As an early employee of Bill Gates's Microsoft admitted later, "We sold promises."

In virtually every change-pressured field—from cyberspace marketing to genetic engineering—those who do plunge ahead typically lack precedents to guide them. As early explorers, they resemble Christopher Columbus sailing blindly into uncharted seas, or the Elizabethan adventurer Sir Martin Frobisher vainly attempting to find a Northwest Passage through the Arctic, or Vasco da Gama struggling around the tip of Africa to find a route to India.

Like the Citigroup, Inc., executives trying to merge former rivals into a global financial supermarket, or the ambitious attempts by Mobil Corporation and Exxon Corporation to create a worldwide energy empire, today's achievers frequently have great visions. But getting from A to B is often as dangerous and mysterious as sailing off into unknown waters was in the age of exploration.

Ambition has always required creativity, daring, and timing, to name but a few of its components. Today it requires all these and more. For example, you can't be successful with a new Internet company just because you are incredibly imaginative, have the heart of a lion, and boast a new stock issue that thousands of seemingly irrational day traders bid up 300 percent the moment it hits the market. Most of all, you need extraordinary perseverance and skill to wait out the time it may take for a new technology to progress from a market dream to actual profitability. And, while you hang in, time may suddenly pass you by when some even newer technology pops up to render yours obsolete.

In these demanding times, when the forces of creative destruction have never been stronger, success clearly requires an ambition of exceptional intensity. And, yet, corporations are still largely run by cautious executives marching to the measured drumbeats of Alfred P. Sloan, Jr., long the presiding genius of the General Motors Corporation. It was Sloan who, in the 1920s, saved troubled GM from dissolution by introducing the disciplines of strategy, financial controls, and vertical integration.

Sloan was a brilliant man, responsible for much of what we define as good management today. But what he did to save GM, so right for his time and place, has left the wrong legacy for ours. Even now, most companies employing a Sloan-like ethos of management control create more fear than vision—and stifle ambition in the process.

Fortunately, changing times have favored a new breed of business entrepreneur. But how much their fresh spirit can reshape management is an open question. As soon as their own companies grow large and unwieldy, one price of success, they tend to develop corporate antibodies that can kill the very ambition that launched them. These antibodies include elements of overcontrol, parochialism, orthodoxy, and cynicism. Howard Schultz of Starbucks says that he would not rule out hiring someone "because they came from a bureaucratic company. But I would be more skeptical and more probing to see if that person can escape that culture."

What happens to society when ambition is blunted, especially in large organizations? One possibility is that, over time, the dwindling number of companies and individuals that retain zesty ambition will become fewer and ever more powerful and eventually control the world—as did the barons of the last industrial revolution. If ambition becomes the dividing line of business between the world's haves and have-nots, then wealth will become even more concentrated in the hands of a few.

We are not socialists. We believe that extraordinary accomplishments deserve extraordinary rewards. History, however, has shown that if wealth or power becomes too concentrated in a few institutions or a few people, the result is often arrogance, abuse, and eventually failure. Such experiences may explain the ambivalence that many people feel about ambition.

Ambition, we think, needs a better reputation.

No society can afford to belittle it, especially now that technology promises ever-greater opportunity. Moreover, history confirms that ambition is more often good than bad. Good ambition is the lifeblood of human advancement.

But what is it that distinguishes good ambition from bad? What sort of achievements should we admire and strive to emulate?

Perhaps the worthiest ambition is the one that goads us to make the best out of whatever talents or conditions life hands us. We see no virtue in a gifted person who squanders his or her gifts. We rightly admire even a modestly talented person who strives to surpass all expectations.

Why do sports fascinate us? Is it because we love competition, skill, economy of motion? All these, yes, but the biggest reason may be the ceaseless drama of athletes seeking to be the best they can be and then some. As Sam Snead, the superlative golfer, once said, "Forget your opponents and play against par." When we watch great athletes in spellbinding action—Wayne Gretzky, Steffi Graf, Tiger Woods—we can't help pondering what it takes to reach such peaks of performance. What it takes, of course, is incredibly hard work, persistence, and sacrifice. In the brilliant results we find metaphors that we dream of applying to ourselves, and sometimes do.

At the end of the day, then, most of us still believe in the quaint notion that winning isn't everything. We value an athlete's skill and spirit infinitely more than his or her salary. We don't think much of those who mainly seek lucrative endorsements. We appreciate performance, not hubris.

We expect ambition to pay off in something beneficial, whether it is a good new law or a good new product. We respect ambition that adds value to a business, to a community, to knowledge, to life itself.

Making money offers ambitious people a clear objective, but as the New Testament puts it, "What is a man profited, if he shall gain the whole world, and lose his own soul?" Good ambition demands that wealth be created in a way that benefits and inspires others. For the new (and often sudden) rich of our day, there are compelling exemplars from the past—John D. Rockefeller, who established a foundation for social research; Andrew Carnegie, who endowed 2,800 public libraries; Leland Stanford, who funded Stanford University; plus countless lesser-known philanthropists who discovered that giving may provide the most lasting gratification.

The conundrum is that money begets power. And power, depending on its use, can be a force for good. But those who have it must also be wary of its corrupting influence. Humankind seems to be permanently burdened with a long line of power abusers—megalomaniacs ranging from Ivan the Terrible to Saddam Hussein to Slobodan Milosevic to any retrograde executive who still thinks fear is a management method. Authoritarians who use power mainly to subjugate others represent the darkest, most frightening side of ambition.

To be sure, ambition that focuses only on personal gain does little for society and at best profits only a small handful of people. The 1999 replay of the 1849 Gold Rush—the Internet investing mania—is yet another case of dreams aimed at instant gratification. We fear that dreamers keep starting companies for no better reason than to sell them for incomprehensible sums as fast as possible. According to James Daly, editor-in-chief of the new Internet magazine *Business 2.0:* "No longer are entrepreneurs interested in becoming the next America Online or Yahoo or Microsoft. Instead, they want to be purchased by AOL, or Yahoo, or Microsoft. Usually within two years. For about $100 million. . . . I can't help thinking we are losing something vital, as entrepreneurs morph from dreamers into sellouts."

We have yet to see whether the sellouts are pioneers adding value to a digital economy or prisoners of their own delusions. If the past is any guide—and these days it may not be—short-term thinking isn't always the road to getting richest the quickest. The companies that we most admire in this digital economy are those that have stood the test of time, like Intel, Microsoft, and Dell.

In this book, we offer a new vision of the creative process that transforms dreams into reality: the arc of ambition. And we argue that ambition—key to the human condition—can and must be far more widely disseminated and encouraged. Ambition, however, cannot simply be taught. Nor is it a birthright. But the art of realizing one's ambitions can be learned—learned from the experiences recounted as we move through the arc of ambition described in this book.

Everyone travels through this arc. Some rise higher. Others fall faster. At each stage along the arc, one risks underachieving or overextending. The trick is to strike the balance that enables an individual to achieve his or her own highest aspirations and realize his or her fullest potential. This book is, then, for all of us, because we all have some ambition.

To write it, we have read about, examined, and discussed many facets of ambition. Out of this search has grown an ambition of our own: We hope to show the ways in which you can learn from the experiences, the trials, the mistakes, and the lessons of others, both past and present. We seek to sharpen your sensibilities and awareness of your own actions so that you can examine them honestly and apply the lessons you have learned to your journey along the arc of ambition. We believe that by gathering your strengths and knowing your potential, you will be able to determine your own destiny.

In the pages that follow, we trace the arc of ambition, from rise to fall, as a series of stages:

- *See what others don't.* Fast or slow, the arc begins with a fresh insight, a discovery. It is some perception unseen by others and perhaps not even imagined. No doubt millions of such original thoughts perish year after year.

What saves the few that propel human progress is the spell of ambition—the urging of a dream transformed by the mind's eye into a belief that something is possible, and from there into a conviction that hard work must and will make it actually happen. Ambition, we note in Chapter 2, is disciplined dreaming, the faith that fierce effort will inevitably turn shadow into substance. Among our cases in point: Dhirubhai H. Ambani, Michael Dell, Judy George, John P. Mackey, Patrick J. McGovern, and the Wright brothers.

- *Follow a steadfast path.* In the mind of an ambitious person, a dream becomes reality infinitely faster than the time it takes to read this sentence. In real life, success more often derives from a series of setbacks confronted and overcome. At the outset, the conditions necessary for success are never quite right. Dreamers invariably encounter missteps, failures, unforeseeable bad luck. A few such obstacles are enough to stop all but those intrepid souls who can't be discouraged. "All I have is stubbornness," the physicist Albert Einstein once confessed, probably to unbelieving ears. To progress along the arc of ambition, we argue in Chapter 3, requires perseverance and optimism, unquenchable hope that the moment of opportunity will come. Our cases in point include George Lucas, Nelson Mandela, Thabang Motsohi, and Samuel Moore Walton.

- *Seize the moment.* Dreamers become potential achievers, we explain in Chapter 4, when they surmount the next step along the arc of ambition—that incandescent moment when opportunity suddenly looms like Everest out of a fog, and the dreamer responds with courage and chutzpah. Hesitating only long enough to make sure that he or she is not hallucinating, the aspiring achiever feels massively imbued with an unflinching impulse—go for it. Among our cases in point: Thomas Jefferson, Martin Luther King, Jr., Ray Kroc, Robert Johnson, William Poduska, Arthur Wellesley, and Margaret C. Whitman.

- *Temper ambition.* The next stage, reaching the apex, entails gaining momentum without losing balance—akin to letting enough wind into your sails to race ahead full speed without tipping over. The key requirement, we argue in Chapter 5, is setting ambitious goals and ensuring disciplined execution. If you execute well but stretch too little, you can wind up with the greatest little coffee shop in Seattle, but not Starbucks. If you stretch far but execute badly, things come apart. Our cases in point include Lawrence J. Ellison, William Jefferson Clinton, and Alfred J. Dunlap—with some advice from Gary C. Wendt.

- *Inspire with a greater purpose.* To continue soaring along the rise of the arc, we need to transform our personal ambition into a broader purpose so that others can join in and contribute to the effort. In Chapter 6, we show that this may not be as difficult as it seems. Some ambitious people see the world as a zero-sum game; they just don't get the idea that victories are more assured when their benefits are shared. Among our cases in point: Cesar Chavez, Mohandas K. Gandhi, Giuseppe Garibaldi, and Robert B. Shapiro.

- *Never violate values.* There will come a point where to move ahead one will be tempted to cut corners, to compromise to satisfy one's ambition. Beware of this temptation, we say in Chapter 7, because it will only hasten the decline of your arc of ambition. Surely it does not pay to be dishonest, unethical, or abusive, for example, nor can any organization long sustain repeated violations of its core values. Compromise can work only in unique instances—and for a short period of time. Recognizing true north is the only way to keep your arc pointing upward. Our cases in point include Arjuna, Andrew S. Grove, John R. Lewis, Azim Premji, and Diego Rivera.

- *Keep control by giving it up.* As an achiever who leads an organization, you need people doing their best to achieve the goals you set for them. How do you get their best? Not by asserting your control over them through force or threats, we contend in Chapter 8. The reality is that the only way to keep control is by sharing it with others. Isolated achievers are dangerous to themselves and their organizations. Fear chills minds and kills companies. Nor do you want to be flattered by courtiers playing on your ego. The smartest achievers know that they can only benefit when their colleagues do great work. They have the confidence not to feel threatened when other people flourish. Among our cases in point: William Gross, George Hastapolous, and Abraham Lincoln.

- *Change or die.* The conditions that enabled the rise of the arc don't last forever, we argue in Chapter 9. Things change: The external environment becomes less favorable, you become more complacent, others emulate you and whittle away your unique claim to fame. Unexpected rivals—just as ambitious as you once were—find ways to change the rules and creatively destroy things you built to last. To stay on the arc, one must change or die. Our cases in point include Louis V. Gerstner, Jr., Peter the Great, Colin Powell, James Rogers, Margaret Thatcher, John F. Welch, Jr., and Deng Xiaoping.

- *Leave gracefully.* Alas, we are mortal. We get old and we die. The power of having achieved greatly, of leaving an immortal legacy, can sometimes make it difficult for ambitious men and women to accept this truest of human truths. They keep searching for the fountain of youth, and not finding it think that by just acting young they can be young. They hang on to the view that the organization's life cannot go on without them. The last passage, we say in Chapter 10, requires us to recognize that ambition can allow us to achieve immortality in history, but not in our own lives. The only good way to confront this fact is to embrace it: Take charge of the truth, and live it out with all the grace, style, and humor that befit a great achiever's great ambitions. Our cases in point include Gilbert Amelio, Sewell Avery, Andrew Carnegie, Roberto Goizueta, Robert Haft, Steven P. Jobs, Dean F. LeBaron, Peter Lynch, John Sculley, and Michael Spindler.

In this book, we pose—and answer—a fundamental question: What is the quintessential human trait? Is it the ability to love, to conceptualize, to imagine? We know that some of these traits are shared with other species. But, in our view, one trait above all others is uniquely human. That trait is *ambition,* the urge to achieve or create, a driving need to improve the known world and perhaps replace it with something better. This is the challenge that great achievers have met in the past and, we believe, will meet in the future. The human story is fundamentally about people overcoming obstacles and rising triumphantly on the arc of ambition. The story has a cast of millions, in which we all have a part.

2

Talent Hits a Target
No One Else Can Hit;
Genius Hits a Target
No One Else Can See

See What Others Don't

~

What did Dhirubhai H. Ambani, Michael Dell, Judy George, John P. Mackey, Patrick J. McGovern, and the Wright brothers have in common? The eyes to see and the faith to believe what others did not, the ambition to own a dream and dare to make it come true.

FOR CENTURIES, human flight was a tantalizing fantasy. Imagination had to suffice for our earthbound ancestors until the unreal became real. Hence, flights of fancy abounded, the most famous being the Greek myth of Daedalus and his son Icarus.

Daedalus, as you may recall, was an architect working for Minos, the tyrannical king of Crete. After Daedalus finished a huge new palace, the king ordered an addition—a maze to contain his dreaded, man-eating pet, the Minotaur.

Daedalus followed orders, but he could not bear the Minotaur. He told one of the king's enemies how to find his way through the labyrinth and kill the beast. The king found out. Enraged, he imprisoned Daedalus and his son.

What to do?

Daedalus, the intrepid hero of this classic Greek legend, dreamed of flying to freedom like a bird. He not only dreamed: He actually created wings made of feathers set in beeswax, and he and his son Icarus soared away.

What happened next is the better-known part of the legend: Icarus ignored his father's warnings, flew too close to the sun, and fell to his death when his wings melted. But there is more to the story—much more. Daedalus survived, hunted down Minos, and contrived to scald him to death in his bath. But we digress.

As we read the legend, it implies that a creative mind (Daedalus) can achieve the impossible (human flight), providing it sees what others cannot (how to make wings), and providing it avoids the danger of hubris (Icarus).

It is a metaphor of ambition.

Humankind's age-old ambition to emulate birds remained unrealized until the Renaissance freed people to explore the unknown. The beginning was slow. First, Leonardo da Vinci, who left us drawings showing machines in flight, observed that air actually offers resistance. Then Galileo Galilei figured out that the resistance varies, depending on how fast an object is moving through the air.

Eventually, the secret of avian flight was revealed. When birds fly, the air pressure under their wings is slightly greater than the air pressure above their wings. The disparity provides the lift as the higher pressure pushes upward, displacing the lower pressure. This dynamic keeps a bird aloft, floating on—and propelled by—its outstretched wings.

From that historic insight emerged the first rudimentary manned gliders, the first propeller-driven puddle jumpers, the first supersonic jetliners—the whole panoply of human flight that we now take for granted. We are barely aware of the incalculable efforts that went into the development of aircraft. At every step of the way, men and women confronted immense challenges. And they succeeded by nurturing the same kind of know-how we need for meeting our own challenges.

Achievement is about seeing beyond the conventions of the day.

The pattern of achievement in virtually every field is about seeing beyond the accepted beliefs and conventions of the day. Achievers ignore the boundaries of the old and have the courage to explore the new. They see something others don't.

Some dreams are truly original, raising possibilities never imagined before. Einstein's theory of relativity, for example, was a *sui generis* insight that hit the world in 1905 like an intellectual meteorite. Earthshakers like that are rare, however. More typical is an ambitious Creator's use of existing ideas in some brand-new combination. William Shakespeare, for example, was a genius at recycling old plots into exciting new forms made immortal by his extraordinary use of language.

In a sense, having the courage to transform the familiar, creating novel forms and patterns, is basic not only to artists and writers but also to imaginative entrepreneurs, even those who simply dream of creating a corner deli where none existed before. Brilliant execution can turn a worn idea into something wholly original.

A cafe that serves good coffee is hardly new. But building 2,000 cafes that consistently offer superb coffee in attractive settings is distinctly new. Howard Schultz turned that idea into Starbucks, creating a new social institution in the process.

Retail discounting also wasn't new. But Sam Walton saw the possibility of lowering prices further and further, while making service better and better. And he saw that rural America might provide the best markets in which to first realize his dream.

Robert Johnson, the founder, chairman, and chief executive officer of Black Entertainment Television, Inc., (BET), observes that a business coup today is often based on an imaginative rethinking of a familiar idea. "Not a lot of our ideas are totally different or unique," he points out. "Most are variations on a theme. Ted Turner did not create the idea of news. He did create the idea of television news 24 hours a day," Johnson says. Or take movies on cable. "Movies have been on television ever since television began," he explains. "But what Jerry Levin and Chuck Dolan did was to put it all together for 24 hours a day and call it Home Box Office. All of a sudden, they created a whole new business."

*Achievers are united by their ability to
see the world clearly, unhindered
by fear of obstacles.*

What unites all achievers is that they see the world as it really
is—without the fears, constructs, and constraints that inhibit
others from daring to act out their dreams, much less believe in
them.

Most people dream big dreams, at least when they are young.
But most people are also quick to see obstacles, which they view
as insurmountable. The dream dies in the light of reality. Perhaps the dreamer fears fiscal, physical, or moral loss. More
often, the dreamer's ambition simply isn't strong enough to overcome the perceived obstacles.

According to some Asian religions—Buddhism, for instance—the key to enlightenment is to accept one's circumstances and go with the flow of life, the great chain of being. To
Westerners, this sounds like a recipe for apathy, if not disaster.

The truth probably lies somewhere in between. But our own
faith in the benefits of ambition-plus-action precludes much patience with people who refuse to even question, much less
change, their circumstances. Taking the path of least resistance
strikes us as a recipe for underachievement. It blinds you to
myriad opportunities that you might well be quite competent to
handle. It is up to you—not your critics—to decide what you are
capable of doing. Although you should certainly be open to advice, only you have the power to say can't—or can.

Achievers are fully aware of that personal power and how to
use it. They look at an obstacle and either dismiss it or see it as
an opportunity. They find a way to act, either by directly con-
fronting the obstacle or by taking an incremental first step

around it. Often, achievers are more inclined to act than to think. But the most successful achievers act and think at the same time.

To ponder the interplay of ideas and action, one can do no better than to read up on Abraham Lincoln's search for a great general to lead the Union armies during the Civil War. Constantly disappointed by commanders like General George B. McClellan, who feared to attack because he feared defeat, Lincoln finally discovered the extraordinary Ulysses S. Grant, an unpretentious genius of few words and almost preternatural clarity and courage.

As in the battles of Vicksburg, Mississippi, and Richmond, Virginia, General Grant never hesitated to confront even a seemingly superior enemy. And objectivity gave him an edge. Knowing that both sides were afraid, he used fear as an equalizer. As Grant wrote in his memoirs, "I never forgot that he [the enemy] had as much reason to fear my forces as I had his."

Before action, though, comes the dream. We believe that the genesis of every great human enterprise can be traced to the power of someone's dreams. The dreamer has seen what others have not: a way to improve his or her world. All of us have such dreams, large or small, for imagination is one of humanity's unique gifts. Beyond the ability to dream, though, we need the courage to ignore the odds against us and absorb the inevitable hardships and frustrations that await those who challenge accepted ideas and the status quo.

Only a few of us ever get this far. Most dreams are stillborn, dissolving in the first encounter with the real world. All through our lives we have been told to be practical. Stop dreaming. Get down to business. Stay grounded in reality. That is the common refrain, and it takes its toll.

Genius resides in the imagination.

The title of this chapter derives from a quotation by Arthur Schopenhauer, the nineteenth-century German philosopher: "Talent hits a target no one else can hit; genius hits a target no one else can see." In other words, genius resides in the imagination, in the dream. The fifteenth-century Portuguese navigator, Ferdinand Magellan, dreamed of sailing around the world and did. Thomas Jefferson's vision of a young United States was not bounded by the Appalachian Mountains but stretched across the immense breadth of the American continent. He, too, realized his dream, as we discuss in Chapter 4.

Schopenhauer was a pessimistic philosopher, whose view of the human condition has ironically served to bolster the kind of optimism this book espouses. He argued that humans have a distorted view of the real world because we have dressed it up with unreal constructs, including space, time, and cause-and-effect. In Schopenhauer's view, humans are miserable because we strive endlessly to conform to meaningless concepts. We are prisoners of blind wills seeking false goals. To even approach true reality, he argued, we should reject worldly ambitions and seek wisdom in the study of philosophy and art.

Of course, for someone preaching withdrawal and contemplation, Schopenhauer did well for himself with his outpourings of books and essays. What is more, his ideas eventually became part of the underpinnings of a new philosophy, existentialism, which holds that we all stand alone in our brief lives on earth, without hope of mercy from above or below, and we are thus individually responsible for what we make of ourselves. Or, as we might prefer to put it, we make our own reality.

Achievers dare to fly in
the face of disbelief.

Take, for example, the history of human flight that began this chapter. In the long line from Daedalus to the supersonic Concorde, the most technologically advanced passenger aircraft (at least for now), the Wright brothers, Wilbur and Orville, best illustrate our principle—that is, see the world differently and dare to make your dream come true. Their ultimate achievement, the construction and flight of the world's first powered, heavier-than-air machine, is known to every seventh-grader. Just how the Wright brothers arrived at that point, as well as their subsequent achievements, is less familiar.

The Wrights grew up in modest circumstances in Dayton, Ohio. Neither Wilbur, born in 1867, nor Orville, born in 1871, graduated from high school. Machines turned them on, and vice versa. Pursuing their natural gift, they built a printing press and soon were publishing their own newspaper. Next they turned to bicycles, quickly progressing from selling two-wheelers to manufacturing their own brands.

Clearly, they had the imagination to see themselves evolving from business to business, plus the ambition, drive, intellectual curiosity, and courage to try something new. Moreover, bicycles were too earthbound to satisfy their appetite for the new and unusual.

In 1894 they read an article in *McClure's* magazine about a German aeronautical engineer named Otto Lilienthal—the first person to pilot a glider successfully. After 2,000 attempts, Lilienthal was killed when a burst of wind caused his craft to veer and crash. At first glance, Lilienthal's fate would hardly seem a recommendation to go and do likewise.

How many of us leap to pursue a failed idea, much less one that killed the last person who tried it? This is what makes the Wright brothers' reaction notable, to say the least. They read Lilienthal's obituary not as a dire warning to keep their feet on the ground but as a call to get airborne as soon as possible.

With their gift for both dreaming and designing machinery, the Wrights saw gliding as a challenge they could master. In one swoop, their minds soared from simple bicycles to the world of the unknown and experimental.

To help ensure success, the brothers set out to learn everything they could about aerodynamics in general and gliders in particular. No detail escaped them. In May 1900, Wilbur Wright sent a letter to Octave Chanute, a Chicago, Illinois, engineer who had designed gliders. Wilbur simply wanted Chanute's advice about the country's best gliding areas, but his letter reflected the brothers' consuming passion. "For some years," he wrote, "I have been afflicted with the belief that flight is possible to man." He likened his belief to a virtual disease, the cure for which would be success—the miracle of literally flying in the face of everybody else's disbelief.

Following Chanute's advice, the brothers built a biplane kite. And, in 1900, they began manned glider experiments on Kill Devil Hill, a strip of sand near Kitty Hawk, North Carolina. When the craft failed to meet expectations, the brothers were undaunted. They simply threw out the existing tables of air pressures over a curved surface, set about constructing a wind tunnel, and then tested wing designs until, two years later, they found the right configuration. Their next glider worked fine.

Wilbur and Orville had still another dream in mind, though. They yearned to take the next logical step—to powered flight.

Theirs was a world-caliber dream. They imagined they could design and manufacture gliders with engines. They visualized these airships carrying mail and even passengers—safely, speedily, and directly to their destinations, as the crow flies. They looked into the future and saw their flying machine revolutionizing transportation around the world.

On December 17, 1903, the brothers took turns flying their first-ever powered aircraft, and Wilbur claimed the longest ride—59 seconds and 852 feet. The first stage of the brothers' dream was now reality, though the world paid no heed to their startling achievement. The first eyewitness account of one of their flights didn't appear until two years later, in a magazine called *Gleanings in Bee Culture.*

It must have been a bitter experience. The Wrights had mastered a challenge as old as humankind. They had beaten far more educated experimenters in solving the heavier-than-air problem, which had eluded flight pioneers ever since the first lighter-than-air balloon ascensions in the 1780s.

But the only serious attention the Wrights got was from aspiring rivals who tied them up in draining patent suits. The world at large either yawned or laughed at those crazy Wright brothers, who seemed unable to keep their feet on the ground. It was four years before the brothers began, slowly at first, to be recognized as pioneering inventors. They ran into the kind of roadblocks so familiar to many achievers as they butt up against ingrained, accepted ideas. We might even call them prejudices.

Far from giving up, as many of us might have, the Wrights persisted in their vision of the flying future. While constantly refining their design and defending their patents, they arranged to manufacture their aircraft both overseas and in the United States. By 1908, a full five years after their now historic flight, the United States War Department was sufficiently interested to award the Wrights a contract to build army planes capable of flying forty miles an hour. Wilbur died of typhoid fever four years later, but Orville lived until 1948, long enough to participate in the revolution the brothers' invention had kindled.

Big dreams aren't always big, but all are worthy of pursuit.

You don't have to invent the airplane or create an empire to pursue a big dream of your own. Audacity is an equal opportunity trait. We knew an airline executive who was good at his job but saw himself as something quite different. What our friend really wanted was to run the perfect restaurant. It was not a pretentious one, just a restaurant that people could enjoy as much as they enjoyed their homes. His dream was simple and specific. Eventually, our friend summoned the resources and, more importantly, the courage to quit his job and pursue his dream. The restaurant was hard work, but he enjoyed it. He found happiness in achieving his dream.

For some, the pursuit of happiness is a matter of striking out on their own. Others find the same satisfaction and fulfillment in working as part of an enterprise, large or small. Within the enterprise, they find the spirit and the vision that offers them the opportunities they crave.

The story of John P. Mackey, founder, chairman, and chief executive officer of Whole Foods Market, Inc., the nation's top chain of natural foods supermarkets, is a case in point. It is a story of a dream and an ambition come true.

Mackey told us that he is not sure exactly where his dream originated: "It came from somewhere within me . . . I was searching for the meaning of life, so to speak. I went to work in a small retail store in Austin, Texas, back in the late 1970s. I fell in love simultaneously with retailing as well as with the idea that what you ate could affect how you felt—your health and well-being. I caught on fire with that idea."

Soon, with only $45,000 in start-up capital, he opened his first store. His company now operates more than ninety Whole Foods Market, Bread & Circus, Bread of Life, Fresh Fields, Merchant of Vino, Nature's Heartland, and Wellspring Grocery stores in about twenty states and the District of Columbia.

For a dream to be of enduring value, it must include a target. The best targets are specific: They provide focus—the discipline of knowing what result you want to create so you can reach it most efficiently.

The power of targeting informs the story of Dhirubhai Hirachand Ambani, the son of a schoolteacher in a remote Indian village, who rose from nowhere to create Reliance Industries Limited.

Reliance is a $3 billion company that produces synthetic fiber, textiles, and petrochemicals. It has become the largest, most powerful enterprise in all of India, outstripping even Tata Steel, Limited, traditionally the country's richest company. At the same time, Ambani himself has become one of the wealthiest people in the world. Doubtless, Ambani nurtured dreams throughout his growing years, but what helped him navigate the obstacle course of life, kept him pushing with all his strength, and made him the extraordinary person he has become, was his ability to find a target for the dreams of his youth.

Ambani's achievements were nothing less than inconceivable when he was born on December 28, 1932, in the village of Chorwad, not far from Porbander, the birthplace of Mohandas K. Gandhi. Ambani's family was too poor to send him or his older brother to college after they graduated from high school.

Like many of their countrymen, the brothers took jobs in the Middle East. Ambani was only seventeen when he joined his brother in Aden—now a part of Yemen, but then a British colony—and found work pumping gas. He had higher ambitions, though. Within months, he was a clerk at a subsidiary of Burma Shell PLC, a global petrochemical company.

As Ambani recalls, he soon found himself envisioning a future that seemed laughable, if not somewhat mad. "I had dreams of starting a company like Burma Shell," he says. Sane friends and wise elders urged him to heed reason and common sense. Unlike many other dreamers, he paid no attention whatsoever. He had decided on his target, and nothing would deflect him from it.

In 1959, after eight years in Aden, Dhirubhai Ambani returned to India with a small nest egg and the determination to start his own business. He combined his own savings with a small loan, for a total capitalization of about $1,000, and set up Reliance, exporting ginger, turmeric, and other spices to the Middle East, where, during his years in Aden, he had the foresight to cultivate all sorts of useful connections.

To accomplish the impossible,
you must first begin with the possible.

As with the Wright brothers, Ambani's grand dream took flight because he was able to translate it into a doable first step. The impossible will remain impossible if you don't begin with the possible. For the Wrights, the first step was replicating glider flight so as to learn the basics. For Ambani, it was starting his own business, however small it appeared relative to the dream of building a Burma Shell. Seeing and taking the first step, and then, as we discuss in the next chapter, having the perseverance to stay the course, is the key to translating dreams into reality.

Though he started off like any other small trader in India, Ambani's drive and intense focus on his dreams soon propelled him away from the crowd. He moved into fabrics and yarn, importing rayon and then nylon. His profits were substantial, even though he found his export growth limited by a shortage of local high-quality fabrics.

Some might have been frustrated. Not Ambani. He saw opportunity. In 1966, he took a giant leap into a whole new world, setting up his own weaving and knitting factory to provide the missing fabric.

In the 1970s, when polyester began to displace nylon, Ambani quickly moved into that trade, too. And before long he expanded his factory to process and upgrade imported polyester yarn and produce polyester fabric for export. Once again he dared greatly, this time by investing in high-cost, state-of-the-art machinery. When demand for polyester fabrics soared in India, as he had envisioned it would, he was positioned to become the market leader.

That ability to see beyond the immediate horizon, to dream of a wider world, has characterized Ambani's entire career. Hindered by India's traditional textile distribution system, from manufacturers to wholesalers to retailers, he moved into yet another new enterprise by establishing hundreds of showrooms across the nation and then supporting them with a massive advertising campaign of a kind India had never seen before.

When Indians suddenly began buying more polyester filament yarn, Ambani built a new factory that departed from his country's industrial norms. Tradition dictated a wait-and-see approach to future demand. But Ambani made extravagant projections, and instead of simply gearing up to meet them, he equipped his new factory with huge extra capacity. He then figured out how to stimulate the demand that validated his projections, which turned out to be a lot more accurate than skeptics foresaw.

To raise capital for his ambitious undertakings, Ambani again broke with tradition. Rather than raise money from conventional Indian financial institutions, which questioned his plans, Ambani appealed directly to the public, raising capital by advertising the company's new equity issues on billboards, just as he advertised his products. The public reaction was equally unexpected. Ambani's action triggered a pent-up demand for equity investing never seen in India before. His equity offerings were all oversubscribed, and he gained access to cheaper capital than any other Indian industrialist could match.

Dhirubhai Ambani, a truly inspired entrepreneur, epitomizes our arc of ambition. Instead of accepting the bleak world of his birth, he created his own world, breaking through barrier after barrier, rising ever higher on the arc. Undaunted by the risk of failure and ridicule, he bet everything on a worthy dream that drove his life. His unquenchable resolve made the dream come true.

A similar resolve drove Judy George, founder of Domain, Inc., a chain of furniture stores based in Norwood, Massachusetts, just outside Boston. She remembers clearly the curious path that led her into the business of selling home furnishings. It began early. "My parents right after the war were entrepreneurs," George says. "They left me with strangers. Right from the start, I began dreaming about creating a home."

While her friends were tacking up pictures of movie stars in their rooms, she started to hang up pictures of beautiful scenes. "I needed to create a safe haven," she explained. "To me, home is everything." Anyone who walks into a Domain store responds to the atmosphere of comfort and serenity it offers, bearing witness to a dream that has evolved into a successful enterprise.

Judy George spent ten years building someone else's furniture company, Scandinavian Design, into a $100-million-a-year success story. Then she was fired—on the spot. Unbowed, this forty-five-year-old mother of four impressed venture capitalists with her passion to launch her own furniture chain and with her unusual approach: She aimed at enriching family life, not just selling sofas. "I wanted to improve the quality of how people live. I wanted to build something that helped people feel good." George raised more than $3 million and established her first Domain.

The invaluable contribution of people like Ambani and George is that they question conventional wisdom. They see the world in a fresh light. They teem with better ideas—new formulations, new solutions, new ways around old problems.

Doers like the Wright brothers, John Mackey, Dhirubhai Ambani, and Judy George teach us that ambition starts with a dream—sometimes grand, sometimes simple. The Wright brothers fantasized human flight. Mackey focused on the idea that what we eat affects our health and well-being. Ambani wanted to build a Burma Shell, and Judy George set out to affect the quality of other people's home lives.

Both Mackey and George further teach us that obstacles can be opportunities around which to rally. Mackey once almost lost his fortune in a flood. George did lose her job. And the Wright brothers and Ambani teach us about the value of continually moving toward a target. Taken together, these lessons illustrate the early and invaluable ingredients of ambition.

Then there are those—often in the sciences and the arts—who see the world as stalled, as mired in vast bogs of orthodoxy.

Even a cursory glance at history suggests the primacy of un-orthodoxy, the engine that drives change in virtually every aspect of human affairs. Scientific discoveries and creative innovation grow out of the ability of unconstrained minds to re-imagine reality—that is, to perceive natural phenomena from a fresh perspective, to transcend tradition, and often to defy common sense. Great artists, inventors, and writers follow similar paths to great achievements.

The quest for improvement means that few,
if any, givens are permanent.

For better more than worse, as we see it, all this questing for improvement means that hardly any given is permanent. This is hard on purists who insist that truth is immutable. They tend to loathe dissent and even become history's despots. Still, dissent, impermanence, and the quest for improvement have dominated human thought from the beginning. Imagine, if you will, the Athenian school of Greek sages established by Aristotle in 335 B.C. Don't bother sitting down: Aristotle never stopped walking when he lectured—his followers were duly known as Peripatetics.

A giant among the sages of his time, Aristotle applied pure reason to his analysis of the universe and how it works. He arrived at many firm conclusions, two of which made perfect sense to a mind unarmed with scientific tools. He was sure first that the sun and the planets revolved around the earth, and second that all forms of life on earth were permanently in place. With the best intentions and reverence for life, the Roman Catholic Church in the Middle Ages embraced Aristotle's two certainties and elevated them to the status of religious dogma.

Anyone who questioned these putative truths was best advised to keep a low profile.

Nevertheless, dissenting thought could not be suppressed, even if its expression wasn't widely broadcast. So it was that the sixteenth-century Polish astronomer Nicolaus Copernicus counted himself among the skeptics. Based on his own observations of the heavens, he concluded that Aristotle and the church were dead wrong. The earth actually revolved around the sun.

Copernicus kept his heretical notions to himself for decades, and they weren't published until 1543, when he was on his deathbed. Nearly a century later, the church's inquisitors forced the great Italian mathematician and astronomer Galileo to recant his own belief in Copernicus's line of reasoning. Fortunately, this theological embarrassment for the church didn't stop Galileo from pursuing fact rather than faith, and he persevered in his revolutionary discoveries of the laws that govern the universe.

Copernicus and Galileo both opened their minds to truths that others could neither see nor accept. And in the mid–1800s, their questing spirit was matched by Charles Robert Darwin, a British naturalist who challenged Aristotle's second conclusion about the permanence of living species.

Darwin was, at best, an indifferent student of medicine, and his years at divinity school, too, were spent more in convivial company than in learning. Not until he switched to science at Cambridge University did he catch fire intellectually. In 1831, fascinated with natural phenomena and fresh out of Cambridge, the twenty-two-year-old Darwin enlisted as an unpaid naturalist aboard the British navy's *HMS Beagle*. He spent the next five years observing the flora, fauna, and geology of the Canary Islands, South America, and the Galapagos Islands. It was a voyage of discovery that changed scientific knowledge forever.

Although Darwin's major focus was on geologic formations, he was intrigued by the fossils he observed in his rock samples. They seemed to represent extinct species, yet they were quite similar to species still in existence. He also found that animals observed on different islands, thought to be varieties of one species, were actually different species. In other words, Darwin's observations seemed to contradict the prevailing belief that God created species to fit their environments, replacing one with another as He deemed necessary or desirable.

The rigors of the long expedition and the discipline of research transformed the young Darwin into a scientist of the first rank—a painstaking student of nature and an open-minded analyst who, during the months of voyage on the *Beagle,* assessed the implications of his finds. Darwin's journey and subsequent papers on geological theory won him respect and standing in the scientific community of his day. But he burned with greater ambition: to solve what he called "the species problem." He was well aware that his views would be harshly criticized by the scientific and religious establishment, that he might even be found guilty of blasphemy, but he persevered. In the end, his courage changed forever our understanding of the world.

His seminal book, *On the Origin of Species by Means of Natural Selection, or the Preservation of Favored Races in the Struggle for Life,* was published in 1859. In it, Darwin suggested that it wasn't divine intervention but, rather, competition among the members of a species that led to the development of a new species. Competition, he asserted, created a natural selection in succeeding generations of those attributes best adapted to the species' particular environment.

A year later, Darwin's friend, the biologist Thomas Henry Huxley, defended the theory of natural selection at a scientific meeting in a debate with Samuel Wilberforce, the bishop of Oxford, England. The bishop was so enraged that he wound up inquiring whether Huxley was descended from an ape on his mother's or father's side. Yet, despite fierce opposition, Darwin's ideas gradually prevailed. By seeing the world in a new way, and courageously pursuing the truth as he saw it, he had, in turn, changed the world.

The arts, like the sciences, are media that invite achievers to rethink givens and uncover patterns that others have not yet seen. Paintings and sculpture, music and dance allow us to express our joys and fears in the face of the unknown. So it has always been. From the strikingly realistic animal images that Ice Age tribesmen painted on cave walls, to the abstract constructions adorning our own era's museum walls, artists have sought to distill the essence of life using the tools of their talents. Throughout the millennia, the world has produced artists and craftsmen so gifted that their work is a constant reminder of human possibility.

Consider Pablo Picasso, the Spanish painter, sculptor, graphic artist, and ceramist widely considered to be the greatest artist of the twentieth century. Throughout his long life, Picasso repeatedly broke with tradition and with his own previous styles. Always seeking new ways to interpret both the seen and the unseen, he shocked the art establishment and forever altered our definitions of art.

In his blue period, from 1901 to 1904, Picasso employed a traditional interpretation of the human form and face, but in

1907, he plunged ahead with a radically different style. His *Les Demoiselles d'Avignon* was the first great signpost on the road to cubism and abstract art. His work with collage confirmed these forms of consideration as major art. In 1937, Picasso's *Guernica,* depicting the agony of war and the evils of fascism, demonstrated the power of myth to inspire and terrify.

Today, his achievements are recognized as works of genius. But in his acerbic, uncompromising way, Picasso never stopped battling philistines—sticks-in-the-mud, who insisted that only traditional art was genuine art. Smug and righteous, such closed minds defend the status quo in every human endeavor, including business. Individual achievers like Picasso find a way to overcome that often heard refrain—"It can never be done." Two stories illustrate Picasso's commitment.

A wealthy Parisian once commissioned the painter to create a portrait of his wife. Picasso refused to let the man see the work until it was completed. When he finally unveiled the fragmented, Cubist portrait, his client was horrified.

The man exclaimed, "But she doesn't look anything like that!"

Deadpan, Picasso asked, "What does she look like?"

The man pulled a snapshot of his wife from his wallet and showed it to the artist.

Picasso shrugged and replied, "I didn't realize she was so small."

The expatriate writer and cultural doyenne Gertrude Stein also complained bitterly when she first saw Picasso's rendering of her.

"I don't look like that," she informed him.

"Don't worry," he replied. "You will."

And she did.

As in science and the arts, business achievement derives from open minds and fresh ideas. We once asked Michael S. Dell, founder, chairman, and chief executive officer of Dell Computer Corporation, if he had dreamed of a future in technology when he was young. He confessed that he had not. But he did recall receiving inspiration from something he saw as a small boy being driven to school. The car passed many new buildings under construction in Houston, his hometown. Each had flags flying out front of them. It was Dell's youthful ambition to own such a building with a flagpole. When we inquired if Dell had what he wanted, Dell answered, "Yes—and I've got three flagpoles." His far-fetched childhood ambition had come true.

The fresh idea that led Michael Dell to create his company had its first incarnation when he was a freshman at the University of Texas in 1983. He started a business dedicated to finding out what his potential customers wanted in the way of rebuilt, upgraded personal computers, which he then sold to them directly. He did so well that he quit his studies and launched his own company. To mollify his alarmed parents, Dell swore that he would resume his studies if the company bombed. But when sales hit $80,000 the first month, Michael Dell said goodbye to college.

Up to that time, personal computers had been sold through giant retailers or small specialty shops. Dell had the talent and the vision to see a different way of producing and distributing computers. He called it the direct model, and it was a spectacular success. Michael Dell took the company public when he was all of twenty-three years old. Within a year, Dell Computer (based in Round Rock, Texas, near Austin) had sales of more than $250 million.

The direct-model idea was revolutionary. By eliminating middlemen, the company started out with a substantial cost advantage. And because Dell was dealing directly with largely corporate customers, the company learned their needs firsthand.

Dell had another fresh idea: built-to-order computers. Rather than cranking out standard models and then ballyhooing their virtues in a bid to interest customers, he built computers to correspond to each customer's tastes and needs. Farewell to the massive, costly inventories that plagued traditional computer manufacturers.

Constantly looking for ways to cut costs and underprice his competition, Dell next considered outsourcing more computer components. Nothing unusual about that. The new twist was that Dell transformed his suppliers into partners. He had the foresight to recognize that the usual arms-length relationship with suppliers would not allow him to maintain his unrelenting drive for better and better computers. The computer industry had never before heard of such a thing.

Today, components of Dell computers are produced by outside companies that work under long-term, mutually beneficial contracts. Dell brings them into the early planning stages of every new product—in fact, they are spliced into Dell's electronic network. Information and innovations are freely traded up and down the supply chain. Dell's workforce stands at about 15,000—or some 65,000 fewer employees than it would need worldwide if it made each component itself.

Driven by a dream and confident of his ability to see beyond the conventional approaches for production and distribution, Michael Dell was sure that he could make his dream happen. And as someone dedicated to going beyond making a better mousetrap, Michael Dell is a model of modern ambition, an entrepreneur's entrepreneur in the Information Age.

Much like Henry Ford, he is a true Creator. Dell didn't invent the computer, nor was he involved with its early marketing. He simply saw a radically different way to manufacture and distribute the machines.

A *dream without courage goes nowhere.*

Perhaps there were others who shared Dell's idea. Who knows? They lacked the initiative to take action. Talented dreamers, they are immobilized when it comes to action.

Another person who had the dream as well as the courage to act was Patrick J. McGovern. In 1964, McGovern founded International Data Group (IDG), based just outside Boston, Massachusetts. It was still early in the computer age, but McGovern saw the future beckoning and had the visionary talent to realize that people would need to read and learn about these new machines. In 1967 he began publishing *Computerworld,* one of the first computer-focused magazines. He also saw that the computer would emerge as an international phenomenon. IDG, which boasts revenues of more than $2 billion annually, now publishes magazines in seventy-five countries, including Greenland and Antarctica.

Pat McGovern's interest in technology dates back to his high school days in Philadelphia, Pennsylvania. Always a talented computer tinkerer, he began his career by building a tic-tac-toe machine that no one could beat. He then went on to the Massachusetts Institute of Technology, got a job at a magazine with the ponderous name, *Computers and Automation,* the first computer magazine.

Next, McGovern founded a company to do market research, then moved into magazine publishing. Like Michael Dell, Pat McGovern is a Creator. Publishing is nothing new. But he saw a need for publishing a new kind of information and moved forcefully to satisfy that need.

People who never dream suffer a kind of poverty, a lack of imagination that can produce a banal life. The ability to fantasize, to imagine something wonderfully better, is one of life's pleasures and privileges.

Chances are that everyone reading this book is thoroughly familiar with fantasizing. It is fun and quite essential to business success. If the barons of Silicon Valley were not chronic fantasizers, all of our mail would still come in envelopes instead of over wires.

But dreams alone are not enough. Acting on one's dreams—that is the hard part. The good news is that the courage to overcome obstacles is not restricted to those born with it. Daring is more often learned than inherited. To those who respond, life teaches courage, which then multiplies itself as if by compound interest.

Experience suggests that just about everyone is a potential success, given the right incentive and inspiration. Skeptics need only sample the incredible record of human achievements, which illustrates what thousands of ambitious people have indelibly proved: One person can actually change the world, or at least change that piece of the world in which he or she resides.

Achievers like Dhirubhai Ambani, Michael Dell, Judy George, John Mackey, and Pat McGovern are harbingers of the potential greatness existing in each one of us—greatness that is standing by for action, if and when we choose to respond. We, too, can own a dream and dare to make it come true.

In the next two chapters, we examine other points on the arc of ambition—the need to persevere as one's aspirations unfold and the need to recognize and grasp opportunity as it presents itself. When conditions are right, one must be ready—physically, emotionally, strategically.

3

It Takes a Strong Character and a Lot of Willpower to Hold onto a Dream Under Adverse Circumstances

Follow a Steadfast Path

~

Great deeds inspire everyone to admire and some to emulate the example of great heroes, past and present. In almost every case, protagonists somehow overcome adversity on the road to triumph. How do they do it? What can we learn from the lives of George Lucas, Nelson Mandela, Thabang Motsohi, and Samuel Moore Walton? We can learn the power of perseverance, of optimism, and of learning.

SUCCESS DOESN'T COME EASILY. Perseverance is essential.

Think of the nineteenth-century French writer Gustave Flaubert. It took him twenty years to write his first novel, *Madame Bovary*, which was published in 1857 and became a world classic. "Art," Flaubert wrote in one of his better-known letters, "is agony."

For those who complain that it takes too long to make dinner, remember that Julia Child spent over nine years writing the first volume of her classic *Mastering the Art of French Cooking*.

The historian Thomas Carlyle defined genius as "the transcendent capacity for taking trouble [pains] first of all."

The British prime minister Benjamin Disraeli maintained that "the secret of success is constancy of purpose."

The physicist Albert Einstein claimed, "I'm not so smart. It's just that I stay with problems longer."

And filmmaker George Lucas asserted, "If you want to be successful in a particular field of endeavor, I think perseverance is one of the key qualities. I haven't met anyone (who is successful) who hasn't been able to describe years and years and years of very, very difficult struggle through the whole process of achieving anything whatsoever. There is no way around that."

Persistence is critical to
realizing your ambition.

There you have four versions of the same advice: Without the ability to persist, you won't make it up the arc of ambition. That idea may seem old-fashioned, no match for the brio of today's Internet wunderkinds. But stay with us: Perseverance is still the way to go.

Of course, persisting in a course that defies reality won't lead anywhere. King Canute, a Dane who reigned over England in the eleventh century, famously proved this to the sycophants who kept telling him he was the master of the universe, able to do anything. One day, Canute sat on the shore of the North Sea and in his most commanding tones ordered the waves to retreat. They didn't. Again he ordered. Again they didn't. His courtiers finally grasped the idea.

The old alchemists never got that smart. For three hundred years, throughout the Middle Ages and into the early Renaissance, they spent lifetimes striving to turn baser metals into gold. They never once succeeded, of course.

Relentless determination is rare because few people have the grit to keep pursuing an elusive goal. We find little pleasure in futile pursuits and want to avoid appearing foolish in the world's eyes. For all these reasons, those unusual people who do persist against all odds deserve credit and respect. Assume their cause is worthy until it is proven otherwise. Give them the benefit of the doubt. Some of them may be tomorrow's prophets in disguise.

A certain respect for zealots is merited. History is full of achievers who began as crusaders, refused to bend or quit, and wound up changing the course of human history. Consider the remarkable life of Nelson Mandela, a saga of persistence in a perilous cause.

Throughout his twenty-seven years in a bleak South African prison, undaunted by vicious treatment, Mandela stayed cool and emerged triumphant. A classic Creator, he never allowed himself to succumb to the prospect of failure and continued to believe, against all odds, in the ultimate defeat of apartheid in his country. Unlike Caesar, Mandela's ambitions were not for power for himself but for the dignity and welfare of an entire nation.

Dreams and determination combine to produce greatness.

Under such adverse circumstances, it takes the flintiest character to even imagine victory, much less sustain the will to achieve it. Dreamer and doer: Such is the alloy of greatness. Nelson Mandela's dream of transforming the racist society of South Africa into a multiracial democracy lasted more than fifty years. His determination to advance that dream, to keep fighting despite intense torments to both his people and himself, carried him to a day in May 1994 when he became the president of all South Africans, united in theory and even in practice as one republic.

To be sure, Mandela is a figure larger than life, a hero rare in history and not exactly imitable for ordinary people. Still, his story is a parable of faith and tenacity, of human possibilities, ours included. It illuminates one achiever's moral fortitude in the face of unjust government oppression. It illustrates how great people keep moving ahead—honing their talents, strengthening their causes, focused on their ultimate destinations.

Rolihlahla Mandela was born in 1918 in a thatched hut with no electricity or running water in the village of Mvezo in the black homeland of Transkei. *Rolihlahla* means "troublemaker." A teacher tacked on the name Nelson, perhaps thinking it less menacing. When he was twelve, Mandela's father died, and he left the family farm to become a ward of the Paramount Chief of the Tembu tribe. He attended a missionary college but was expelled when he joined a protest against efforts to weaken the student council.

Mandela put aside one opportunity—the likelihood that he would eventually become Paramount Chief himself—and headed for Johannesburg. He worked as a guard at a gold mine, then as a clerk in a white lawyers' office, and studied for a correspondence law degree. He was twenty-four when he joined the African National Congress (ANC), a mild-mannered organization of older leaders, who sought to improve the treatment of blacks via constitutional means.

But Mandela had other ideas, and his timing was right: A new, more impatient generation was waiting in the wings. Two years later, Mandela and a handful of friends created the Youth League of the ANC, intending to rejuvenate and reform the parent organization and also to build a huge, grassroots protest movement. In his first major speech before the membership of the ANC, Mandela declared his extraordinary ambition—he promised that he would become the first president of a democratic South Africa. As prophetic as Mandela's claim turned out to be, at the time it then seemed more like the cockiness of an upstart leader. Many senior members of the ANC appeared more deserving. But Mandela quickly proved his worth and then his indispensability.

Like his counterpart in the United States, Martin Luther King, Jr., Mandela chose passive resistance as his weapon, organizing a series of protests over the next few years. The government responded in 1948 with apartheid, the official policy that aimed at the separation of the races by setting up self-governing enclaves for blacks. The bulk of the country, including its cities and infrastructure, was reserved for whites, who represented just one-sixth of the population. Blacks were required to carry identification passes when moving from town to town or entering white areas. They were barred from obtaining passports, and they were routinely harassed and jailed by police.

For revolutionaries like Nelson Mandela, apartheid and the repression associated with it represented a rich new opportunity, a rallying point for opposition. In 1952, Mandela was named national volunteer-in-chief of the ANC's Campaign for the Defiance of Unjust Laws. He crisscrossed the country setting up marches and strikes.

Four years later, he was among 156 activists arrested and charged with treason. Though the trial ended in the acquittal of all the activists, government pressure on the dissidents constantly increased.

The police massacre of peaceful demonstrators in Sharpeville in 1960 was the spark that ignited outright armed struggle. The government banned the ANC; the next year, Mandela went underground. He led the ANC in a new direction, organizing a military wing and ordering bomb attacks on rail lines and power plants.

"It would be wrong and unrealistic for African leaders," he explained, "to continue preaching peace and non-violence at a time when the government met our peaceful demands with force."

Eventually, Mandela was captured. In June 1964, he was sentenced to life in prison. He spent the next eighteen years in an island prison off Cape Town—toiling from early morning to sunset in a limestone quarry, exposed to the broiling heat of the African summer and the bitter cold of winter, forced to endure the random indignities and cruelties of the prison system.

It might have crushed a lesser person. Mandela recognized it as an opportunity to grow and to inspire a new audience with his political ideals. Early on the prisoners were prevented from even talking to each other during their work hours. Although he had minimal contact with this fellow inmates, Mandela was still able to inspire them through the dignity with which he conducted himself and the dignity he demanded from the prison guards. For instance, he refused to run to the work shift as the guards demanded, choosing instead to walk at a measured pace. Eventually the guards were forced to walk at the same pace. In these little ways, he kept the struggle going.

Constantly moving toward a goal,
even if the steps are small,
will eventually bring success.

Most great achievers realize, just as Mandela did, that there are always ways to advance their ambitions, however modest the actions might appear. The only constant is to never give up.

To that end, Mandela organized cultural programs including plays and concerts to be performed during the prisoners' recreational time—he later told of playing Creon in *Antigone,* by Sophocles. Later in his prison term, he saw to it that each gang of workers included one prisoner who would serve as the gang's instructor for the day in economics, philosophy, or politics. The prison actually came to be known widely as Mandela University.

His years in prison turned Mandela into the undisputed leader and symbol of the struggle for black freedom in his country. As other nations increased economic pressure on South Africa to ease and then eliminate apartheid, the government was forced to negotiate. That meant negotiating with—and eventually freeing—Nelson Mandela.

Many on both sides of the racial divide insisted that a fair and peaceful resolution was impossible. Some ANC leaders wanted to keep fighting to bring the government to its knees. Mandela had a different vision of the future. He was convinced that a real opportunity existed to achieve victory without more bloodshed, through compromise and economic and political pressure. He set about to calm both his fellow blacks, who feared the government would once more betray them, and the white citizens, who feared they would be stripped of their property and even their lives by a black-dominated government.

Finally, in the spring of 1994, Mandela was elected president of South Africa. Despite the occasional rough patch, the nation is well on its way toward achieving his dream of unity and democracy. Time after time, Nelson Mandela demonstrated the ability to keep going despite the political maelstrom about him. Patiently, insistently, year by year, taking one calculated risk after another, he advanced his cause.

Optimism begets success because it keeps the mind open to all opportunities.

What does Mandela teach us about pursuing a good cause? That optimism wins because, unlike pessimism, it keeps the mind wide open to opportunities, however fleeting. Mandela exemplifies at least three virtues of positive thinking. First, he views all setbacks as temporary, even if temporary means twenty-seven years. Second, he doesn't fall prey to stereotyping: Rather than viewing all whites as enemies, he sees some as potential allies, an opportunity to which he would be blind if he pessimistically assumed that all whites were racists. Third, he doesn't internalize defeat. In response to being arrested, he could have said, "I have failed. What good can I do now?" But even behind bars in a maximum security prison on an escape-proof island, he still saw himself as a leader responsible to his people. Every day, he carried out his mission in their behalf.

As the quintessential optimist, Mandela reminds us of the work of the psychologist Martin E. P. Seligman, author of *Learned Optimism*. Seligman argues that we all interpret events in ways that stamp us as optimists or pessimists. For example, pessimists feel that bad things have permanent causes and will keep on happening. It is a crippling attitude. Worse, it is a self-fulfilling prophecy. If you are sure you can do something, you probably will. If you are sure you can't, you are probably right.

Optimists, by contrast, tend to see personal setbacks as temporary. Failure may depress them, but they expect to feel okay in the morning. As Seligman notes: "It's like a punch in the stomach. For optimists, it hurts, but the hurt quickly goes away. For pessimists, the hurt lasts, it seethes, it roils, it congeals into a grudge. They remain helpless for a long time."

Pessimists also tend to explain their failures in universal terms. When they fail in one area, they give up on everything. If they launch a new business and few customers bite, they cast doubt on their entire business model. Optimists, on the other hand, tend to isolate the cause of bad events. Confronted with a shortfall in customers, they look for specific reasons such as inadequate promotion. They don't just impulsively dump the whole business.

Finally, pessimists tend to internalize causes or blame themselves when things go wrong. As a result, they often suffer from low self-esteem and their self-confidence declines. It is just the opposite with optimists. They externalize bad news, sure that it derives from forces beyond their control. They may take responsibility but not blame. This preserves their self-confidence and gives them the ability to try again.

Optimism can be learned.

Like Seligman, we believe that optimism can be learned. It just requires a concerted effort to change how we explain things to ourselves. Some huge proportion of success—perhaps 60 percent—is surely a matter of attitude, of positive thinking, of insisting and literally seeing in the mind's eye that things are bound to come to a good end. The rest of success derives from perseverance begetting luck. It is said we make our own luck, and that was clearly true for Nelson Mandela.

Out of the crucible of South African apartheid come other examples of perseverance and optimism. One we came across was Thabang J. Motsohi. A classic Consolidator, he is now general manager of transformation for Trans-Net, a huge government organization that runs South Africa's railroads, harbors, roads, metro rail, and postal services.

During the worst years of apartheid, while Nelson Mandela struggled to survive in jail, Motsohi was still a schoolboy. He grew up in a poor family like Mandela's. They lived in the town of Frankfort, not far south of Johannesburg, in the Orange Free State, which, by the way, wasn't free at all for Africans. Motsohi's father had begun by working in the mines, but illness forced him to find another occupation. With the help of a benefactor, he became a school principal. A farmer at heart, he passed on his love of growing things by encouraging his children to help tend the family garden.

It was from these duties, Motsohi told us, that he derived "a sense of pride of working on the garden and the fruit trees." It was then, too, that the first seeds of ambition began to grow in the boy. Motsohi dreamed of going to the university and becoming a doctor. "I was always driven by the pursuit of the good," he explains. "From my childhood, I have always tried to achieve."

For an ambitious achiever, the road ahead in South Africa led nowhere. So Motsohi's father sent him to the neighboring country of Lesotho, then called Basutoland. Even there, life was not easy. "The first two years at school," he remembers, "were very difficult. The school was demanding—physically and mentally."

As a foreigner, Motsohi was looked down upon and called "a fence jumper." He had a hometown friend to keep him company, and together, their sense of isolation drove them to make extra efforts. By the last year of high school, Motsohi was at the top of his class. His academic success went hand-in-hand with a growing inner self-confidence and, as Motsohi describes it, "mental fortitude."

When the police arrived one day to search the school, he was the only student present who stood up to them. "Unless you have a warrant," he told them, "you can't search the school." His challenge led to an end of the search and a negotiation for a settlement with the school authorities. "That day," Motsohi remembers, "I was a hero."

He finished university. But too politically active to please Lesotho's government authorities, he was denied a scholarship to go on to study medicine. Instead, he taught science and math at his old high school.

Although Motsohi enjoyed teaching, it did not assuage his dreams or his ambitions. He switched to a civil-service job in the department of geology and was sent to Denmark to get a diploma in analytical chemistry.

When he returned to Lesotho, he found he was as restless and frustrated in this job as he had been as a teacher. But Motsohi was never pessimistic. When things didn't work out in one area, he persevered. Not missing a beat, he immediately looked for another opening—and as most optimists do, he found one. Through a friend, he got a job in Lesotho's civil aviation department. At last he was fulfilled in his work, traveling around the world, meeting people of different cultures, and learning to fly.

"For a young man with ambition," he recalls, "travel brings its own development. Airplanes were supposed to be the province of the white. When I was flying I felt I had conquered this great divide."

In 1979, Thabang Motsohi was made director of the Department of Civil Aviation. In this job, he found himself rewriting civil aviation policy, once again flying around the world, meeting with experts, enlarging his horizons.

Motsohi had risen fast in Lesotho's government hierarchy and was some fifteen years younger than most of his peers; he aroused resentment and jealousy among them. "Why is a foreigner in this job?" they asked.

When the country embarked on the construction of a new airport, Motsohi ran afoul of the transport minister and was suddenly removed from the Civil Aviation Department. Instead, he was named deputy secretary of the Department of Energy.

Still later, after a brief interlude as general manager of the Lesotho airline, which gave him a chance to develop business skills, Motsohi once again ran afoul of ministerial authority. This time, he moved into the private sector. Motsohi spent the next four years as executive director of an insurance brokerage company.

"But I found life boring and routine," he remembers now. "I had no power. I could not influence things. I wanted to influence things."

A pessimist might have lost hope, deeming his situation permanent, without any redemption. It would have been easy to blame oneself—to say, if I had been more politic, this would not have happened to me. But like other achievers, Motsohi was always willing to look forward, to continue the struggle, to invest in himself and his future.

Motsohi read the fix he was in as an excellent chance to invest "in building my own intellectual capital. I began to school myself in management literature and read avidly. . . . This preparation built the foundations for what I was able to do later."

As Motsohi studied, he watched events in South Africa, where the demise of apartheid was approaching. His long exile from his homeland ended with the 1994 elections that made Nelson Mandela president. Motsohi's experience with aviation led to his first job with Trans-Net, where he was made regional manager for Southern Africa.

After that, his rise within the organization was rapid. He has, of course, faced difficulties; certain factions in the country wanted Trans-Net and its numerous divisions to be privatized. The government decided that Trans-Net had to be reorganized, and Motsohi was put in charge of this massive undertaking. He had previously run PX, the Trans-Net subsidiary concerned with parcel distribution, during its reorganization. This work gave him an insight and familiarity with the problems he would encounter in this even bigger undertaking.

Although the transformation is not yet fully in place, Motsohi is already looking ahead to new challenges. "Leaders can never be satisfied," he says. "My wife jokingly tells me, 'The powder in the gun has not yet dried, and you are off on the hunt again.'"

Thabang Motsohi never allowed hardship to bully him into settling for less. Like Nelson Mandela, he remained optimistic, saw setbacks as temporary, and didn't personalize defeat. In fact, he saw his losses as opportunities to move on.

In his own words, "Life is full of commas. Everyone has set-backs. But what you do during these periods is the key. If you view them as periods of preparation and don't allow the fire of ambition to die within you, you will be ready when the opportunity arises."

Business achievers pursue goals different from those of Nel-son Mandela or Thabang Motsohi. But, in many respects, all high achievers are alike. They firmly believe they will prevail, no matter what stands in the way. So, they do prevail.

> *Achievers share an appetite for learning—*
> *from the successes of others and*
> *from their own mistakes.*

One reason for their confidence is that successful achievers are less often born geniuses than born scavengers of terrific ideas. They all share an insatiable appetite for learning anything they need to know, whether from other people's successes or from their own mistakes.

A penchant for lifelong learning is perhaps crucial in the trial-and-error work of pursuing new ideas and elusive goals. It was certainly essential to Mandela and Motsohi.

Those who excel in business are no different. In business, as in all fields, those who claim superior knowledge may impress some people some of the time. But those who never stop learn-ing are the ones who keep moving forward.

Consider, for instance, the lifework of Samuel Moore Walton. The original small-town merchant, he became one of the rich-est men in business history. Application and dedication lie at the heart of his rise from rural poverty to business triumph as the founder of Wal-Mart Stores, Inc., the world's largest discount chain with revenues of more than $118 billion and 3,046 stores across the globe.

"Somehow over the years, folks have gotten the impression that Wal-Mart was something I dreamed up out of the blue as a middle-aged man," he wrote near the end of his life, "and that it was just this great idea that turned into an overnight success. . . . Like most other overnight successes, it was about 20 years in the making."

Like his competitors, Walton looked for new ideas. But when he saw something he liked, when his experience told him it was something special, he set out to make it even better. In that sense, he was a classic Capitalizer.

Walton saw ideas as common property like air. It was what you did with them that made you different. He competed by improving whatever he admired.

Born in 1918, Walton grew up on a small Missouri farm. It was, he once said, "a pretty hardscrabble" childhood. Before school, he milked the cows. After school, he delivered the milk his mother had bottled. At the age of seven, he had a newspaper route and sold magazine subscriptions. He was already in training for a future of hard work.

After graduating from the University of Missouri in 1940, he began as a salesman for J. C. Penney Company, Inc. But no sooner had he hit his stride (he was obviously a born salesman) than World War II intervened. Drafted into the United States Army, he spent three years as a captain in the Army Intelligence Corps.

At war's end, Walton was eager to sell for himself. He bought a Ben Franklin franchise—a five-and-dime store—in Newport, Arkansas.

With his own brother Ben's help, Walton turned miniscule margins into six-figure revenues and, in three years, more than doubled the store's business. He learned to appreciate the value of an eye for detail when he displayed his wares. He knew the wholesale price of everything down to the last half-cent and could calculate his profit margin with ease.

The value of volume sales became clear to Sam Walton early in his business career. He put it this way: ". . . say I bought an item for 80 cents. I found that by pricing it at a $1.00 I could sell three times more of it than by pricing it at $1.20. I might make only the half the profit per item, but, because I was selling three times as many, the overall profit was much greater." Within five years, the Walton brothers—Sam and Ben—ran the most profitable Ben Franklin store in a six-state region.

In another unusual move, Walton shied away from depending on his franchiser for all his merchandise. He bought directly from manufacturers whenever possible, driving as far as New York to find cut-rate goods. He also paid attention to what his competitors were doing and learned from it: How were they displaying their goods? How did they price them? How did they promote their stores?

After five years at Newport, Walton was forced to sell the franchise to his landlord. It seems that when he leased the store space, he had neglected to ask for an option to renew. Both wiser and richer, with the $50,000 sale price burning a hole in his pocket, Walton opened another Ben Franklin store in Bentonville, Arkansas. The location presaged his future strategy of basing new stores in small towns with populations under 10,000 (not to mention that Bentonville gave this avid hunter access to excellent hunting opportunities in four adjoining states). In

Bentonville, Walton stressed self-service and low prices. His promotional skills and natural friendliness bought customers in droves.

Ambitious achievers continue to
build on their own successes.

By 1962, Walton had a total of six Ben Franklin stores in Arkansas and Kansas, but his ambitions were far from satisfied. Against opposition from his franchiser, he opened his own discount store, calling it Wal-Mart.

"It's true," he wrote, "that I was 44 years when we opened our first Wal-Mart in 1962, but the store was totally an outgrowth of everything we'd been doing . . . another case of me being unable to leave well enough alone, another experiment."

Gradually, he expanded, setting up Wal-Marts around the country, buying small chains of stores, converting them to his philosophy. By 1979, Wal-Mart owned 230 stores and, for the first time, sales reached $1 billion.

But discount retailers were no longer something out of the ordinary. Walton saw that his opportunities for expansion were dwindling. So he decided that his company had to move east of the Mississippi River before his competitors took over the south. In 1981, he set up a Wal-Mart in Jackson, Tennessee.

From that beachhead, his company quickly and inexorably spread across the region. New stores were opened at the amazing rate of 100 to 150 a year. For all this frenzy, Wal-Mart never lost sight of its core slogans, "We Sell for Less" and "Satisfaction Guaranteed."

Despite his success, Sam Walton was ever the Capitalizer. He never stopped monitoring other people's good ideas.

Kmart Corporation, probably his chief rival in discount retailing, furnished many of those ideas. According to Kmart founder, Harry Cunningham, Walton "not only copied our concepts, he strengthened them. Sam just took the ball and ran with it."

In later years, Walton himself admitted as much. "Kmart interested me ever since the first store went up in 1962. I was in their stores constantly, because they were the laboratory and better than we were. I spent a heck of a lot of time wandering through their stores talking to their people and trying to figure out how they did things. I've probably been in more Kmarts than anybody else in the country."

He was also particularly impressed by the success of a California discount merchant named Sol Price. It was Price who founded the eponymous Price Club, a huge operation that sold goods in big packages at rock-bottom prices in a warehouse setting.

In 1983, Walton opened his own version, Sam's Club, in Oklahoma City, Oklahoma. He complimented Price by admitting that he had "stolen—actually I prefer the word borrowed—as many ideas from Sol Price as from anybody else in the business."

The format worked so well that Walton extended it to other towns. Soon, Sam's Club was a multi-billion-dollar business of its own.

In the last years of his life, Sam Walton was the richest man in the United States, at least according to *Forbes* magazine. Yet, neither age nor affluence sated his ambition—or appetite for competition. At seventy-four, when he died, he was busily planning Wal-Mart's overseas expansion.

Sam Walton's method had a dollop of the age-old truth that imitation is the sincerest form of flattery. Instead of fretting about a competitor's threatening innovation, he was more likely to see it as an opportunity.

He was not a big thinker. He simply turned the obvious into success.

From Leonardo da Vinci to Sam Walton to Warren E. Buffett, a diverse array of achievers over the generations have displayed the same powerful traits—perseverance, optimism, learning. When opportunity knocked at their doors, it was no accident. They were ready. Like the doers we meet in the next chapter— among them, Thomas Jefferson, Martin Luther King, Jr., Ray Kroc, and Ted Turner—such people display the courage to act fast and live greatly.

One can make the worst of life, as some do, or make the least of it, as too many do. Or one can seize every chance to create, grow, enjoy.

"There is," wrote William Shakespeare, "a tide in the affairs of man which taken at the flood leads on to fortune. Omitted, all the voyage of their life is bound in shallows and in miseries." Or, in the irrepressible manner of winners in every field, in every century, one can seize every chance.

4

Opportunity Knocks with All the Temerity of a Brown Trout Hiding in an Overfished Stream

Seize the Moment

~

Those who embrace opportunity create it. Those who fear disaster court it. There is no substitute for preparation. Witness the wave-riding sagas of Thomas Jefferson, Martin Luther King, Jr., Ray Kroc, Robert Johnson, William Poduska, Arthur Wellesley, and Margaret C. Whitman.

In 1803, Thomas Jefferson was president of a small republic with no power, scant cash, and fewer prospects—all of which pleased him. He dreaded bigness. A land of small farms, modest taxes, and minimal government was his idea of the perfect state. Even so, Jefferson was a man of boundless imagination and intelligence. Faced with an unexpected opportunity to vastly enlarge his country, he seized it.

The world's greatest buccaneer, Napoléon Bonaparte, emperor of mighty France, had just gained control of Louisiana, the huge western territory abutting the United States. He envisaged a New World French empire, stretching from Canada to the Caribbean. Unhappy with having Napoléon as a neighbor, Jefferson set out to at least secure New Orleans, mouth of the Mississippi River and a vital *entrepôt* for United States trade abroad.

Neither Jefferson nor Congress had any constitutional authority to buy foreign territory, but they took a deep breath and agreed to offer Napoléon $2 million for New Orleans, a sum almost incomprehensible to Americans of the time. Jefferson dispatched a trusted envoy, Virginia's Governor James Monroe, to Paris to help Minister to France Robert R. Livingston negotiate the deal.

When Monroe got to Paris in April 1803, he and Livingston found themselves with a challenge that far exceeded their instructions from President Jefferson. France was at the brink of a draining war with the world's other powerhouse, Great Britain. Napoléon was unsure that he could hold Louisiana against the British: He had sent troops to Haiti, where most of the men succumbed to tropical fevers.

Napoléon needed francs, and if the British seized New Orleans, he would be left without even America's $2 million for the city. So he made a counterproposal. How would the United States like to buy the entire Louisiana Territory, all 830,000 square miles of it? Price: a mere $15 million.

Monroe and Livingston had every reason to back off: $15 million was a fortune for the United States, the deal was unconstitutional, and the New England states were sure to oppose the acquisition as a threat to their political dominance.

But Jefferson's negotiators also knew that Napoléon might well cut a deal with another nation in the time it would take to get instructions from the president across the Atlantic Ocean in Washington, D.C.

Armed with daring and a large vision of America's future, Monroe and Livingston took it upon themselves to sign the Louisiana Purchase treaty in Paris. When Jefferson got the news, he applauded the deal, then did some fancy political footwork to hush up its unconstitutionality and coax the Senate into ratifying the treaty.

Monroe and Livingston had the nerve to risk disavowal in order to pursue their country's true interest. Jefferson had the courage to look beyond his constitutional powerlessness in order to enhance national security in the profoundest sense. In a unique deal they knew could never occur again, President Jefferson and the Senate literally doubled the size of the United States, increasing its potential as a world power. And the cost? Less than three cents an acre—the best bargain in American history.

History offers few parallels to this case of risking so much to gamble on national greatness. Things could easily have turned out quite differently. What if Jefferson had lost his nerve and failed to support the Monroe-Livingston deal with Napoléon?

What if the British had then acquired Louisiana by conquest? For one thing, the future American West would have become the British West—the United States would have stopped at the Mississippi River. For another, historians would also dismiss Jefferson as a wimp instead of a national icon. And Monroe would never have become the fifth president of the United States.

What makes this story all the more arresting is that opportunities rarely occur so unexpectedly and are seldom "seized" so impulsively. Achievers are far more often masters of long, careful preparation.

> ### *Preparedness allows achievers to seize opportunities.*

Knowing precisely what to look for, achievers see opportunities far ahead of other people. When they act fast and win some victory, we often credit them with mystical luck or superhuman talent. In fact, their foresight and hard work fixed the odds and ensured their success.

The French chemist Louis Pasteur, inventor of vaccines, put all this in a nutshell when he remarked, "Chance favors the prepared mind."

A brilliant exemplar of this approach was just beginning his rise to fame at the time Jefferson & Company bought the Louisiana Territory. He was Arthur Wellesley, the British general (and future Duke of Wellington) who twelve years later crushed Napoléon Bonaparte at the decisive Battle of Waterloo.

One reason Wellesley wound up defeating the era's most indomitable soldier may be that he was the tortoise to Napoléon's hare. For most of Wellesley's youth, no one expected anything of him, a condition that can be quite liberating.

Wellesley was the unpromising second son of impoverished Irish aristocrats. He flunked out of Eton, joined the British army for want of anything better, and appeared fated to confirm his mother's acerbic put-down that he was "food for powder and nothing more."

It took years for Wellesley to get anywhere in the military, but he spent those years thoroughly learning his trade rather than lamenting his glacial progress. At first, he was just a lowly British officer fighting the revolutionary French in Holland in 1793 and sharing the self-inflicted defeat of an incompetent regular army filled with drunks, rogues, and sycophants. From that crucible Wellesley learned "what one ought not to do, and that is always something."

As he rose through the ranks, Wellesley also learned to boost troop morale, demand superb supplies, study the enemy, and memorize every inch of contested ground.

Acquiring the proper knowledge can turn foolish risks into acceptable opportunities.

Terrain was Wellesley's specialty. He trained himself to spot the most advantageous positions before the enemy did. Accordingly, he could take risks that might seem foolhardy to others but were actually reasonable.

Posted to India in 1797, Wellesley's troops fought a series of brilliant campaigns against Indian insurrections, using surprise attacks and well-organized supplies to achieve victory. His careful preparation was evident in all his victories. Wellesley left nothing to chance. Both caring and commanding, he inspired his men by leading all cavalry charges in person.

By 1805, now a brigadier general at age thirty-six, Wellesley was back in London as Britain's Secretary for Ireland, in effect that country's ruler. In words that startled the British establishment, he vowed to desegregate Ireland's warring Catholics and Protestants and to ensure that "government ought to do what is just towards the governed, be the consequences what they may." He was so far ahead of his time that in two years, probably by no coincidence, he was recalled for military duty against Britain's chief nemesis, Napoléon Bonaparte, who by then had conquered nearly all of Europe and put the British Isles in danger of invasion.

In 1807 General Wellesley took command of the British army in Portugal, with orders to drive the French from there and then from Spain, loosing the entire peninsula from Napoléon's grasp. Wellesley's strategy was to keep bleeding the French juggernaut with small battles that drained Napoléon's resources, weakening his campaigns elsewhere in Europe.

The Peninsula War lasted five years, much of which Wellesley spent riding alone through the Torres Vedras mountains, carefully scouting the terrain between Portugal and Spain. A stickler for detail, he slept only three hours a night and spent every dawn perfecting his plans and whipping off memos to his 17,000 troops.

Wellesley commanded his men to improve everything from supply systems to their behavior toward local civilians. Unlike Napoléon's troops, who usually lived off the land, Wellesley's men were under his strict orders to befriend Spanish peasants and to pay for everything, thus ensuring that the British invaders were preferable to the French occupiers.

Wellesley's meticulous planning paid off in 1813 when he defeated the French at the Battle of Vitoria and drove them out of

Spain. Named Duke of Wellington in 1814, he marched into Paris, forcing Napoléon to abdicate as emperor of France.

But no sooner had Wellington begun a new job, representing Britain at the historic Congress of Vienna in 1815, then Napoléon escaped from Elba and gathered a new army. Wellington was dispatched to Belgium to stop the seemingly irrepressible Frenchman.

The deciding battle took place at Waterloo, sixteen miles from Brussels. Wellington reconnoitered the topography of Waterloo with his customary thoroughness. Unlike Napoléon's marshals, however, he made no specific battle plans ahead of time.

Wellington's ability to stay flexible in moments of crisis undoubtedly contributed to his success as both a soldier and a politician. His almost eerie calm in battle earned him the nickname, *The Iron Duke*.

The Battle of Waterloo occurred on June 18 and lasted all day. Napoléon began the day with high, but misplaced, confidence. "Wellington," he declared, "is a bad general"—a particularly odd statement considering that Napoléon had never actually met Wellington in battle before. The Englishman proceeded to confuse the French by placing his troops behind a ridge and luring the enemy into a frontal assault that proved suicidal.

At the end of the day, 27,000 Frenchmen had died, compared with Wellington's 15,000, and the defeated Napoléon was headed back to prison on the island of St. Helena, off the coast of Africa. He spent the rest of his life there.

The Iron Duke returned home with the kind of celebrity accorded today's pop stars. He was inevitably destined for a political career that in 1828 made him prime minister of Great Britain. In that post, he soon provoked the electorate by taking uncompromising positions, notably in opposing parliamentary reform.

His mastery of terrain apparently did not quite translate from war to politics. Even so, Wellington eventually regained immense public respect for his honesty, shrewdness, and uncanny ability to do the right thing at the right time, at least in battle. More than only a handful of other famous generals, he made preparation the key to military success.

Opportunities arrive in different forms;
be alert for those that knock softly.

Some opportunities, like Jefferson's, arise suddenly. They cry out for a quick response. Other opportunities emerge from an accumulation of gradual changes, still others from one's ability to catch a new wave. But most opportunities come and go, as the title of this chapter suggests, with all the elusiveness of a brown trout hiding out in an overfished stream. In other words, they hardly knock at all.

Whether obvious or obscure, all worthwhile opportunities pose challenging questions. Are you ready to reject the status quo? Can you reject a familiar present in favor of an uncertain future? Are you willing to take a big risk on the off-chance of a bigger reward?

Every yes answer is a tribute to the uniquely human gift of daring. If humans had never dared to risk all, the species would still be literally stuck in some primordial mud.

To seize a big opportunity is to dare—and to dare greatly. Nobody ever achieved anything major without the courage or boldness to try the untried, to go where others feared to tread. It should also be noted that daring is not always what it appears to be. The Duke of Wellington appeared to be very daring, but he nearly always acted from certainty. He was certain he knew more than his opponent did. Wellington demonstrated time after time that effective daring entails preparedness.

Timing may not be everything, but it matters.

Daring and timing also go together. You can't seize the right opportunity at the wrong moment, nor will it hang around while you dither at the right moment. When daring is augmented by a shrewd sense of timing, a vision of the future unseen by others, ambition flourishes. When timing is augmented by the courage to persevere in the face of obstacles, achievement thrives.

But the big question, of course, is whether we ourselves can live up to these standards, all these maxims so easily prescribed for others. Vision, drive, opportunity—too often we own all the right assets but flinch at using them when it is time to put ourselves on the line. Once again, ambition dangles success before our eyes, but we lack the courage to pursue it. The risks, in the end, are just too risky. So we let another big one get away.

The angry regret that follows is pernicious. Any good opportunity attracts real risk-takers, invariably braver than we. And when they dare what we feared to try, reaping the rewards we should have reaped, we look for excuses. It was all dumb luck, we say, as if some divine fix were in. Or it was all connections: They just knew the right people. "Why play when the deck is stacked?" we ask in disingenuous response.

In our hearts, we know better. We know the truth of the Persian poet Omar Khayyám's famous passage in *The Rubaiyat*: "The saddest words of tongue or pen is that which might have been." Or to put it in the Brooklynese of Marlon Brando in the movie, *On the Waterfront*: "I couldda been a contenda."

But sometimes an opportunity is so powerful, so right in some large sense, that it cannot be denied. It waves away our fears and sweeps us into its orbit. Destiny commands, we follow.

We have already described Sam Walton's genius as a retailer, but, the fact is, had he not taken risks, his career would have been snuffed out before it truly took off. To the end of his life, Walton retained a clear memory of what happened.

"On July 2, 1962," he wrote, "we opened Wal-Mart No. 1 in Rogers, near Fayetteville, and not everybody was happy about it. Everybody who knew I was going ahead with the discounting idea really did think I'd just completely lost my mind. Nobody wanted to gamble on that first Wal-Mart. I think my brother Bud put in 3 percent and Don Whitaker—whom I'd hired to manage the store—put in 2 percent, and I had to put up 95 percent of the dollars. [My wife] Helen had to sign all the notes along with me and her statement allowed us to borrow more than I could have alone. We pledged houses and property, everything we had."

Business is risky. So is everything else that rewards those who dare against odds that turn back others. Consider all the bold characters who have seized opportunities in matters of art or spirit—like an obscure Alabaman named Martin Luther King, Jr., for instance. Until 1955, King was more or less content with his lot as a young Baptist minister in a black church in a white-ruled southern city. To be sure, he was deeply concerned about the inequalities that plagued the lives of black Americans. And he had read the works of the Indian leader Mohandas Gandhi as well as those of other advocates of change through nonviolence. But equally important, Martin Luther King, Jr., was a resident of Montgomery, capital of both Alabama and the Confederacy. As such, he knew that even peaceful protest would spark overpowering force and that the chances of success were slim.

Then came the startling rebellion of Rosa Parks, a black woman who refused to move to the back of a segregated city bus when ordered to give up her front seat to a white man. Parks was arrested for disorderly conduct. Inspired by her example, a black citizens' group called the Montgomery Improvement Association decided to protest her treatment by launching a boycott of the city's bus lines. Martin Luther King was asked to become president of the association and personally lead the boycott.

Unparalleled opportunity can force painful choices.

King, then twenty-six, faced a painful and altogether unexpected decision. Now safe and secure in his church, he would have to go public in a big way, risking his life and taking responsibility for those who followed him onto the battlefield. He pondered whether it was even appropriate for a man of the cloth to lead a secular protest. But all his misgivings paled beside the chance to serve his people. In the end, King felt he had no choice. "History," as he later put it, "has thrust something on me which I cannot turn away."

The boycott began in December 1955 and ended a year later with total victory: The bus lines were desegregated. And that was only the beginning. King's leadership riveted the nation, triggering a dozen other passive-resistance campaigns that dramatized the unresolved issue of racism and inspired new laws aimed at strengthening the rights of black Americans. Although racism was far from over, its existence as a national evil had at least been acknowledged, leading to a profound self-examination. And it was all because Rosa Parks forced Martin Luther King to heed his conscience. With newfound daring and instinctive timing, he then pursued an opportunity to help change his country for the better. King's remarkable achievement cost his life but left a legacy that was, perhaps, worth the price.

In business, as in society as a whole, opportunity can arrive unsought and unheralded, with its own weight of rich potential and incalculable risk. In general, opportunities arrive less dramatically. They simply appear in the achiever's environment, as the culmination of a variety of forces and trends. Thus, it usually takes many years of preparation, conscious or unconscious, to be able to see and seize a great opportunity. The more successful among us are, in fact, those who have a wealth of experience and knowledge to bring to the opportunity.

Robert Johnson, the founder, chairman, and chief executive officer of Black Entertainment Television, Inc. (BET), gained his key opportunity in just that way—as a payoff for patience, perception, and preparation. "There does come a time," he told us, "when you do see an opportunity, and you have to grab it. In the early 1980s, I saw that cable was going to become a major part of urban America. As a result, someone was going to provide black cable viewers with black-oriented programming, just as John H. Johnson [founder and publisher of *Ebony*] had provided black magazine readers with black articles, and black radio stations provided black music to black listeners. Someone who saw the potential audience for black television was going to act fast and first. Fortunately, I was in the right place at the right time." He continued, "The technology was evolving. The cable industry was ready to penetrate the urban markets, and the industry's need for a broad array of channels gave me that opportunity."

Robert Johnson took his idea to John Malone, now chairman and chief executive officer of Liberty Media Group, and Malone backed him. Was there any risk for Bob Johnson? Not in terms of making a living. At the time, he struck out on his own, Johnson had been a lobbyist for the cable industry for three years, and he reasoned that even if he failed as an entrepreneur, "I could always go to one of the cable operators and ask for a job. So the risk was not so much of being poor. It was a risk of not achieving the goals I had set for myself. I knew that if I didn't seize the moment," Johnson explained, "I would regret it. The fear of regret outweighed the fear of losing a job."

Ambitious achievers make
their own breaks.

When Johnson says he was in the right place at the right time, he means mentally, not just physically. His mind was in the right mode for him to act in the right way. In short, he was prepared. He was so prepared that, in effect, he invented the opportunity which he then seized. That is the essence of pulling off a coup in business or any other field. "You can't sit back and wait for breaks to come your way," says the actor Chuck Norris. "They don't happen by hoping. They happen because of positive actions."

John P. Mackey of Whole Foods Market, Inc., believes that "you create the opportunity through your desire and your vision. It isn't a reactive act. It is a very active, creative act. That doesn't mean that there isn't any luck or serendipity to it, because you can seize an opportunity that doesn't go anywhere.

"I am asked a lot of times if I thought that Whole Foods would grow this big when I started out. No. I didn't think so. I didn't calculate that there was a market opportunity for national organic foods or a demographic trend developing to back it up.

This may happen but it didn't happen in my case. I wanted to go into this business, and I created the opportunity."

Opportunity plays a different role in a big, established company, as Gary Wendt, former chief executive officer of GE Capital Services, points out. "I think in larger businesses, opportunity is more a matter of action than of creation," Wendt says. "We never had a shortage of ideas. But getting those ideas off the ground was something that took a particular talent. Business development was said to consist of the Four S's—search, start, support, scramble. Of these, the most important was to start. In big organizations, you have staff that tends to analyze and analyze."

"The fact is, you never know what the customer wants until you take the product to market," Wendt rightly observes. "What you need in the face of risk is the courage to say to yourself, 'I have to start. I don't have all the facts. There will be some risk but I have to start.'"

Ray Kroc was over fifty when he finally spotted the chance that would make him the country's master franchiser, the man who turned McDonald's Corporation into a worldwide household name. The fast-food chain now boasts some 25,000 restaurants worldwide and sales topping $9.92 billion annually.

A child of working-class parents in Chicago, Illinois, with only two years of high school, Kroc had been variously a failed music-store owner, an ambulance driver in World War I, a nightclub pianist, and for twenty-five long years, a salesman for Lily Cup Company, peddling wholesale paper products aimed at the growing fast-food business.

Kroc was a born salesman, cheerful and helpful, constantly suggesting ways for his customers to improve their businesses. He pointed out to the managers of Walgreen Company, for example, that, since their drugstore's soda-fountain operations were virtually deserted except at lunchtime, they could keep counter people busy and open a new profit line by selling takeout coffee in slack hours—in Kroc's Lily cups, of course. At first, the chain rejected the idea out of hand. Then, months later, somebody in the Walgreen hierarchy allowed one outlet to give Kroc's suggestion a try. Takeout coffee was a hit, for Walgreen's and for Kroc. It soon became a staple of business culture the world over.

During World War II, Kroc ran a small Chicago company that manufactured speedy electric mixers used for making ice cream sodas. When the wartime shortage of copper wire almost put him out of business, Kroc stayed afloat by selling sweetener additives as a replacement for rationed sugar. After the war, his mixer operation thrived again—until the 1950s, that is, when Americans began switching from drugstore milk shakes to soft ice cream sold by two franchised companies, Dairy Queen and Tastee Freeze.

By now, of necessity, Kroc had developed a keen eye for market changes. When he heard about a highly popular hamburger restaurant called McDonald's in San Bernardino, California, he flew there to check it out. At that now famous corner of Fourteenth and E Streets, he chatted with customers and took note of their enthusiasm for the place. The restaurant was immaculate, and the lines moved fast, even though the parking lot was jammed at mealtimes.

"This had to be the most amazing merchandising operation I had ever seen," Kroc later said. "In my motel room I did a lot of heavy thinking. . . . Visions of McDonald's restaurants dotting the country paraded through my brain." One week later, Kroc proposed himself to the founding McDonald brothers, Richard (Dick) and Maurice (Mac), as their national franchising agent.

The McDonald's opportunity was there for everyone to see. Ray Kroc recognized it, because he had been preparing for that moment all his life, through all the ups and downs of paper cups and electric mixers. In our terminology, Kroc was a Capitalizer. He saw an opportunity and seized it, partly because he had the school-of-hard-knocks smarts to do it but also because his fertile and restless cast of mind drove him on, continually, to envisage the next step up the arc of ambition.

There is another quality often exhibited by achievers: They think big when others still think small. They spot big trends— social, economic, demographic.

Trend spotting seems to be a learned skill, and one best honed by constant focus on new developments, sustained by a zest for catching the next wave early. This kind of achiever tends to be active, engaged, a master of what's happening.

The secret of trend-spotting achievers? A combination of sensing and superb timing. Knowing when to act doesn't come as a bolt from the blue. It is neither magic nor mysterious.

Achievers learn to use sharp senses to spot opportunity-laden trends.

Knowing when to act involves sensing. And sensing can be learned. What is important is being out in the world, ear to the ground, nose to the wind, eyes and mind open to signs and portents of what millions will care and talk about before it quite occurs to them to do so. We believe that you can train yourself to listen and watch—and then *act* on what you see and hear. The best place to start is to follow Peter Drucker's advice: "Walk in your marketplace."

As a model for study, we couldn't do better than the spectacular case of Robert Edward (Ted) Turner III, one of the great trend spotters of our time. Ted Turner, as we know him, is like a surfer who knows how to catch the big wave when it is just a little ripple out on the horizon. And over and over, he has had the courage to ride the wave when others feared they might crash.

Ted Turner has spent most of his now sixty-one years barely containing a head of intense emotional steam that has driven him to seize one big moment after another. He is a tenacious, turbulent man, the son of a tenacious, turbulent father. Ed Turner launched his own outdoor advertising business in Cincinnati, Ohio, where his son Ted was born, shortly before World War II. He rode his company upward to a sizeable fortune and then crashed in a tragic way that shaped his son's life forever.

Ted started selling advertising on his father's billboards when he was twenty-three. He did well. Then his father bought into a national company that fell on hard times. Ed Turner, alcoholic and depressed, arranged to sell his business and then committed suicide. Son Ted angrily faced down the buyers, rescinded the sale, and wound up owning his father's company, albeit with a crushing burden of debt.

Ted Turner's angry yet productive ambitions propelled him right past his competitors, as he retained a single-minded focus on winning and achieving his aims. Once he had his own business in order, he started buying other outdoor-advertising companies. Employees were both charmed and inspired by Turner. They loved his contagious enthusiasm, grandiose plans, and liberality with stock options. Those who didn't love him resented his occasional tantrums, but even they came around. Everyone knew Turner was juggling huge debts, but they also somehow sensed that he could master the use of debt to keep growing.

In 1968, Turner bought the first of three radio stations. Then television caught his attention, and he saw opportunities galore—a new advertising medium to explore, a new, fast-growing world to conquer. Ignoring unanimous opposition from his financial advisers, he plunked down $2.5 million to buy a debt-ridden UHF station, WJRJ, Channel 17, Atlanta, Georgia. With typical boldness, he changed the call letters to WTCG, for "Watch This Channel Go."

Turner kept the station alive by filling airtime with old movies and by covering the games of Atlanta Braves baseball games and Atlanta Hawks basketball games. "I don't know where I'm going," he told prospective employees, "but hang onto my coat-tails, and we'll get to the stars and the moon." On his moonward flight, alas, the station was devouring profits from his other company operations.

No matter.

Instead of pulling back, Turner again ignored his financial advisors and bought yet another television station, this one in Charlotte, North Carolina. He had to pay for it with his own money.

"I just love it when people say I can't do something," Turner says. "There's nothing that makes me feel better, because all my life people have said I wasn't going to make it. The secret of my success is this: Every time, I tried to go as far as I could. When I climbed the hills, I saw the mountains. Then I started climbing the mountains . . . ."

In 1973, WTCG made its first (small) profit. Then, in 1974, Ted Turner began negotiating for a hookup with RCA's satellite, Satcom I. Cable television was still only a blip on the commercial screen, but Turner, by this time, was like a surfer floating out from shore, watching and waiting for the next wave.

He figured that a satellite hookup would vastly increase his potential audience and that the $1 million price tag was a bargain. His advisers, of course, were against the deal, pointing out that he was gambling his precious, limited capital on viewers and advertisers who might well fail to materialize.

About that time, the Atlanta Braves were in the cellar, and the team's owners were conducting a fire sale with few bidders in sight. Viewing the Braves as one of his television station's key assets, Turner wasn't ready to see the franchise disappear. He bought the team with $1 million on his personal guarantee. "When you're little, you have to do crazy things," Turner said. "You just can't copy the big guys."

By 1977, Turner was getting sizeable himself, with an estimated worth of $100 million. Applying his unlimited energies to the world of big-time yachting, he gained national prominence by winning the America's Cup race.

Other, less ambitious types might have rested on their successes at this point. But no one would ever classify Ted Turner among the "less ambitious." Accordingly, he was preparing to embark on his riskiest gamble yet—an all-news, only-news cable channel.

Virtually everybody he knew and worked with thought he was headed for disaster. They didn't know that Turner had spotted another wave about to crest.

In those days, the three television networks controlled about 90 percent of the market. Families crowded around their sets each evening at seven o'clock to get their network news.

But Turner saw that the traditional family unit was rapidly changing. Mom and Dad were working different shifts. The number of single and divorced men and women was rising. Family life was more hectic and fragmented. At the same time, network news had created a hunger for graphic, life-as-it-happens reports that newspapers and magazines could not supply. Turner was the first to spot the new hunger for news at any hour, and he saw the opportunity awaiting the entrepreneur who could feed that hunger. He aimed to be that entrepreneur.

CNN's opening broadcast took place on Sunday, June 1, 1980. Turner put $34.5 million of his own money into the start-up. It was a catch-as-catch-can debut. When hookups failed, viewers found themselves staring at a blank screen. In its first year, CNN reached 1.7 million homes, a drop in the bucket compared to the network news' 76 million homes fed by the major networks. Yet, by the end of 1981, CNN was reaching 10 million homes. Today, it dominates broadcast news and is seen in 210 countries around the world.

Wave catchers don't quit just because they rode the big one. As a matter of fact, it just whets the appetite for more. So in 1988, Turner went on the air with cable station TNT—Turner Network Television—to meet what he perceived as a burgeoning demand for movies on television. To make it work, he paid $1.2 billion for the MGM/UA Entertainment Company's film library, taking on a crushing debt.

But once again, Ted Turner's far-reaching vision paid off his wager. By the end of the 1980s, Turner Broadcasting System was worth more than $5 billion. It was sold to media giant Time Warner Inc., in 1996 for $7.5 billion, and Ted Turner became one of the fifty richest people in the United States.

Sam Walton, Ray Kroc, and Ted Turner had the imagination—driven by ambition—to envision opportunities that others either missed or lacked the courage to pursue. They also had enough optimism to plunge into ventures that at first seemed distinctly unpromising. Of course, imagination and optimism require a firm foundation of knowledge—developed through experience—to uncover potential successes where others might see only trouble or disaster. And our trio of achievers had know-how in good measure. But overlaying all, these men had the courage to ignore critics and bet everything on their ability to turn dreams into reality. We believe that they dared because they were prepared.

That each acted at precisely the right moment was crucial, of course—the difference between an opportunity seized and an opportunity lost is not huge. Quite often, it is a matter of exerting just an ounce of courage at the precise moment when one little ounce can move a mountain or, in Napoléon Bonaparte's case, win a battle or even a war.

"I have observed that it is always these quarters of an hour that decide the fate of a battle," Napoléon Bonaparte once said. "In all battles, a moment occurs, when the bravest troops, after having made the greatest efforts, feel inclined to run. That terror proceeds from a want of confidence in their own courage; and it only requires a slight opportunity, a pretense, to restore confidence to them. The art is to give rise to the opportunity and to invent the pretense. At Arcola, I won the battle with twenty-five horsemen. I seized the moment of lassitude, gave every man a trumpet, and gained the day with this handful.

"You see that two armies are two bodies which meet and endeavor to frighten each other; a moment of panic occurs, and that moment must be turned to advantage. When a man has been present in many actions, he distinguishes that moment without difficulty: It is as easy as casting up an addition."

Opportunity is seized by those who stand always at the ready.

Experience—the kind gleaned from staying fully committed to your game, with senses in fine tune—is what alerts you to the moment when you must make your move.

Listen to what William Poduska, a computer-industry legend, had to say on the subject: "When opportunity knocks, I'm ready. I'm always ready to get in the game. Opportunities knock repeatedly, but each opportunity only knocks once. If you don't take it, it's gone. What I tell my colleagues and my children is, 'Boy, be ready.'"

Poduska started, among others, Apollo Computer, Inc., and Stellar Computer, Inc., the precursor of Advanced Visual Systems, Inc. His thoughts above are quoted from a memorable interview, summarizing Poduska's advice on opportunity.

Here's more from Poduska: "What it comes down to is you. There are no alibis; no tomorrows; no well, we would have, could have, should have done this, that, or the other. It either works or it doesn't, and every morning when you look in the mirror, you know why."

You are much more likely to be at the right place at the right time if you are constantly poking around, looking for openings, running small experiments to see what happens, forming relationships that open new permutations and combinations of possibility.

Expect the unexpected. Be prepared for anything. Assume that anything and everything is likely to be the right thing. With this attitude, reinforced by hard training, opportunity is greatly enhanced if never guaranteed. Remember: Even lightning isn't a random event. It strikes when conditions are right.

Consider the enormous fortunes now being amassed by Internet entrepreneurs who seem to be arriving out of nowhere, as if by spontaneous generation. Who *are* these people? Why are they so incredibly lucky when others are so deserving?

But, of course, it turns out that they were born to become what they are. They grew up mastering lore incomprehensible to others. Or (in a growing pattern) their long-honed skills in other fields suddenly became urgent needs for the Internet's pioneering companies.

The latter scenario describes Margaret C. Whitman, the chief executive officer of eBay, Inc. In case you are among the apparently dwindling few who have yet to visit its Web site, eBay is the on-line auction house, based in San Jose, California, that hordes of daily buyers and sellers consider the center of the universe.

eBay's global brand triumph—the company only started in 1995—is largely the work of Meg Whitman, an admitted novice at technology but an acknowledged whiz at brand building. Many have remarked that Whitman's arrival on the Internet scene is reminiscent of Ray Kroc's role in the 1960s, when he turned McDonald's into a global winner, even though he knew little or nothing about running a hamburger chain. Kroc was a classic Capitalizer. Meg Whitman is cut from the same mold.

Whitman grew up in a privileged enclave on Long Island's North Shore, light years from Silicon Valley in mind and spirit. Princeton University and Harvard Business School prepared her for a career that began at the Procter & Gamble Company.

Later she spent eight years learning brand promotion at the consulting firm of Bain & Company in Boston. In 1997, she was dutifully touting Teletubbies at toy maker Hasbro, Inc., when eBay investors sought a brand builder to help make the then-obscure company a household name on the way to taking it public.

Offered the post of chief executive officer, Whitman was at first dubious, then enchanted by eBay's mesmerizing effect on Web users. Millions were so addicted to on-line trading that promoting the company was a pleasure, she says.

On her first day on the job, Whitman also discovered the perils of success. eBay's Web site crashed for eight hours. Crashes may continue to be a problem as eBay confronts the ever mounting traffic of its avid customers. Meanwhile, Whitman has become a familiar television figure in eBay commercials, a frequent Washington lobbyist for Internet issues, and a lively cheerleader reaching out to eBay's distinct customer culture.

Competition is heating up, however. Yahoo and Amazon.com are moving in on eBay, hotly pursuing its most addicted traders. "The challenge," Whitman says, "is to reorganize your business every three months."

For Whitman, the rewards make that challenge appealing. Since eBay's $735 million stock offering in September 1999, the share price has risen more than 1,000 percent, boosting its market capitalization to $22.1 billion. As of June 1999, Whitman's own stock options were worth some $1.3 billion, collectible in 2003. Three years is an eternity in cyberspace, however, and no one can guarantee that the stock won't go down.

Either way, Meg Whitman epitomizes today's open-minded opportunist. A brand-new industry suddenly needed her particular skills, so she took a chance and jumped on board the Internet freight train. Win, lose, or draw, she is better off for having taken the chance of her life to gain experience not available anywhere else.

Looking back at the sudden opportunities thrust upon Thomas Jefferson and Martin Luther King, it seems fair to say that they were as much creatures of history as creators of it. Both men happened to be in the way when the whirlwind of history scooped them up and forced them to respond. When the call came, they had little or no time to consider it at length. Jefferson could not wait for constitutional authority to buy the future of his country. The opportunity would likely have vanished. Martin Luther King could hardly put off his decision to lead the fight for racial justice for a month or two while he canvassed church leaders.

Despite the rush of circumstances, each man was somehow prepared to make the right decision and move in the right direction. In each man, a combination of skill, experience, and temperament was at the ready for use when the situation demanded.

Readiness for greatness doesn't necessarily ensure a willingness to act, of course. We can only imagine how many scores of unknown Kings or Jeffersons flinched from challenge and will never be known. Their windows of opportunity slammed shut as soon as fate perceived their hesitation.

To be sure, for every angler who has successfully hooked the brown trout in the overfished stream, there are dozens who have come home with a creel full of nothing. Why do some strivers succeed and others fail? That is the topic of our next chapter.

5

History Is a Long List of Warnings About the Folly of Overreaching

Temper Ambition

~

Is there such a thing as too much ambition? Does it have limits? The short answer is yes. Ambition is the *sine qau non* of achievement, but unbridled, unmitigated ambition can lead to folly of historic magnitude. Witness the examples of Lawrence J. Ellison, William Jefferson Clinton, and Alfred J. Dunlap. Gary C. Wendt also sheds light on the subject.

FACED WITH HUGE RISKS promising even huger rewards—in sum, a breathtaking opportunity—how do most business people react? They brake to look for pitfalls. Caution prevails, often for far too long. And so, from big dreams, small acorns fall. Such is the course of ambition in most lives. But a few lives are extraordinary.

H. Wayne Huizenga is extraordinary. He may resemble any other sixty-year-old Florida businessman—friendly and unpretentious—but he is different. Aiming at businesses whose owners usually thought small—garbage collection, video rentals, used cars—Huizenga thought big, really big.

He builds giant businesses by consolidating fragmented industries in ways that better serve customers. He loves to create new entities. His ambition drives him into one new field after another, transforming tiny operations into major companies with nationwide markets. He can be compared—in another life and time— to William Crapo Durant, who consolidated a fragmented car industry into the behemoth General Motors, and to Rockefeller who did the same thing in the oil industry, creating Standard Oil.

Huizenga started in 1962 at the age of twenty-four when his father-in-law lent him $5,000 to buy a truck and begin collecting garbage in Pompano Beach. In his early career, he routinely collected garbage from 2 A.M. to noon, then changed into clean clothes to spend the rest of the day outwitting his competitors— scores of other small companies—by selling his collection services door-to-door.

Huizenga has attributed his success to being "in the right place at the right time." But a comment by an acquaintance from a rival corporation is more to the point: "Wayne grew because he worked the hardest and had the clearest vision."

What Huizenga envisioned was garbage consolidation—a single, efficient company owned and operated by him, the best collector of them all. He started buying up his competitors. By 1984, his Waste Management, Inc., was a $1 billion-a-year company—the biggest waste collector not only in Florida but in the United States.

Huizenga next bought controlling interest in a small chain of video stores called Blockbuster. He had sized up the fragmented video rental business, and it fit his formula. Building hundreds of new stores and buying thousands of competitors, he turned Blockbuster into the McDonald's of the video world and once again swept all before him.

Then his imagining eye fell upon retail auto sales, yet another fragmented business crying for consolidation. First he launched AutoNation, a national superstore chain selling used cars; next he built a cross-country chain of more than 400 new vehicle franchises (including twenty big Nissan dealerships) across the country, the nation's largest. Soon he added several car-rental companies (Alamo, CarTemps USA, and National), and built a finance company from scratch.

Huizenga has transformed classically small, local enterprises—the corner store, so to speak—into companies of national dimensions. His early beginnings in the humble business of garbage collecting and his unbridled ambition taught him how to transform small opportunities into big business.

Along the way, he has sometimes run afoul of sudden market changes. But Huizenga is a realist. He has always known when to bet, check, or pass. In fact, as we write this book, he has just put his car-rental business up for sale. Ambition has not yet to land him in any trouble he could not turn into triumph.

The ability to walk a high wire without falling—to risk all without failing—is rare in business or any other area. It is a matter of mastering one's limitations, of being neither cowed nor seduced by heady opportunity. By contrast, many star achievers begin to imagine they are invincible. They pay the big price of big success—self-delusion.

Unlike other creatures, human beings can both imagine the impossible and deny its impossibility in the same rush of ambition. We at once perceive and deceive all at once. We see an obstacle yet believe it doesn't matter.

Success ensnares as many achievers as it enriches.

Imagining and denying the impossible at the same time is a paradox that may be uniquely human. But knowledge doesn't always breed wisdom. Generation after generation reinvents folly. Year after year, success probably ensnares as many achievers as it enriches.

To be sure, prudence is not exactly a call to action, nor do we expect any pioneer to do anything with the word *caution* other than forget it.

But creation and consolidation are different stages. On the arc of ambition, there is a time to free your dreams for soaring and a later time to tether your dreams to reality. At some point, great innovations must become efficient operations—or die for lack of common sense grounded in practicality.

Shakespeare articulated this rule in his classic play *Hamlet,* when the protagonist directs his own little play onstage. Listen to Hamlet's admonition to his actors: ". . . in the very torrent, tempest, and . . . whirlwind of passion, you must acquire and beget a temperance that may give it smoothness." Such temperance is indeed what distinguishes true achievers from transient ones.

A startup business must be propelled by its founder's ambition, imagination, force of ego, perhaps even greed. But it can't succeed unless he or she pays attention to detail, to the nuts and bolts of delivering superior results day in and day out. Business is grounded in reality. Try telling your largest customer an order will be late because you aren't feeling inspired at the moment.

Or try telling your sales force that their jobs depend on 100 percent growth every year, and ignore how they achieve it. That was the error of Larry J. Ellison, cofounder, chairman, and chief executive officer of Oracle Corporation, the giant of database software.

Ellison is noted for seeing what he wants to see, a trait that has propelled him up and down and up, rising and falling and rising again like a yo-yo of the software industry. Ellison has overcome obstacles that would have been the end of any less driven achiever. But hard experience has also inclined him to revise the truth and then believe the revision. This gift/habit has served him for good and ill.

Back in the early 1980s, Ellison and a small band of fellow Oracle techies pioneered the concept of relational databases, which allowed the user to store data in one form and then recall it in another. Ellison sold the idea to two hot prospects: the Central Intelligence Agency and the United States Navy.

Only then did Oracle get around to creating a product. The strategy worked. Soon Ellison was running a half-billion-dollar company with 1,000 employees serving clients in fifty companies.

He was also fixated on besting his perceived nemesis, Microsoft Corporation's Bill Gates. To that end, Ellison sought to impress Wall Street investors by racking up 100 percent annual growth. He did it—mainly by doubling the size of Oracle's sales force every year, while turning a blind eye to quality control and customer service. As a result, some Oracle sales people began reporting fictitious sales to fictitious customers and pocketing big commissions they didn't deserve.

In early 1990, a straitlaced accountant named Stephen Imbler joined Oracle and quickly tracked $15 million in false sales. In the end, Ellison agreed to tell stockholders that Oracle had a "revenue recognition problem," which necessitated revised balance sheets and caused Oracle to post a $34 million loss.

In March 1990, Oracle stock began plunging from a high of $28.38 a share to an eventual $4.78. Angry stockholders sued, alleging that Oracle insiders had sold their own stock at the high just before the crash. Oracle eventually had to settle one suit for $24 million.

All this forced Oracle to lay off more than 400 people. Ellison's personal worth (nearly all Oracle stock) shrank from $954 million to an un-Gates-like $164 million. Fortunately, he has since instituted numerous reforms, notably good accounting and good customer service.

Oracle is still not the fount of innovation that Ellison wants it to be. But in 1999 it grossed $8.8 billion as the world's largest supplier of database management and services. And Ellison hasn't remotely stopped dreaming. As he recently put it, "Today we are the Number Two software maker in the world. Microsoft is Number One. We'd like to turn that around."

Genius and pragmatism must co-star lest growth derail the rising arc of ambition.

The need for realism and discipline in times of giddy growth is why many great organizations, from Hewlett-Packard Company to Microsoft, are founded by two complementary achievers—one who is the creative genius and one who handles the more pragmatic side of things.

Growth is the life force of ambition. We all want more—more recognition, more money, more power, more pleasure. Loath though we may be to admit it, however, growth has its limits. Those who violate the limits get punished.

So what are the limits of growth? In nature, examples abound. The blue whale and the brontosaurus aren't just the largest creatures that ever existed. They are two of the largest creatures that ever could exist. Laws of physics, mathematics, and the geometry of space ultimately limit the size any living organism can attain.

In human affairs, fewer limits exist—the mind is a magnificent tapestry capable of incorporating the theory of quantum mechanics, the paintings of Mark Rothko, the writings of Virginia Woolf, the infinite realm of cyberspace. Right now, scientists are again pushing the limits by striving to map the entire human genome, the chromosomal code that defines human beings. When first announced, this goal seemed like such an enormous dream that only a few experts considered it even possible. And, yet, as of this writing the project will be completed in less than a year, with surely profound consequences for science and technology.

Our imaginations routinely defy limits—and occasionally we demonstrate an almost miraculous ability to transform that defiance into performance. For generations, running a mile in under four minutes seemed beyond human capabilities. In fact, it became a symbol of man's limits. Then on May 6, 1954, in Oxford, England, the great English runner Roger Bannister—driven as much by his imagination as by his body—ran a mile in 3 minutes, 59.4 seconds.

For Alexander the Great, the insurmountable obstacles included the Zagros Mountains of Persia and the Sinai Desert, barriers that had effectively stopped all conquerors before him. With an imagination backed by fierce will, Alexander—like Bannister—performed the seemingly impossible and built an empire that covered the Middle East, from Greece and Egypt in the west to India in the east.

But humans aren't exempt from nature's laws of growth, much as we assume we are, and the perilous course of overpopulation in underdeveloped countries reinforces all those pessimists who have scheduled and rescheduled Armageddon for era after era. On the other hand, humans constantly demonstrate an apparently limitless ability to find or invent new resources and to recycle old ones. Indeed, the richest 15 percent of the world's inhabitants, meaning the United States and Europe, might well see the population crunch as an incredible opportunity to redistribute resources and achieve both profit and stability in the process.

Today's business world provides examples of attempts to create the hitherto impossible—the recent mergers of CitiCorp, Inc., and the Travelers Group to create Citigroup, Inc., of the British Petroleum Company, Plc., and Amoco Corporation to form BP-Amoco, Plc., and of Exxon Corporation and Mobil Corporation to create Exxon Mobil Corporation portend organizations of a size previously considered not viable. Will the world of commerce be able to support these behemoths? Are they the shape of the twenty-first-century organization? Or will they be ungainly, unable to ward off nimble competitors a tenth their size? In business circles, there is an intriguing new mantra, "It's not just that the big will eat the small. It's that the fast will also eat the slow."

Ambition is often
undone by greed.

For every success story of overcoming limits, from Wayne Huizenga to the Genome Project, there exists a corresponding cautionary tale. Greed and megalomania—common human failings—are often ambition's undoing. One need look no further than Washington, D.C., circa 1996 for a striking example of grandiosity run amok—and its consequences.

Speaker Newton Leroy Gingrich—who had led House Republicans to a victory of stunning and historic proportions only two years earlier—later admitted that he childishly shut down the United States government because he had been requested to exit the president's jetliner, Air Force One, by the back door. After the press reported his tantrum, Gingrich's public-approval ratings never exceeded 30 percent and usually hovered in the high teens. Although Newt Gingrich had once envisioned himself as president, this fiercely ambitious politician was permanently damaged. He was forced to resign when members of his own party refused to support him for another term as speaker.

As if in bipartisan support of political stupidity, President William Jefferson Clinton allowed his libido to rule his brain in undertaking his rash affair with Monica Lewinsky. Although he survived House impeachment by winning Senate acquittal, Clinton's indiscretion did him irreparable damage. In addition to paying a high marital price, he managed to alienate millions who had genuinely admired his presidency and to incline future historians to question his character. One can almost hear his regrets echoing over the next century.

Overreaching achievers ultimately encourage inertia among the less ambitious.

High achievers who overreach and fail damage more than their own careers. They contribute to the ambivalence we feel about ambition. They subvert one of the key human assets, the drive to create new things and improve old ones. And when the mighty fall by their own hands, both the fearful and the envious are encouraged to rationalize their own inertia. Human enterprise is the ultimate loser.

There may be no fool like a political fool, but every field (academia, the media, entertainment) has its megalomaniacs, and business is no exception. The most chilling recent example of business-world grandiosity is Albert J. "Chainsaw" Dunlap. This once acclaimed manager first attracted media attention when he took over the troubled Scott Paper Company and performed the dirty but necessary deed of firing some several thousand employees.

Success went to his head. When the directors of the Sunbeam Corporation hired him to cure their even sicker company, Dunlap again slashed the payroll but started loving his power. Reveling in his ruthless image, he even produced a boastful autobiography titled *Mean Business*. But few complained—not when the stock price kept on climbing.

To maintain the momentum, though, Dunlap allegedly began cheating. Sunbeam engaged in secret bill-and-hold deals with retailers: It sold products at large discounts but then held them at third-party warehouses for delivery later. By booking these sales before the goods were delivered, Sunbeam reportedly boosted revenues by 18 percent in 1997. In effect, it was shifting sales from future quarters to current ones.

Dunlap didn't inform his board, let alone his shareholders. In spring 1998, an audit unmasked the deception. In a June 9, 1998, board meeting that one director later described as "surreal," Dunlap was confronted and became so emotional that board members feared for his stability. Four days later, he was fired.

Dunlap's behavior may seem extreme, to say nothing of self-destructive, but greed and overreaching does occur in the executive suite. They can harm any company that chooses to overlook inevitable clashes between hubris and honesty.

Consider the close call that Salomon Brothers suffered in 1991. United States Treasury Department regulations limit any one company from purchasing more than 35 percent of the Treasury securities being offered at a given auction. On more than one occasion in 1990 and 1991, Salomon's hard-driving managing director Paul W. Mozer bought Salomon's 35 percent allotment and then made separate bids under the names of certain Salomon customers—without their knowledge or authorization. Then Mozer put the securities these phantom bidders had supposedly won into Salomon's account. His illegal actions came within an inch of bringing down the entire $150 billion-a-year firm. Only intervention by the investment tycoon (and Salomon director) Warren E. Buffett kept the firm afloat.

Achievers are at risk of drowning in egotism.

In truth, there is a little of Dunlap and Mozer in most of us. Achievers tend to be gifted, dynamic people who have earned their large egos. Self-knowledge can be low on their list of priorities. It ought to be at the top.

Harold S. Geneen, former chairman and chief executive officer of ITT, Inc., believed that "the worst disease that can afflict business executives in their work is not, as popularly supposed, alcoholism . . . it's egotism. The egotist may walk and talk and smile like everyone else," Geneen said. "Still, he is impaired as much by his narcissism as the alcoholic is by his martinis."

The danger of excess, of going too far beyond some ideal line, moral or material, has concerned humanity for millennia. Our moral history, as we noted in the title of this chapter, is a long list of warnings about the folly of overreaching. These cautions range from Buddha's admonition that desire causes suffering to Adam and Eve's expulsion from Eden for disobeying God, a sin that doomed humankind to earn its bread by the sweat of its brow. "Pride goeth before a fall," warns Old Testament Christianity. In Greek mythology, Prometheus offended the gods by giving fire to humans. His punishment was to be chained to a rock and have his liver pecked by a buzzard—forever.

Classic Greek tragedy was built around the concept of hubris—overweening pride, spiritual gluttony inviting retribution. The Chinese philosopher Confucius stressed a dynamic harmony and said that disruption of that harmony led to disease, disorder, and doom. Kautilya, or Chanakya, minister to the Indian king Chandragupta Maurya, and often called the Niccolo Machiavelli of ancient India, cautioned rulers not to pursue every victory, that some battles weren't worth fighting. And every culture has proverbs advising us not to bite off more than we can chew.

History provides innumerable examples of suicidal overreaching. After the Napoléonic Wars of 1805, 1806, and 1807, Napoléon Bonaparte ruled virtually the entire European continent. That wasn't enough. Ambition tricked him into thinking he could conquer the entire vastness of mighty Russia. Like Adolf Hitler a century and a half later, Napoléon failed to recognize what he was up against. Overconfidence numbed his sense of self-preservation. And so, in 1812, Napoléon invaded Russia, and that winter his army suffered disastrous defeat, decimated as much by the cold as by the Russian forces. By ignoring the obvious realities of climate, this brilliant general went up against natural law—and lost. Hubris can be as blinding as the equator's noonday sun.

How do we push beyond perceived limits and yet not exceed our limits?

Devise a checklist of dream-killing realities.

Gary C. Wendt, the former chairman and chief executive officer of GE Capital Services (General Electric Company's financial services arm) is a master at balancing ambition and reality. He believed that companies can be highly successful whatever their size provided they maintain a sense of equilibrium. Under Wendt, GE Capital grew at a spectacular 20 percent a year and relentlessly pursued other companies in accordance with Wendt's mantra, "More markets, more products."

However, Wendt was careful to recognize and manage the limits of growth. He argued that these limits differ for every company. Many find it hard to raise capital, for example, whereas GE Capital had "so much money we can't use it up fast enough," Wendt once said. But he developed a reality checklist that he integrated into his entire operation. It included the following items.

Time. "I spend a lot of time taking care of shareholders, the people who own us," he said, speaking before his resignation.

"We need approval for every major move. Just to buy some tin mine in Australia, we have to go ask someone." Meaning a big someone, General Electric. The result was that Wendt often found himself with too little time to study the good ideas his people generated, all of which needed his approval before they could be launched. How will your ambitions be affected by time limitations? There are only so many hours in a day, and decisions made after forty-eight sleepless hours are rarely solid ones. Time may be an ambitious person's scarcest resource. And never having quite enough time leads to impatience, corner-cutting, and potentially critical misjudgments.

Talent. "I can't find enough good people I trust—repeat trust—who can run newly acquired businesses all over the world, often in exotic cultures, while still working within my organization," Wendt lamented. "As [the] Coca Cola [Company] proves, single-product businesses with universal appeal work fine anywhere. But things get complex," he went on, "when you move beyond simple operations and acquire businesses attuned to local cultures and markets. I can't just send people across the globe and say do whatever feels right. You need people with the ability to quickly grasp and adapt to the realities of a foreign country. That's where truly gifted managers are scarce." Lack of talented people endangers ambitious leaders in other ways, we believe. For example, they tend to start doing too much on their own, thereby spreading themselves too thin and allowing things to slip through the cracks because no one is paying attention.

Momentum. "When managers no longer have a vision—a purpose they preach to their people and a passion to carry it out—

they go stale and begin doing the same thing over and over," Wendt said. "That's when you know they've lost their zest, their ability to excite others. They've reached their peak and begun coasting. Momentum stops dead in its tracks. Whatever they're responsible for will stop growing until you replace them." Even the most ambitious people may lose energy—the infectious force that keeps them going and allows them to exhort others. Such a loss can't be allowed: Momentum is too important. What enables some people to maintain energy is their inner conviction in the importance of what they are doing, or the sheer pleasure they take in doing it.

Risk.   "Like all financial-services companies, we're sensitive to risk," Wendt observed. "But the bigger and more diverse we get, the harder it is to judge risk. That's what I lose sleep over. Take one that blew up on us—automobile leasing. We had a great business financing those leases. One year it hit $350 million, but next year it plunged to $90 million. Reason? We thought car leasing was risk-free because of the combination of the lease revenue and the price we sold the car for at the end of the lease. It didn't work that way. We leased too many cars just as the automakers overproduced and unloaded inventory. Today you can lease a new Jeep Cherokee for less than we have to charge for leasing a two-year-old one coming back to us. Beyond this particular mistake, which we'll soon write off, risk is a chronic problem. It gets bigger as you grow, but you can't grow unless you keep moving into new areas that pose new risks." No enterprise is risk-free. On the other hand, risk is a great adrenaline booster. Gary Wendt's performance at GE Capital is a model of how to calmly balance ambition and realism amid the pressures of a high-risk business.

History is littered with defunct organizations that failed to sustain ambition's friends, such as talent, trust, judgment, and momentum, while succumbing to its enemies, notably greed, egotism, distrust, and expediency.

Consider this tiny sampling: the Roman Empire, the British Empire, the Third Reich, the Soviet Union, the United States Army in Vietnam, the Nixon White House, and Japan, Inc. Scores of others could be added.

Whatever happened to all these once vibrant entities and all their once ambitious participants? Surely none of them courted disaster, or remotely expected it. Yet, all of them, however different in other ways, were accidents waiting to happen.

Why? Because arrogance snuffed out their ability to see danger ahead. They scoffed at anyone who resented their high-handedness. They dismissed warning signs and consequences. They expected to dominate their worlds forever. But, suddenly, they were like a car that loses its headlights while speeding down a mountain road on a dark night. These once vibrant entities succumbed to blinding ambition.

The theme of this chapter, temper ambition, should not be misunderstood as a plug for humility or even modesty—admirable as those virtues may be. In our view, ambition clearly needs a certain immodesty, although a little goes a long way.

> *For ambition to survive,*
> *a sense of balance is needed.*

What ambition does need in order to save itself from excess is a sense of balance. The Greeks are thought to have invented not only the concept of hubris but also its antidote—that is, the habit of seeing things as parts of a whole, of never forgetting that because everything is interdependent, whatever gets too far out of line is bound to incite countervailing power and probable retribution. The Greeks had a firmer grasp of this perspective than we do. After all, they originated the root word for ecology.

But we need not rely only on Greek wisdom to save ambition from itself. Twenty centuries of wrenching human experience confirm that moderation usually outlives extremism. To that end, let ambitious leaders get everybody's blood racing for some exciting purpose, but never forget to respect all hands at all levels, and especially to share the rewards of power.

Focus your ambition on benefiting others, not just yourself, and you're most likely to escape the trap of overreaching. Happy is the achiever who creates a worthy purpose and then delivers on it. How you might reach that crucial level in your own ascent of the arc of ambition is the subject of our next chapter.

6

Greatness Must Be Driven by a Purpose Beyond Money

*Inspire with a
Greater Purpose*

~

People who reach exceptional heights may differ from each other, but one thing they all share is a clear goal born of some organizing purpose that summons their talents, aims their efforts, and steers them in the right direction. A compelling purpose is the ambitious person's true north, keeping him or her on course. What kind of purpose is worth pursuing? The most satisfying purpose empowers its pursuer to enlist others in a quest for some higher good. In this chapter, we examine several achievers and their inspiring causes—Cesar Chavez, Mohandas K. Gandhi, Giuseppe Garibaldi, and Robert B. Shapiro.

THOSE IN HOT PURSUIT of an ambitious goal seldom pause for self-analysis. Introspection is distracting, as Hamlet reminds us. Even so, it may be that an unexamined ambition isn't worth achieving. A pause to check your direction can improve self-knowledge. Best of all, it helps ensure that your purpose is compelling, realistic, effective. Like a pilot's checklist, these are must-confirm items.

Like ambition itself, a purpose is both the goal you strive for and the goad that animates and disciplines your efforts. Pursuing it flat-out makes you purposeful in the best sense. You need a strong purpose for the obvious reason that you need a valued cause to guide you through adversity. The right purpose works like a ship's gyroscope, holding a steady course in the roughest seas.

But a "right" purpose is more than a stabilizing guide to action. It should enrich life, give it meaning—preferably a meaning higher than becoming the wealthiest person in town or the company's chief executive officer, heady as that may feel.

The right purpose for the right meaning goes beyond personal glory or power. How? By its appeal to others. The right purpose can get many people working together for a vital cause that gives all of them a new sense of meaning.

The need for meaning drives achievement.

The need for meaning drives every human to create, to build, to pursue achievement. At one time or another, most people also yearn for a purpose larger than solving their own problems, especially when those seem insoluble. Hence, the enormous appeal of a worthwhile cause.

Casting aside the negatives in one's life, one joins others in doing something positive, something bigger and nobler than oneself. To join others in such a cause is transformative. It offers the rare feeling of being selfless, and solidarity for a greater purpose can be thrilling.

Of course, it can also be cruel and destructive. The dynamic just described is so powerful that it can animate all sorts of hatreds—ethnic, tribal, religious—to say nothing of world wars in which all sides consider themselves defenders of decency and justice. Even so, the inspiration of working for some higher good is the source of human greatness, indeed, of civilization.

The more you heighten your purpose, the more you can inspire others to invest themselves in your dream. By "heighten," though, we refer to purposes that benefit people rather than destroy perceived enemies, that do good rather than evil, that make all hands feel they have left at least one corner of the world a better place.

Just as a fresh tide lifts all boats, so a worthy purpose evokes everyone's best instincts. And what is genuinely good for society (in a moral or material sense) is likely to spin off an institution that outlasts its founder and bequeaths his or her heirs, followers, or employees the same passions that drove the founder's own quest for excellence.

The most successful people in history have been utterly committed to their work, yet not so grimly intense as to alienate their followers. Many have looked upon their goals as a kind of calling and exuded a sense of mission. A charmed few have also gained enough confidence to share their emotions with others and to treat people with that seductive mix of grace and generosity we call charisma.

Your purpose need not be extravagant or all-encompassing.

But you don't need a fancy purpose to leave something transcendent that people will admire long after your departure. Your gift to the world might be an honest car dealership, the greatest little diner, or a highly reliable hardware store, all of them social institutions in your town. It could be a child who overcomes barriers to learning. It could be a fount of consumer value, like the local J. C. Penney or Wal-Mart store, dedicated to everyday prices for everyday goods. It could be Howard Schultz's Starbucks, gentrifying the old corner coffee shop and liberalizing labor relations in an illiberal field. On the other hand, your legacy could also be as big as such things get—let's say a company aimed at literally saving the world.

That is the unembarrassed purpose of Robert B. Shapiro, chairman and chief executive officer of the Monsanto Company, the former chemical maker now emerging as a powerhouse of biotechnology. Shapiro is an unusual industrialist, known for thinking big and carrying a small ego.

In 1994, he focused on the harsh probability that the world's current population—5.8 billion, one quarter of them in abject poverty—will roughly double in thirty to fifty years. Calling in his best and brightest from Monsanto's global branches, Shapiro asked them to analyze the implications and suggest what Monsanto should do for both the planet and itself.

As a result, Shapiro sold Monsanto's core business—its $2.7 billion chemicals division—and reinvented the company as a pioneering researcher into biotechnology applications in agriculture, health, and nutrition. The purpose is to provide some new solutions to humankind's central problem: The earth's environment is already overused and cannot handle twice as many people. "There is no more land," Shapiro says. "The land has been used."

Of the many challenges ahead, Shapiro highlights four:

- Most of the world's additional people will be born in the poorest places. To grow food, they will slash and burn land; when crops dwindle, they will seek nonexistent jobs in increasingly overpopulated cities.
- Developing countries will seek to improve lives by re-capitulating the industrial revolution—a fabulous success for the world's wealthiest nations, but a model so wasteful and polluting that expanding it will permanently damage the ecosystems on which all life depends.
- Rich countries will pay an ironic price for affluence—more and more people will live far longer and therefore require unprecedented medical care on a scale increasingly beyond those countries' means. Who will pay the health costs for increasing numbers of aging North Americans, Europeans, Australians, and New Zealanders? The young who still work and pay taxes? Don't hold your breath.
- Shapiro says that none of these issues can be adequately addressed with existing technologies, which cause "destructive subsistence, destructive development, and destructive affluence." Example: For a 98-pound woman

to drive herself to work in a two-and-a-half-ton Toyota Land Cruiser is a ludicrous waste of resources. Example: The earth is losing about 25 billion tons of topsoil a year. Floods, construction, manmade erosion, and chemicals are destroying this crucial food source much faster than it's being created. To produce one ton of soybeans, Brazilian farmers lose five tons of topsoil a year. If you fly over the Mississippi Delta, you can see much of Iowa gushing into the Gulf of Mexico.

Bad as all this is now, what happens in a world with twice as many people and a quantum leap in ecological damage?

Shapiro argues that "we as a species . . . [must] reinvent the technologies by which we feed, clothe, and house ourselves." It is no longer feasible "to use enormous quantities of stuff in order to create modest economic value . . . The trick is going to be to multiply value to people to enable them to lead better lives, without multiplying stuff."

Shapiro sees evolving answers in information technology, biotechnology, and nanotechnology, the new science of miniaturization. All three maximize value while minimizing environmental impact.

Consider what's involved in sending letters the familiar way. Trees have to be cut to make paper; the writer has to type a physical object, which is then transported by air, rail, and truck between various depositaries from which it's eventually walked to the recipient's mail slot.

By contrast, e-mail is instantaneous and requires nothing more than a silent movement of cheap, renewable electrons. E-mail is what Shapiro calls "scale-neutral." It doesn't require heavy machinery. Like smart seeds versus dumb tractors, e-mail gets huge results with minimal efforts.

Monsanto is now focused on bioengineering to create new food, health, and nutrition products aimed at "sustainable development," meaning impact-free ways to run the human household. For example, the company has already reengineered the potato, altering its DNA to produce a spud with more starch and less water content, thus sharply reducing the saturated fat in French fries. Monsanto has also developed cotton plants genetically instructed to protect against harmful insects. In just a couple of years, these plants have reduced pesticide usage in cotton fields by 60 percent or more.

For Robert Shapiro, these are small steps toward what he hopes will become a vastly more benign and well-run human society. Well aware that bioengineering may have unintended effects requiring appropriate caution, he guards against "the sin of hubris" and ponders the follies it may strew in his successors' path.

Some people believe that parts of Shapiro's dream are more marketing than a greater purpose. But we see his ambition as authentic. Whatever its results, Shapiro will have bequeathed a singularly big purpose—a far bigger ambition than most people ever dream up, much less carry out. After all, how many companies get a chance to save the world? As cosmic as Shapiro's purpose may sound, history is full of examples of people who have dedicated their lives to a similar great purpose, such as transforming a nation or creating a country.

Consider Giuseppe Garibaldi, the nineteenth-century Italian patriot and revolutionary. Not only in his lifetime but to this day, he was and is Italy's greatest hero. Hardly a city in Italy is without its Garibaldi statue or its Via Garibaldi. There is good reason. Garibaldi spent nearly every waking minute of his adult life pursuing the cause of *Italia Unita*—Italian unification—and his devotion to this cause was almost saintly.

Born in 1807 into a family of northern Italian seafarers, Garibaldi went to sea at seventeen and soon began absorbing nationalist ideas. Italy was then ruled by Bourbon kings in the south, the Papal States in the center, Austria in the north, and the royal House of Savoy in the northeast. But a determined minority, persecuted as much for its republican ideals as for its nationalism, was gaining strength, and small uprisings on behalf of Italian unification occurred throughout the country. Garibaldi joined a nationalist group in 1833.

Already suspect for his proselytizing among sailors, he was condemned to death and forced to flee Italy. Making his way to South America, he spent the next thirteen years gaining experience as a guerrilla, fighting for various independence movements. In 1848, with revolution breaking out all over Europe, he returned to Italy.

Garibaldi organized a small force of 500 men and began pitting his guerrilla skills against the Austrians in northern Italy. Soon he was so admired by the general populace that when he reached Venice to aid an uprising there, he was greeted by a torchlight procession. He won more fame when he miraculously extracted his troops from Rome after an uprising there failed.

A *purposeful ambition survives* *even great hardship.*

Once again, Garibaldi was forced into exile. He worked as a candle maker in New York, then moved to Chile to take command of a small trading ship. He sailed from one Pacific port to another but never relinquished his ambition for a unified Italy. To a friend he wrote that he was "terrified at the likely prospect of never again wielding a sword in her name."

He need not have worried. In the 1850s, with 1,000 volunteers in tow, Garibaldi sailed from Genoa intending to wrest Sicily from the Bourbon king of Naples. A ragtag group of idealists with little if any military training, his troops were dedicated to Garibaldi's goal of unification, and to Garibaldi. After landing, they marched across the island toward Palermo, the capital, joined by hundreds of peasants.

At the town of Calatafirmi, Garibaldi met determined opposition from Neapolitan troops, but when one of his aides suggested withdrawing, he replied: "Here we shall make Italy—or die." Waving his sword and under heavy enemy fire, Garibaldi led his troops to the top of a steep hill and won the battle.

Word spread quickly. At the next town, jubilant crowds fell on their knees before their hero. In Palermo, the 20,000-man Neapolitan army was waiting. Outnumbered and outgunned, Garibaldi still managed to push the enemy back, forcing the Neapolitans to seek a truce and, eventually, to withdraw from Sicily.

Life's turning points reveal an ambitious person's true purpose.

In the interests of unification, always his prime concern, Garibaldi handed over Sicily and Naples to the king of Piedmont. Better proof of his dedication to a greater purpose would be hard to imagine. Unlike most power seekers, Garibaldi did not use his victories as a springboard to make himself undisputed ruler of a unified Italy. He used them to ensure a unified nation in which he could simply be another citizen.

Such turning points reveal an ambitious person's true purpose. Some go for personal glory; others for a greater glory. It is the latter that ensures the admiration and respect of future generations.

Full Italian unification was completed in 1871 and a government was established in Rome, with Garibaldi as a member of the Parliament. It had taken more than four decades, and he had faced death time after time, but Garibaldi had persevered in a purpose larger than himself. He was a hero, yes, but more important, he had helped to create a nation for millions of others.

What helps achievers like Garibaldi persevere is clearly their attachment to a higher cause, one so animating that, for them, life without it would have been unimaginable. Moreover, they are reinforced by their ability to share this excitement with others. They know they can't achieve their ambitions alone. No one can: Even solo artists need patrons.

They also know or soon learn that nothing attracts dedicated supporters better than a truly selfless higher purpose. A chance to do good can be a powerful recruiter. Those who sign up tend to be especially strong, ever ready to rally around in adverse circumstances.

This may seem counterintuitive in our sometimes narcissistic era, but the appeal of selflessness has been pivotal in the creation of every great movement, nation, and religion. The dynamic remains unchanged: Finding at least some committed supporters is remarkably easy when you are clearly driven by a higher purpose.

Some years ago, our friend Peter Drucker wrote about the unnoticed magnitude of the volunteer economy in the United States. How many of us are involved in charitable activities or other social causes, even though we are working flat-out in our professional lives? Why do we do it? Because it fills us with a sense of purpose.

Many people find purpose both within and outside their work. And for some people, when work becomes problematic or loses its sense of purpose, they put intensity into other causes. We have a friend who was working seventy hours a week at what was then Digital Equipment Corporation (DEC). The company was experiencing extreme business difficulties, putting tremendous pressure upon her and others at work. Yet she found great meaning by volunteering an extra five hours at a nearby soup kitchen.

When the stress of a particular project at DEC seemed to become unbearable, we asked her why she didn't give up the soup kitchen and get more time for herself. She replied that the volunteer work was too important to her sense of belonging to the community. So she went to the soup kitchen—and she stayed up until three in the morning completing new marketing materials for a fund-raising campaign that she had volunteered to design.

Perhaps all great selfless leaders are essentially volunteers writ large. They volunteer not only their time but their very lives in pursuit of a goal that attracts others willing to give themselves with equal devotion. History keeps repeating this pattern.

Just two years before Garibaldi's vision became a reality, for example, Mohandas Karamchand Gandhi was born near Bombay in the Gujarat region of India. Like Garibaldi, he would devote his life to a revolutionary purpose and suffer on its behalf. Unlike the Italian warrior, Gandhi would pursue his goal through nonviolent means.

Gandhi's early years carried no hint of potential greatness. After an arranged marriage in prepuberty (he was thirteen), he drifted through school, eventually studied law in England and became a certified barrister at twenty-two. Back in India, he spent three years vainly seeking work as a barrister and helping with menial tasks in his older brother's office.

In 1893, an Indian businessman, a member of the large Indian population in South Africa, needed an English-speaking barrister to handle a lawsuit. He hired Gandhi. In pursuit of the case, Gandhi boarded a train to Pretoria, in the Boer province of the Transvaal.

Despite his first-class ticket, Gandhi was ordered to move to the car for "colored" people. When he protested, a policeman threw him off the train. That night, sitting in the waiting room of a train station in South Africa, Gandhi started on the crusade that would transform India. Then and there, he vowed to dedicate his life to ending discrimination of every kind.

Issues of human dignity stir the soul to higher purpose.

Gandhi had thereby picked one of the great issues of human fulfillment, most of which (freedom, justice, equality, expression) involve the fundamental right to individual dignity. Nothing seems to win our support more than an unselfish battle against some unjust deprivation of human dignity.

We have always celebrated such causes, ranging from the creation of Greek democracy in place of tyrants to the focus of World War II on erasing Nazism from the human condition. With their battles against racism and foreign subjugation, Garibaldi and Gandhi are squarely in the tradition of great causes that summon humanity's best instincts.

Gandhi spent the next ten years defending the rights of Indians living in South Africa. He began by organizing opposition to a bill in the Natal provincial legislature aimed at disenfranchising the colony's 40,000 Indian residents. The law passed, but Gandhi went on combating racial discrimination. He founded the Natal Indian Congress to fight for the rights of Indian workers.

In letters to the local paper, he asked white readers nagging questions: "Will you re-read your New Testament? Will you ponder over your attitude towards the colored population of the Colony?"

This tactic reflected one of the less noticed powers of a higher purpose. If the cause is basically irrefutable, as in the fight against racism, it will always secretly impress a small core of potential sympathizers within the oppressors' ranks.

That they even exist, in turn, helps validate the cause in the eyes of its less brave supporters. If those seeming enemies can see things our way, a leader can say, then someday the rest are bound to follow. Moreover, such covert sympathizers often belong to an educated elite that rules an oppressive society and may potentially lead it to change.

At the same time, Gandhi tried to persuade Indians both in Africa and back home to disavow the traditional Hindu caste system, a birth-based pecking order that kept the poor in poverty and the lowest of the low, the so-called Untouchables, in misery.

Gandhi's consistency in fighting oppression by anybody, including his own people, earned him great credibility and respect for his greater purpose. The world increasingly perceived him as a freedom fighter in the largest sense of the term.

All through these years, Gandhi remained loyal to the British Empire, even organizing an ambulance corps to aid British troops during the South African Boer War. But in 1906 he had enough. He announced that he would no longer obey laws directed against Asians. Thousands of Indians rallied to his civil disobedience campaign; he was twice imprisoned.

By the time he returned to India in 1914, Gandhi had a huge following there not only because of his courageous leadership against discrimination but also because of his devotion and his conviction that a return to traditional handicrafts and away from industrialism was the path of righteousness for his nation. This latter stand was not so much one against industrialism per se as it was an anticolonial protest, aimed at freeing Indian enterprise from British domination serving British needs. Gandhi's insistence on homespun cloth and homemade salt was more a symbolic appeal to Indians, urging them to determine their own economic needs, than it was a vote against the industry that eventual independence would obviously require. To that end, he became convinced that India must achieve at least partial independence from Britain, and he began a momentous drive for home rule.

Gandhi helped organize the Indian National Congress party in 1919, and the next year he led a nonviolent campaign asking Indians to boycott British goods, as well as the courts and government. As a result, he was again imprisoned, this time for two years.

During World War II, Gandhi demanded complete independence for India as a reward for its contributions to Britain's war effort. And it came to pass in 1947, with the partition of the country to create the two nations of India and Pakistan, Hindu and Moslem.

One of Gandhi's most powerful weapons was his willingness to starve himself so that the eyes of the world would focus on his country's struggle for independence. But he also fasted to pursue his goal of erasing discrimination in all its forms. In

1932, for example, he fasted for twenty-one days trying to convince Hindus that "the blight of Untouchability" should be ended. He fasted again to halt the rioting in New Delhi and Calcutta that followed partition.

Known universally as the *Mahatma*—the great soul—Gandhi won the support of millions for his humane, peaceable goals. Despite constant setbacks, sacrifice, and suffering, he hewed to his greater purpose and carried his nation to freedom. And he inspired other leaders around the world, including Martin Luther King, Jr., to pursue freedom through civil disobedience and other nonviolent means.

For leaders in every field, that sense of mission, of a greater purpose, can be expressed in a variety of ways, all legitimate as long as they are unequivocally selfless. Garibaldi exemplified the bulldog tenacity of an honest revolutionary. Gandhi displayed the often cunning purity of an Asian leader skilled in teaching millions how to conquer the mighty British Empire.

Like so many successful leaders before them, Garibaldi and Gandhi motivated others to join their cause by offering them a larger, inspired vision of the world as they saw it, the world as it could be. A sense of purpose, as Garibaldi and Gandhi showed us, leads to great achievements that benefit society far and wide.

Consider the story of a penniless young Mexican American, born in Arizona in 1927. He was a farmer's son who was forced to quit school in the sixth grade and support his family as a preteen migrant worker. His name, Cesar Chavez, is now synonymous with the cause of farmworkers. After serving his rather indifferent country in the wartime United States Navy, he began devoting his life to helping other migrant workers achieve fair treatment by those who abused them—their employers, plus all manner of police, welfare officials, and immigration agents.

Soon, Chavez had a dream: Organize a farmworkers' union empowering migrant workers to seek their rightful share of the richest agricultural bounty on earth. Many laughed; it was an impossible dream, at best an invitation for agri-tycoons to crush Chavez & Co. like a plague of boll weevils.

Chavez persisted. By 1965 he was running the nationally known United Farm Workers Union (UFWU). Its clearly greater purpose was supported by numerous church groups and sympathetic politicians, including Robert F. Kennedy.

When big farmers refused to recognize the union and its 300-mile march on Sacramento failed to impress them, Chavez organized a nationwide consumers' boycott of California table grapes—the biggest such boycott in the history of the United States.

It worked. In 1970, most grape growers signed union contracts, freeing the UFWU to organize the nation's pickers of everything else, from lettuce to oranges.

Chavez, who died in 1993, achieved his greater purpose in part by cultivating a remarkably pure reputation. He insisted on non-violence, no matter how well armed the forces against him. He hired interracial organizers, not just Mexican Americans. And he limited his union salary to $900 a month, a virtually unique vow of poverty compared with other union leaders prone to feed on their members' dues. His biggest achievement, however, was to prevail over universal doubt and prove that farmworkers could not only get organized but actually win their fight for equal justice.

We expect people in public life to be driven by greater purpose, although unfortunately some are not. For those of us who pursue a life in business, there is equally the need to define the nature of our greater purpose. B. C. Forbes wrote in the first issue of the magazine he founded, "Business was originated to produce happiness, not to pile up millions." Although this definition may seem a little naive in a more cynical age, it has a message that is worthy of examination.

Whether you are looking for a greater purpose as an individual or to bring others to your cause, we have found eight ways that may help you elevate your ambition:

- *One, achieve excellence in whatever you do.* Individual achievers—artists, athletes, adventurers—almost always seek to excel in what they do. They seek recognition for their performance. Imbuing a company with the same sense of excellence is more challenging, however.

  Many Creators do succeed in convincing their organizations—and their customers—that the company's service or product is the very best. When Steve Reinemund, Chairman and chief executive officer of PepsiCo, Inc.'s Frito Lay division, talks about a Dorito chip, for instance, you might think he is describing a piece of art, not a crunchy snack. Creating a consistently high-quality product is central to Frito Lay's purpose.

  When Xerox Corporation managers speak of printing, you might believe that every sheet is a masterpiece. Like the people at Frito Lay, they share a value about quality. When a company succeeds in instilling a deeply shared purpose, that purpose transcends the original founder and lives on as a company tradition.

  It is, by the way, usually the company founder—a Creator in our terms—who first establishes a higher purpose, a belief in, say, excellent quality. And it is often a Consolidator—a person who is overly focused on making the numbers—who kills it. That is because excellence requires a constant focus and can't take a back seat to another purpose, such as numbers on a profit-and-loss statement.

- *Two, create great value.* People who seek to create excellence typically create great value as well. There is a close relationship between value and quality. Take the founders of Wal-Mart Stores, Inc., Staples, Inc., and Home Depot, Inc. In building their companies, they all recognized the need for excellence, while remaining relentlessly focused on creating great value for their customers. And when the sense of excellence and value is so strong as to take the form of consumer activism, then the organization's higher purpose can be seen in its extraordinary level of customer service.

  Wal-Mart, Staples, and Home Depot all take pride in the combination of product quality, customer value, and service that they deliver. But then as the late Sam Walton said, "We exist to provide value to our customers, which means that, in addition to quality and service, we have to save them money. Every time Wal-Mart spends one dollar foolishly, it comes right out of our customers' pockets. Every time we save them a dollar, that puts us one more step ahead of the competition—which is where we always plan to be."

- *Three, empower the individual.* Empowerment allows people to achieve their own dreams, to exercise their human potential, to exceed previous limitations. Individual achievers generally have no problem in feeling empowered. They know that they are on their own to succeed or fail.

  But for the last ten years, there has also been a popular management movement to "empower" individuals in larger companies. It is rooted in the belief that customers and companies are better served when people are allowed to make decisions on their own based on the facts as they see them. As one manager told us, "when intelligent people are given the right information, they will make the right decision."

But a greater purpose is achieved when a company can produce a service or product that empowers its customers. Few examples of this kind of empowerment exist. Steven P. Jobs and Apple Computer, Inc., provide a notable representation.

Apple's Creators saw their machines not just as computing devices but as a way for people to create and learn on their own and then to share that learning. So the Apple operating system was designed from the start to facilitate such creativity and learning. Apple machines became the favorite devices for most artists and designers and the computer of choice for many classrooms. Apple's commitment to the empowerment of its customers provided a handsome return when loyal followers helped to sustain it through difficult times.

- *Four, improve the human condition.* Thousands of individual achievers dedicate themselves to this worthy cause. Health care professionals, teachers, religious and social workers, and, yes, even politicians find a greater purpose in working for the betterment of humanity. Many do it quietly, recognized only by those people whom they directly help. Others—like the late Mother Teresa of Calcutta—achieve an almost mythical status.

A greater humanitarian purpose is what drives health care organizations, schools, colleges, universities, and government agencies. It is unusual, however, to find a profit-making corporation putting concern for the human condition at the forefront of its endeavors. Pharmaceutical companies are a notable exception. That's why we consider the case of Robert Shapiro and Monsanto also to be exceptional.

• *Five, create fun and pleasure.* Celebrated individual performers almost always bring great pleasure to their audiences. But it takes a unique personality to build an organization that continuously delivers fun to its customers. Walt Disney was just such a person, and the organization he built, of course, is the Walt Disney Company.

Walt's amazing imagination—hand-in-hand with his perfectionism—perhaps brought more enjoyment to audiences than any other moviemaker before or since. And the Disney Company has continued to further its founder's purpose of giving customers the best possible entertainment by making sure that everything that emerges from the studio lives up to the highest standards of production.

Excellence in entertainment is the higher purpose for Disney. Walt's standards and his values continue to serve as a guiding influence thirty-three years after his death. The trust that audiences place in the Disney product is indicative of the company's achievement.

Other entertainment executives have created great production companies or studios, too, of course. Louis B. Mayer, George Lucas, and Steven Spielberg are some of the names that come to mind. But as every director knows, a permanent tension eventually develops as the creative process and the process of making money begin to come into conflict.

The tension can actually be healthy for a company, as long as the Capitalizers who typically run the major television networks and cable production companies recognize that there will be no profits unless the greater purpose of creating fun and pleasure for audiences is maintained. When the purpose of these companies becomes purely profits, the work of an original Creator is subverted, and the company begins a decline.

- *Six, invent the future.* To discuss inventing the future, we might look to the past for examples, men like Thomas Alva Edison, Guglielmo Marconi, and the Texan Willis H. Carrier. They were men who believed in the benefits that science and engineering could bring to the public good.

Marconi, of course, gave us wireless telegraphy and went on to win the Nobel Prize in physics in 1909. Carrier is—or should be—revered by anyone who works in a warm climate. The Texan invented the air conditioner and founded the Carrier Engineering Company. Now the Carrier Corporation, a subsidiary of United Technologies, Inc., it is still the world's leading maker of this great boon to humankind.

Thomas Alva Edison's multiple inventions—he acquired some 1,093 patents in his eighty-four years—had an immeasurable impact on humankind and the practical course of daily life and are reflected in the General Electric Company's slogan, "We bring good things to life." Those words eloquently exemplify our phrase, "invent the future," which Edison did almost single-hand-

edly with his electric light bulb, sound recording devices, motion picture projector, and alkaline storage bat-
tery, to name but a few of his remarkable achievements.

In every age, inventions change the way we live and
work. And in every age, including the current one, inventions can lift humankind to a higher purpose. Today,
we have the inspiring example of Walter H. Gilbert, who
won the Nobel Prize for inventing the technique to se-
quence genes. He was among the ten founding scientists of the biotechnology company Biogen N.V., which
was created to exploit the myriad applications of genetic
engineering. Although Biogen under Gilbert's leadership
as chief executive officer was unable to successfully
commercialize many of its initial ideas, Gilbert paved
the way for the exploitation of biotechnology in fields
ranging from pharmaceuticals to agriculture.

- *Seven, use profits for the public good.* The use of private
profits to promote the public good is a controversial
topic among business people today. The conflict usually
focuses on—and this is especially true in large publicly
held companies—whether profits should be reserved ex-
clusively for the benefit of shareholders. We believe
shareholders enjoy long-term benefits when a company
exercises a public conscience and shares some of its
success and wealth.

Examples of ambitious achievers who believe as we do
include Bennett Cohen and Jerry Greenfield, founders
of Ben and Jerry's Homemade, Inc., and Anita Roddick,
founder of The Body Shop International PLC. In the
business world, these three are sometimes looked on
with raised brow—in part because of the sums they

have spent on their larger public purpose and also because their profits have sometimes fallen below shareholder expectations.

Such situations have led us to postulate a principle about using profits for the public good: Taking care of the world is commendable, as long as you also take good care of your shareholders. In order to allocate funds to pay for your greater purposes, you may have to work harder to achieve a better performance in your business.

- *Eight, improve the environment.* There is probably no more public example of someone who has focused on the environment than Tom Chappell. His "Tom's of Maine" line of products—everything from soap to toothpaste—contains no ingredients that can damage our environment. Chappell founded his company on the belief that people and nature deserve respect. In framing his greater purpose and imbuing the company with a sense of his mission, Chappell has strengthened both the organization and its ties to him as its founder. He has persevered in his policies despite pressure to relax his strict standards for his products.

We agree that Chappell's accomplishment is to be devoutly wished for. Unhappily, it is far from automatic. Many people yield to the temptation to forget about greater purposes and the value system that supports them when it becomes inconvenient to do otherwise. Experience suggests that moral restraint is prone to evaporate whenever impulse is free to thumb its nose at consequences. It happens in business; it happens in politics and every other form of human activity.

But that doesn't mean we should give up. Far from it. People like Tom Chappell—and Robert Shapiro of

Monsanto, for that matter—remind us of our responsibility to the environment. They challenge us to do likewise.

What is it, then, that keeps businesspeople, politicians, and other ambitious achievers true to their chosen paths of higher purpose? They are imbued with a sense of purpose born out of an understanding of society's needs and a deeply held conviction that each of us is in some way responsible for the greater good of society.

This sense of purpose can often take the form of financial support of the environment, of culture, or of education. And all of us are beneficiaries of the greater purposes pursued by such achievers, past and present. They have nourished our minds, our bodies, and our souls.

Today, when the media is focused on celebrity wealth, it often seems harder and harder to find people, both in public and private life, who are driven by anything other than personal gain. And so we become cynical about ambition itself, especially when there seem to be few limits on what are acceptable methods and means for pursuing these selfish goals.

But we say, take heart. Life's most enduring achievements are clearly driven, as this chapter illustrates, by a sense of purpose, a mission bent on giving something back to society. There are Garibaldis among us yet today. They share with those who have gone before the desire to lead lives with rich meaning.

The truth is, as we said at the beginning of this book, you get more if you give more. So add your name to the rolls of people who live life with purpose.

In the next chapter, we argue with equal conviction that ambition is best realized when achievers are guided by strong values.

7

Compromise Is
Bad for Ambition

Never Violate Values

~

As an ambitious person striving in a complex
world, you inevitably face right versus wrong
dilemmas. The right decision may be costly; the
wrong may be easy. Take our advice: Your integrity is too precious to squander on short-term
gains. When you violate moral or ethical values
you claim to believe in, you are headed for a slip-
pery slope, sliding from bad to worse. Self-
betrayal is a recipe for failure. In every field, successful people are those who live by their values.
Consider the examples of Arjuna, Andrew S.
Grove, John R. Lewis, Azim Premji, and Diego
Rivera.

O N   A   W A R M ,   S U N N Y   D A Y   in the fall of 1989, Georgia
Congressman John R. Lewis arrived in Montgomery, Alabama. He was there as an honored guest at the dedication of a
memorial to the civil rights movement.

Inevitably, he recalled an earlier visit. It was May 20, 1961,
when he rode into town from Birmingham on a bus, one of a
group of students, black and white, who were known as Freedom Riders. These men and women were challenging racial segregation laws, and they expected a hostile, even abusive
reception. But they weren't prepared for the viciousness and ha-
tred that awaited them at the downtown Montgomery bus
depot.

On the bus trip, they were accompanied by Floyd Mann, the
state's public safety commissioner, a committed segregationist
but just as committed to upholding the law—all of it. Montgomery's police chief had assured Mann that all would be
peaceful.

But when the bus arrived, a crowd of screaming, threatening
whites—including children as young as ten—rushed toward the
Freedom Riders' bus. More than three decades later, in the
spring of 1999, Representative Lewis described the onrush.

"Men, women and children. Dozens of them. Hundreds of
them. Out of alleys, out of side streets, around the corners of office buildings, they emerged from everywhere," he says, "all at
once, as if they'd been let out of a gate."

The crowd turned on two of the young black students, knock-
ing them to the ground. One was William Barbee, the other
John Lewis. At the time, both were students at the American

Baptist College, a theological seminary in Nashville, Tennessee, and both were adherents of the nonviolent philosophy of Mohandas Gandhi.

Soon Barbee and Lewis were lying unconscious on the asphalt. Lewis later said, "Everything turned white for an instant, then black."

*The strength of long-held moral values
prompts right actions even
when one might least expect it.*

Some three hundred people in the crowd attacked and mauled eighteen Freedom Riders as local police stood and watched. Then Floyd Mann, the state officer, marched straight into the screaming, hate-driven crowd toward Lewis and Barbee's attackers. He was no supporter of integration, but the local police had double-crossed him. And perhaps more importantly, Mann could not tolerate the lawless mob. "We're going to keep law and order here," he yelled, pulling out his pistol. "There'll be no killing here today."

When some of the crowd ignored him, Mann sent two shots up into the air. He put his gun to one's man's head and declared, "One more swing, and you're a dead man." The surly crowd moved back.

Save for Floyd Mann's actions, Bill Barbee and John Lewis would certainly have been severely injured, if not killed.

It was twenty-eight years later when Congressman John Lewis returned for the dedication of the memorial. Erected in the shadow of Alabama's Capitol, in front of the Southern Poverty Law Center, the black granite is inscribed with the names of those who lost their lives in the civil rights battles of the 1960s.

A thin sheet of water runs over the surface of the monument, as if to wash away the horrors of the past.

While waiting for the dedication ceremony to begin, John Lewis was approached by an older man. He looked familiar, but Lewis could not place him. "You're John Lewis, aren't you?" the older man asked. "I remember you from the Freedom Rides."

For another instant, Lewis's mind was blank, and then, suddenly, he recognized the man. The face and voice belonged to Floyd Mann, who had stood up to the howling mob.

"You saved my life," Lewis said, overcome with emotion. He held out his arms, and the two men embraced. Letting go of one another, Mann looked at Lewis and said, "You know . . . I'm right proud of your career."

It was a dazzling moment of reconciliation.

The two men had stood on opposite sides of a bitter struggle, separated by the realities of the segregated South. Mann had believed in the laws of segregation and was sworn to uphold them. Lewis had put his life on the line to change those laws.

Yet, the two men shared a basic decency, a respect for human life. In 1961, that sense of decency and his belief in the need for law led Floyd Mann to save the Freedom Riders. By 1989, he had also come to share Lewis's commitment to racial equality. In one sense, Mann had changed dramatically, but, in fact, he had never changed his bedrock values. He remained true to himself whatever the circumstances.

Floyd Mann is a living example of the wisdom Shakespeare expressed through Hamlet's words five centuries ago: "This above all: To thine own self be true/And it must follow, as the night the day,/Thou canst not then be false to any man."

In all walks of life, people behave not simply in response to pain or pleasure, fear or hunger, powerful as those stimuli may be. At the most important moments, people behave largely according to their fundamental beliefs and values. These criteria govern our relationships, both in terms of what we expect of others and what we expect of ourselves. They set the limits of what we can tolerate in the way we treat other people and in the way they treat us. They help us draw a line between moral and immoral conduct.

Because beliefs and values are a reflection of the things we hold most dear, the things we are willing to fight for, they define us to the point that we may become literally indistinguishable from our values.

Strong values can help establish business purpose.

It is plain to see that not all businesses are governed by moral values of the kind we are discussing. Yet, sometimes in business, beliefs about quality and excellence can be so strong that they take on a moral quality. Amorality and profit are not incongruous concepts. On the other hand, there is no question that strong moral values spur a business to treat its customers fairly and help it earn their loyalty in return. Such values also determine a company's behavior with regard to issues of quality, innovation, and the environment. In short, they fit hand in glove with individual or corporate purposes.

It can be hard to hold onto values when all around you others think differently. But if you violate these values in the pursuit of ambition, your trustworthiness becomes suspect. When you allow these values to be violated in an enterprise you are building, its performance is likely to decline.

But achievers we admire have a firm value system that puts a limit on what they are willing to do to realize their ambitions.

These admirable people also make sure that their personal values permeate their organizations.

Any number of leading organizations have developed explicit, written statements of values. They may be called "our basic beliefs," "our code of conduct," or something similar. Whatever they are called, the statements put limits on the means an organization can use to achieve its business ambitions. They are intended to guide all workers in their daily dealings and to help them resolve potential value conflicts.

Ethical conflicts are not insoluble dilemmas.

Dealing with ethical conflicts is no abstract exercise. What, for example, should a company do when a highly valued executive is discovered taking favors, however minor, from a vendor seeking more orders, or is abusive to an employee, or is found to have lied about his background? It is a blatant violation of the company's stated values. But the executive is almost irreplaceable. What to do? Fire him or her? Doing nothing is unthinkable. Losing a talented person is unappealing. Yet, a slap on the wrist will make a mockery of the company's rules and raise serious questions about what the company truly believes in.

It is all about values, and value dilemmas force ambitious leaders to make uncomfortable, risky decisions that can derail their careers. Honesty or acts of humanity can throw up roadblocks alongside what would otherwise be a road to easy profits. Doing the right thing at a high cost can be a task worthy of Solomon.

When moral dilemmas take stage center, the financial penalties of a principled decision are often sky-high. Doing the right thing is apt to cost money—and lots of it. What's more, it can be almost impossible to quantify the advantages of preserving a company's image and reputation.

Leaders have no trouble calculating the cost of recalling a product. It is bound to be huge—far bigger, in fact, than the harm (in monetary terms) the product may actually do if not recalled. But doing nothing could also trigger the even bigger price tag of the loss of public trust. Moral puzzles like this can't be wished away. Do managers really want to spend millions to correct an error that may affect only a handful of people? Can they defend to their directors a decision to sacrifice current profits for incalculable goodwill?

If morality seems expensive, consider the even higher cost of immorality.

A pause for reflection: Is it possible these are the wrong questions? Morality is expensive, but immorality is not cheap, either. In the long run, immorality may cost the earth and destroy a company in the process.

Take it as a maxim of corporate wisdom: Never let money muddy your concern for your company's integrity. This is the perspective we heard not long ago from Azim Premji, one of modern India's most thoughtful industrialists. "Once you start calculating the numbers," he told us, "it is almost a foregone conclusion that you will end up compromising your values."

If Dhirubhai H. Ambani is the overachiever of India's industrial age, Azim Premji may well be the overachiever of India's information age. As chairman of Wipro, Premji has transformed a traditional industrial enterprise into one of India's fastest growing and most successful software development companies.

Headquartered in Bangalore, the Silicon Valley of India, Wipro has been growing at about 50 percent in revenues and net income throughout the 1990s. The darling of Dalal Street (India's equivalent of Wall Street), Wipro now has a market value in excess of $5 billion. As 80 percent owner of this enterprise, Azim Premji has become one of India's richest men, and some reporters have dubbed him the Indian Bill Gates.

Unparalleled integrity need not be at odds with uncommon success.

What makes Azim Premji's accomplishments even more remarkable is that he enjoys a reputation for unparalleled integrity in Indian business circles. In a country where corruption is commonplace and most leaders are expected to be corrupt, Azim Premji stands out for having held fast to a higher set of values.

Premji inherited his family business under adverse circumstances. When he was only twenty-one and still a student at Stanford University in Palo Alto, California, his father died unexpectedly. Premji had to abandon his studies and rush home to run the family business. What he discovered was a virtually insolvent enterprise because his father had been so preoccupied with various social and civic obligations that he had neglected his business.

With his mother's help, Premji set about fixing the business. Early on, he resolved to build an enterprise that was based on strong moral values. "I had seen such hard times," he says, "that I wanted to build something that would have the strongest foundation possible. I wanted it to be pure. Initially, it was almost an aesthetic sensibility. Only later did I realize what a powerful business advantage integrity could be."

To build a foundation of integrity, Premji has displayed uncommon rectitude in the face of misdeeds that other Indian managers generally ignore. For example, one of Wipro's union leaders submitted an expense account for first-class travel, to which he was entitled. It turned out that he had actually traveled second class and pocketed the difference.

By Indian standards, this was the pettiest of petty graft. But not in Premji's eyes: He fired the man forthwith. He was not about to let someone in a leadership position set such an example. It was a costly decision. Wipro took its first-ever union strike at its corporate office. The strike lasted four weeks and caused much disruption. No matter. Premji would not relent.

Premji's insistence on integrity is not restricted to blue-collar workers. Early in his career, he fired two of the company's five top executives because they failed to live up to his standards of integrity. "They were highly performing executives," he told us, "and losing them was not easy because of the difficulties the business was in. Yet, we got rid of them. It was one of the most difficult yet important decisions I made early in my career."

Premji has also never allowed himself to get dragged into the bribery that infects much of Indian bureaucracy. He has refused to pay bribes to government officials—on occasion at considerable cost to the firm. In one case, a government official put up some bureaucratic roadblocks that threatened to delay a shipment of computer hardware during the last quarter of the year. He demanded a bribe of half a million rupees (about $11,500). Premji refused to pay.

The official knew that if the shipment was delayed until the next fiscal year, Wipro's customers would be unable to depreciate their orders. As the corrupt official expected, Wipro's customers were irate. They threatened to cancel their orders if they didn't get their deliveries on time, and in many cases did. Some of Premji's senior managers buckled under the constant haranguing by their customers and asked him to reconsider his decision. He still stuck to his principles. The whole incident cost Wipro approximately $4 million in lost profits (more than 260 times the bribe being demanded).

In yet another bribery situation, Premji faced down the New Delhi bureaucrats who issue the interminable licenses necessary to do business in a country that has sometimes been accused of having replaced the British Raj with the License Raj. "When we initially refused to pay the bribes the license people demanded, we were met with disbelief," Premji relates. "The bureaucrats thought we were bluffing. They couldn't believe we were serious. It took them a long time to accept that we were in fact dead serious about our integrity. It has cost us some time and some opportunities," he admits. "We still have a lower batting average than some others, but we are able to do business with integrity."

> *Once your strength of character is known,*
> *others will flock to your side,*
> *sometimes from the most unexpected places.*

When we asked Premji how he is able to do business at all, he replied: "Most people overlook two important things. One, there are always a few people, even in the Indian government, who share your sense of integrity. If you have integrity, you will find them and they will find you. They then become your champions and advocates and help you get what you want. Two, even corrupt people understand how to prioritize their time. They know who will pay them off and who will not. After a while, if they recognize that you are in the latter category, they stop asking and just give you what you need so that they can focus their energies where there is more likely to be a payoff."

What about the cost of all this straight shooting? Rather than being "a drag," Premji says, "I believe that our reputation for integrity has been a huge competitive advantage. It helps us have much more trusting relationships with all our stakeholders, and that greatly reduces the transaction costs of doing business. It has been a huge asset when we have competed for business in international markets. It has allowed major firms to overcome their hesitancy in doing business with a foreign vendor. It has also been an enormous source of free advertising. It has gotten us accolades that are disproportionate to our achievements relative to our competitors. I deeply believe that one of the reasons why we trade at a multiple that is higher than our closest competitors is precisely because of the reputation we have for being true to our values. Quite beside these corporate benefits, there are personal benefits. You sleep better. You wake up in the morning and look yourself in the mirror and feel good. You don't have to keep looking over your shoulder."

The final question we asked Premji was how he was able to maintain this sense of integrity throughout the organization. How did he discover infractions? His reply was this: "An organization with high integrity has a very different muscle tone. In such a company you discover infractions very quickly—everyone has pride in the reputation they have built for themselves and the company. They are just as determined as you to prevent a few rotten apples from spoiling the organization's reputation. The thing you have to do is be a clear role model. That has a massive multiplier effect. If you can be trusted to adhere to the values you have espoused, you will be surprised how many people can be trusted to do the same. But if you slip or compromise, the whole thing unravels quickly."

We think Azim Premji has got it exactly right.

At Intel Corporation, the world's biggest chip maker, in Santa Clara, California, is no stranger to the paradoxical difficulties a moral dilemma produces. A crisis a few years back brought its then chairman and chief executive officer, Andrew S. Grove, and his organization face to face with some tough values issues.

In November 1994, a report circulating on the Internet disclosed that a mathematician had discovered a flaw in Intel's Pentium processor. The company, still growing by 30 percent a year, had invested heavily in the processor, its newest product. Advertising flooded the media, and the company's four plants around the world were geared up to churn out the processor as fast as possible. Now, chat rooms across the planet were buzzing with talk of the processor's problems.

Intel itself had actually discovered the flaw a few months earlier. The problem was located in a part of the chip known as the floating point unit (FPU), and it affected abstruse mathematical calculations. The company's tests showed that the error occurred once every 9 billion times in a calculation. Not exactly a big deal, Grove and his team decided, and they pushed ahead with the chip and its promotion.

Even the most highly principled people sometimes make a wrong turn.

Here was a highly principled and widely admired leader who, when confronted with one of those muddy values decisions, initially came down on the wrong side. The cost of halting the Pentium campaign and production while the flaw was being corrected would clearly be tremendous. On the other hand, the number of people who would be affected by the flaw was miniscule. The eventual benefits to be gained by taking the high ground were incalculable but probably minimal.

What seemed so logical and right to Grove's mind turned out to be all wrong once the story broke. As news of the Pentium flaw moved from the Internet to the trade press and beyond, Andy Grove began to have second thoughts. He later recalled, "I've been around this industry for thirty years and at Intel since its inception, and I have survived some very difficult business situations, but this was different. It was much harsher than the others. In fact, it was unlike any of the others at every step. It was unfamiliar and rough territory."

Intel's reputation was taking a terrible beating. If the processor had this one flaw that the company chose not to disclose, who was to say that there might not be other flaws? Each of them might be small in Intel's eyes, but one of them might just affect you in the middle of a big project. The trust people once had in the Intel name was leaking away like helium in a rubber balloon.

Something had to be done.

Grove's first impulse, naturally, was to replace the chips only for that handful of customers whose calculations might be affected by the flawed microprocessor. On the face of it, fair enough, but, once again, it was a decision that failed to reflect the company's value system. It was an engineer's approach, oblivious of the power of imagery and a reputation for integrity in the marketplace.

As a supplier of chips to the computer manufacturers, Intel traditionally had little concern about—or direct involvement with—the public. Now, all that changed as individual computer owners bombarded the company with irate letters and calls. Employees from all divisions of the company became volunteer telephone operators.

Then the International Business Machines Corporation announced that it would no longer ship personal computers run by Pentium microprocessors. This was Big Blue talking. IBM's vote of no confidence was devastating.

When you rediscover your values, wrong choices can be reversed.

Grove saw what he had been missing before. He reversed his position, announcing his decision to replace each and every one of its shipped chips. It was a major undertaking. "We developed a logistics system," Grove recalls, "to track these hundreds of thousands of chips coming and going. We created a service network to handle the physical replacement for people who did not want to do it themselves." When the six-week-long crisis was over, the company took a write-off of $475 million.

It was money well spent, both for the crisis it ended and the lessons it taught. For all his technological smarts, power, and success, Andy Grove now understood that his company was nothing without public confidence. Many ambitious achievers never learn that lesson until it is too late.

Long after the smoke cleared, Grove shared another lesson that he, personally, had taken away from the experience. For companies facing similar response-to-crisis dilemmas, he said, "your tendency will almost always be to wait too long. Yet, the consequences of being early are less onerous than the consequences of being late. If you act too early, chances are the momentum of your previous business is still healthy . . . [but] even if you're wrong, you're in a better position to correct course."

In our work, we are seeing an increased awareness of the importance of keeping true to values. Although it is still difficult to quantify the benefit of doing the right thing, the cost of not doing it is becoming more visible. That cost is compounded by the speed of communications, notably the Internet, which makes it ever harder to keep bad news out of circulation.

But we also believe that even among ambitious achievers, there is a renewed belief in integrity and morality. At Viacom, Inc., for example, movie producers and directors are now encouraged to address the moral issues of the day no less attentively than the imperatives of the bottom line.

Listen to what Viacom's chairman and chief executive officer, Sumner M. Redstone, says about values: "All too often we use spreadsheets and stock prices as our compass, instead of looking to our sense of humanity to guide our judgment. The bottom line may be the nature of the beast, but as Katherine Hepburn says in *The African Queen,* 'Nature is what we have been put in this world to rise above.'"

Ethical awareness is also a way of life at Nordstrom, Inc., where employees are indoctrinated in a value system that puts customer service above all other considerations.

The same goes for Levi Strauss & Company, where profit is pursued, but within the context of the organization's dedication to human values. "We've all heard the expression that the business of business is business," explains Robert Haas, Levi Strauss chairman and chief executive officer. "In my view, that's unrealistic, and it's entirely too narrow. Business exists in the context of society. For a business to prosper, we need to help that vital, vibrant society."

Haas points out that you can't be a successful downtown retailer if there is crime in the streets and people don't come into the city to shop. You can't win in global markets if workers aren't educated.

"We can't get the full energies of our people," he says, "if they're dealing with health problems, a chemical dependency, or child-care worries."

> *Look for a pragmatic solution when*
> *it seems that one moral imperative must*
> *be sacrificed to another.*

The tension between money and morals, profit and principle, is as old as humankind, and it is ever-present in the affairs of individuals as well as organizations. The same can be said for another kind of dilemma people encounter when it seems that one moral imperative must be sacrificed to another.

One of the most famous of those dilemmas is set forth in the *Mahabharata,* a Hindu epic made up of more than 90,000 couplets and one of the longest poems in history. You will be pleased to learn that our version is much abbreviated. To wit . . .

Arjuna is a leader of the Pandavas, one of two branches of a family that are vying for control of the kingdom. When his family loses a game of dice to the Kauravas, the other branch, the Pandavas must go into exile for twelve years. On their return, Arjuna and his brothers demand that their territories be returned, but the Kauravas refuse. The Pandavas decide to go to war.

As the day the fighting is to begin dawns, Arjuna hesitates. He cannot bring himself to bear arms against his cousins, even though he believes in the justice of his cause and will benefit greatly from a victory. At that point, Arjuna's charioteer, who is actually the god Krishna in disguise, speaks up. The dialogue that follows, which covers the arena of religion and ethics, is the heart of the epic and is known as the *Bhagavad-Gita.*

Krishna understands Arjuna's quandary. Killing one's kin is morally objectionable. On the other hand, Arjuna has a duty as a soldier and leader to enter the fray. Krishna offers a pragmatic solution: Arjuna should fight, but if he renounces the rewards of victory and offers them in devotion to God, he still has a chance at salvation. Arjuna, much relieved, wields his sword, and he and his brothers are victorious. The story ends happily when, some years later, they renounce their kingdom and are eventually admitted to paradise.

Confronted by a moral dilemma, the *Bhagavad-Gita* suggests, Arjuna is advised by Krishna to find a reasonable, practical answer that will also allow him to hew to the major tenets of his value system. By doing so, he is able to inspire his troops and lead them to victory.

Neither mythology nor business have a monopoly on dilemmas caused by conflicting beliefs. Ambitious people in art and politics face the same issues.

The famed Mexican painter Diego Rivera describes this kind of dilemma in his autobiography, *My Art, My Life*. He writes of his youth in Paris where he was studying on a subsidy from the Mexican government: "My compatriots considered acceptance at the official French Salon d'Automne as the apex of artistic recognition. Consequently, I made that my goal. Yet, I couldn't help feeling that I would be compromising my artistic integrity. Every true master of modern French painting had been rejected by this or similar academic salons which fostered pompous mediocrity and academicism. However, if I succeeded in getting my work shown, my subsidy would be extended another two years. I needed this time to carry out a plan I had formulated: to digest all the forms of modern painting the better to eliminate them from my own artistic idiom. Thus, I decided to make the sacrifice."

In Rivera's case, the compromise of his antiestablishment values was only a momentary glitch on the way to international fame as a muralist. His work can be seen at the Detroit Institute of Fine Arts, where it was initially criticized as being irreligious, and at Rockefeller Center in New York, where it was criticized for including positive images of Vladimir Lenin and other communist heroes. Rivera's art was so powerful that conservative patrons were willing to allow him to express his strong leftist political beliefs. He would not compromise his values to further his artistic career, as he had during those early days in France.

Consider another man of ambition, a politician-general. He was forced to make a choice between two of his most deeply held beliefs. His decision forever defined him in his own eyes and in the eyes of the world.

Moshe Dayan was the glamorous general with an eye-patch who won two wars for the state of Israel. A stalwart of the Labour Party, he was offered the post of foreign minister in the cabinet of Menachem Begin, leader of the rival Likud Party. He knew the offer would give him a chance to broker a historic peace with Anwar Sadat, then the president of Egypt.

"The inner struggle over whether to accept or refuse the appointment, which engaged me for the next three days, was the toughest I had ever known," Dayan later wrote. "Abandoning my party and joining the government of our rival would mean a final break with my remaining Labour friends. There would be renewed demonstrations against me by bereaved parents whose sons had fallen in the Yom Kippur War . . . I would be denigrated from all directions . . . I was also aware of the impact on my personal life. I was cutting myself off from my friends and from the circle to which I belonged."

But, in the end, the invitation to play a major role in achieving peace with Egypt could not be denied. It spoke most powerfully to Dayan's most deeply cherished ambitions for his nation. He could not refuse.

In each case, the artist and the general compromised one value in the interest of others, in the determination to pursue the value that was uppermost in their minds. The decisions were reasoned and pragmatic. Each of the men believed that he essentially had no choice. And to be sure, ambitious people may have to face such moments when the compromise of their beliefs is in fact necessary.

However, those moments should really be few and far between. Far too often, corporate leaders treat a clash of values without taking enough time or applying sufficient effort to finding a third way. There is almost always some resolution that will not compromise one's value system. The truth is, we almost always do have such a choice, and it behooves us to find that solution.

If you find that you are constantly being faced with conflicts about your moral and ethical beliefs, it may be that your ambition has led you into the wrong career, the wrong business, the wrong company, or the wrong politics.

Often, you may be the right person in the wrong situation. It takes some self-knowledge and honesty to come to a decision to look for another situation where such corrosive conflict will disappear. We know of one professor in a business school, who, coming from a working-class background, questions many of the tenets of capitalism. He loves his job but his conscience cannot let him rest easy. His question and that of others in the same position will always be how and when to disengage and go on to seek the next opportunity.

Our advice: the sooner, the better.

Guard against the common tendency to rationalize moral lapses.

The excuses leaders offer for moral lapses often have a familiar ring. "When in Rome, do as the Romans do," they say, or "Everyone else does it, so I have no choice." In the world outside business, such rationalizations can bring about episodes like the Salt Lake City Olympic Committee scandal of 1999. There, a group of outstanding citizens—ambitious leaders all—justified the bribes they offered the International Olympic Committee (IOC) by saying, in effect: "We personally hate to do business that way, but what else could we do if we really wanted to get the Winter Olympics for Salt Lake City? It was the way the IOC always operated. Our city would have lost out if we didn't play along."

A similar logic is used by business leaders around the world to justify bribery, underpaid child labor, and various forms of exploitation. Many a company in the garment and footwear industry, for example, says in effect, "If we didn't give children jobs in sweatshops in third-world countries, they would die of poverty, neglect, or physical abuse."

Nike, Inc., and Liz Claiborne, Inc., have been among those charged with this kind of betrayal of their larger values. Contrast that behavior with the record of Levi Strauss & Company, which has shunned such exploitative practices despite competitive pressures.

Yes, it is easy to base ethical decisions on the lowest common denominator, but it is the wrong way to go. The true leader's ambition is not to stoop down and march with the crowd but to raise others to a higher standard.

Perhaps the most common excuse offered by those who have violated their values is that they were obeying orders. We defer to those in authority. Isn't that the way companies—and countries—operate? Unfortunately, that excuse has been used to justify many crimes against humanity.

Bowing to authority does not have to be automatic. Many Germans struggled against Nazism. The story of Floyd Mann and John Lewis, which we presented at the beginning of this chapter, is another example of individuals having the courage to face up to their better selves and face down authority when ethical values are being denied. Throughout history, men and women have had the courage to stand up against authority when they believed it was wrong.

Let us be very clear: When we talk about the value system of a leader or a company, we are not simply preaching the gospel for gospel's sake. Ambitious business leaders whose moral compass is somewhat askew might still succeed, but they often find that they cannot attract others to join them if they are not true to a shared set of values. People who cut corners in one way are likely to cut them in other ways, and smart employees know what that kind of environment can mean to their futures. We are stating categorically that achievers, if they hope to succeed, should have a great purpose in mind and pursue it according to a set of values.

We have sought in this chapter to provide a realistic view of the forces and enticements that make values so fragile and so difficult to uphold, while at the same time making them so significant. As an ambitious person rises along the arc of ambition, confrontation with a value dilemma is often the greatest challenge he or she will face. In writing this book, we have been heartened to meet so many people—an unexpected number throughout the world—whose fundamental values have emerged in some ugly crisis and led them strongly and surely to make the right choice, the principled choice.

8

Power Comes from Other People

Keep Control by Giving It Up

~

Clinging to power is a temptation that is hard to resist. But sharing power is the only way to open an enterprise to its full potential for growth. Replacing autocracy with partnership releases creativity and the human potential. In this chapter, we examine achievers like William Gross, George Hatsopoulos, and Abraham Lincoln, who prove that letting go of control is the secret of real control.

No ONE CAN BE TRULY effective until he or she understands that a person can't succeed alone. Power derives mainly from an ability to inspire others. People need each other to carry out their ambitions. Divided, they can easily cancel out each other. United, they can achieve their shared ambitions.

Every achiever should become a master in the beneficial exercise of power. Here's some advice on how to do it.

Don't assume that no one else on the premises can match your own ambition, competence, and vision.

Maybe you started the business, have amassed great wealth, have appeared twice on *Fortune*'s cover, and are one of the key campaign fund-raisers for the next president of the United States. None of this matters if you habitually treat your in-house dissenters with disregard.

Learn to accept jolting opinions, or even being called part of the problem. Just make sure your advisers are honest, independent, and preferably smarter than you. Condition them to tell you what you need to know, not what you want to hear. But never let them—or yourself—forget that you are the person ultimately responsible for the toughest decisions.

To attract the best, create conditions that allow them to pursue their own dreams and ambitions. Recognize that they seek not simply wealth but the opportunity to realize their own dreams. Treat people as owners and entrepreneurs, free to pursue their most compelling ideas.

165

Do it partly with group incentives (equity holdings, shared bonus pools, and so forth). But more importantly, develop bonds of trust, reciprocity, and mutual support. Here's where the role of the greater shared purpose discussed in Chapter 6 comes into play. These emotional bonds enable each individual to join in sowing and reaping the brilliance of all.

> *Recognize that a healthy balance of*
> *freedom and control sets the stage*
> *for peak accomplishment.*

Don't trouble yourself too long with Machiavelli's famous riddle: Is it better to rule by fear or by love? The quick answer is that neither works, at least in excess. Autocracy winds up alienating talent and destroying whole companies. Conversely, being too "soft" may prevent you from making hard decisions.

If there is an answer to Machiavelli's riddle, it lies not in the extremes of love and fear but in the exercise of mutual respect and caring. Do it by inviting your people to set fair, achievable performance standards that, by consensus, all agree they can meet if everyone pays attention and works hard. Also, inject healthy helpings of empathy for the stresses and strains people are going through, while instilling just a bit of fear about the consequences of a venture's failure.

How does all this work in practice? How do you share power in ways that set minds afire without burning out? How do you free individuals to run with their ambitions but not run amok? How do you make their dreams pay off for the company as well as for themselves? In sharing power, what is the right mix of sweet and sour?

To find answers, we can do no better than to examine the new culture of Internet start-ups, specifically, the initiatives of William Gross, founder and chairman of idealab!, Inc.

Based in Pasadena, California, idealab! is a kind of intellectual hatchery–cum–holding company. It exists solely to create and spin off Internet businesses, an esoteric field that has made Gross an expert on the subject of business parenting and partnering.

By the time Bill Gross arrived at the California Institute of Technology also in Pasadena, he was already an accomplished and experienced entrepreneur. At the age of twelve, he had designed a parabolic dish for concentrating sunlight. While still in high school, he founded his own company, Solar Devices, Inc., and made a tidy sum by selling kits that enabled customers to assemble their own solar dishes.

In 1980, with a few years of college behind him and some on-the-job experience in mechanical engineering and electronics, he founded his second company, GNP, Inc., specializing in electronic products. Then, in 1991, Gross launched Knowledge Adventure, an educational software company that has since evolved into one of the industry's biggest players.

Along the way, the company developed three-dimensional visualization and navigation technology for a program called Science Adventure. Gross found the 3-D technology so impressive in itself that he decided to sell it separately to other software companies. But there was a catch—his organization had no experience in consumer sales.

What to do?

Several directors offered a solution: Create a separate company and maintain ownership. But also give the company substantial independence by distributing 80 percent of the equity to its employees.

The upshot was Worlds, Inc., a pioneer in creating 3-D Web sites. But Gross was not immediately enamored of the idea. In fact, at the time, he was appalled.

"I rejected the idea out of hand," he recalls. "Why? Mine was the typical reasoning of any owner or manager." For one thing, he wanted to keep his hands on what he believed would be a huge revenue stream. For another, he was violently opposed to surrendering the lion's share of the Worlds equity to its employees.

Gross had carefully selected his board members for their experience, knowledge, and independence, however. So, eventually, he backed down and accepted their advice. He never regretted the decision.

Within a year, the fledgling was almost as large as the parent. "We put in $250,000," says Gross, "and today the company's worth about $75 million."

How did it happen?

The new company, Gross says, "seemed to rise to entirely new heights of creativity and passion—putting in Herculean efforts to close deals, to improve product, and to recruit new star employees."

Why did it happen?

Sharing power unleashes a new level of performance.

Certainly, Worlds's leaders had sharpened their market focus by the time they went out on their own, which served to attract investors with fresh money. But Gross has no doubt that the chief reason for the new company's startling achievements was the "magnification" of human potential.

"We gave employees near total ownership of Worlds," he says, "and unleashed a new level of performance."

In Gross's view, what he calls the "new math of ownership" is all about relinquishing ownership to employees, giving them significant equity, and freeing them to use their abilities fully in their own interests, which beautifully coincide with the company's interests.

For Gross, "significant equity" means that each person should have at least 1 percent ownership of the company—an astonishing notion that other companies can barely imagine. "The problem with 1-percent owners," Gross goes on, "is that you can have only 100 of them."

It is an equation that isn't really a "problem" at all, as far as Gross is concerned. As he sees it, 100 is a perfect number to make people feel they belong to a strong "tribe," while the 100 limitation encourages him to keep "spinning out" new projects that lead to new companies.

This is the premise of idealab!, which Gross founded in 1996 as a "business incubator," meaning that it systematizes the process of freeing smart people to turn projects into small new companies, which they largely own. Each company is intensely focused on one dynamic new idea, enabling its staff to "make unbelievable things happen."

"In our Pasadena offices," Gross relates, "I work with a core staff of twenty people to develop ideas for new Internet-based businesses. At any given time, we have four or five embryonic companies in development. Those that seem worthy of flight are then hatched into stand-alone enterprises, whereupon they find their own office space but continue to receive operational assistance from idealab!.

"About twenty companies have left the nest so far," he adds. They range from GoTo.com, a search engine, to eToys.com, an on-line toy retailer.

Idealab! operates with a kitty of $10 million raised from individual investors. About $4 million of that has been reinvested in new companies so far—a seemingly small sum that actually reflects one of Gross's most effective disciplines.

"Our policy is to give each spinout no more than $250,000 in seed money and to take no more than a 49 percent equity stake—usually much less than 49 percent. Indeed, I insist that idealab!'s interest in its offspring be noncontrolling.

"Typically, the spinout's management team and employees get 30 percent of the equity, with the chief executive taking 10 percent of the total. Everyone on the payroll gets something. I also insist on a salary cap for the CEO, usually in the neighborhood of $75,000."

In all cases, the goal is some sort of "liquidity event"—going public or being acquired for at least $100 million. One Gross company, CitySearch, filed to go public at a valuation of $270 million, giving its chief executive, Charles Conn, a potential stake of $13 million.

Gross says he wants to "create a family of independent, yet interdependent companies—and a family of owners." The ultimate results remain to be seen. But early returns are promising.

In 1998, according to the National Venture Capital Association, the rate of return for the venture industry as a whole was 29.5 percent. In its first two years of existence, idealab! generated a return of 155 percent. And most of its offspring had grown strong enough to attract further money from outside investors.

Bill Gross may have been dragged into discovering the advantages of power sharing, but he was open to advice and willing to gamble on the amazing potential lurking inside employees' minds. The results have been so unarguably positive that it is hard to see why some businesses persist in bad old command-and-control management, a sure recipe for repelling creative people.

Such companies are fading in market value and winding up on the uncutting edge of business progress. In today's start-up climate, autocracy isn't merely antique; it's obsolete. By contrast, power sharing has long characterized some of the world's most successful organizations, and the concept of gaining power by sharing it has probably driven most of the era's successful companies.

Bill Gates may be the undisputed chief of Microsoft Corporation, but he would not be where he is now—nor would his company—if he hadn't worked closely with Paul Allen in the early years and relied heavily on the brilliance of other technologists and managers as the company has grown.

Partnerships prove that the whole is greater than the sum of its parts.

Bill Hewlett and David Packard were so closely allied in the Hewlett-Packard Company during Packard's lifetime that it is doubtful either one alone could have led the company to its spectacular achievements.

Partnerships obviously flourish in every field, not just business. From dancing to exploration, from Astaire and Rogers to Lewis and Clark, the power of collaboration keeps proving that in most human efforts, the whole is greater than the sum of its parts.

One might hope that a new business era attuned to partnering has seen the last of the old Hollywood studio emperors like Louis B. Mayer and other founding oligarchs like the Seagram Company Ltd.'s late Samuel Bronfman ("Wherever I sit is the head of the table"). One could envision vanity becoming almost taboo in a time of cautionary tales about inflated egos causing deflated profits.

Yet, although much has been written about empowering people, most organizations are still being managed top-down. There have been times, though, when the history of industry told a different story.

Earlier, we expressed concern that if the controls pioneered by GM's legendary Alfred P. Sloan were overapplied, the ambition of people working in a company could be killed. But Sloan himself was not guilty of such a crime. Indeed, when he and Pierre Du Pont joined together to pull General Motors out of its mud hole, they came up with a reorganization that actually provided greater autonomy and control to lower-ranking managers, a move that saved the company.

The year was 1920, and an economic recession had left GM with more than $200 million of unsold inventory. William C. Durant, the company's founder, was a brilliant automobile man and entrepreneur. But, unfortunately, his massive ego stood in the way of any management skills he might have acquired. The company had been formed out of an association of various car manufacturers, but Durant made no effort to mesh the parts into a productive whole.

Things changed when Du Pont and Sloan took over. As Nicholas Von Hoffman has written, "Suffice to say that Du Pont and Sloan invented a method for combining centralization and decentralization, to get the benefits of both without the drawbacks of either."

They broke apart the previous hierarchical structure of GM, making each separate division freestanding, with the proviso that it show a year-end profit. The financial reins were held tight, but in other respects, a partnership existed between the center and the companies on the rim.

This partnership worked smashingly well until the 1970s, when GM became complacent in its response to the Japanese invasion of the United States auto market. But that is another story entirely.

A complex company cannot be micromanaged from behind a central desk.

Eight decades ago, Sloan and Du Pont understood that a company like GM, complex and diverse in its products, could not be successfully micromanaged from behind one central desk. Yet, the shadow of William Durant still hovers over the business world today. There are old-style corporate martinets—Sunbeam Corporation's demon downsizer Albert Dunlap is an example with which you are already familiar—whose relationships with their employees are based more on fear than love.

Autocrats have no doubt that it is better to be feared than loved. When Winston Churchill asked Joseph Stalin whether he preferred being obeyed out of fear or out of loyalty, Stalin replied, "Fear. Loyalty can change."

The history of man's inhumanity to man, as exemplified by Stalin's slaughter of his political rivals, may suggest that autocracy pays, but that is true only in the short term. If you are cold-blooded enough, you can terrify people into doing pretty much anything you demand of them, but the tyrant, political or corporate, will eventually become so isolated that he is incapable of seeing reality. When that happens, his arc of ambition inevitably curves south.

Subjugation ultimately destroys not only its victims but also its practitioners. You need to be surrounded by people doing their best to achieve their goals (and yours), people who share your ambitions.

You need their respect, not their fear. And to earn that respect, you must first respect their dignity. Only when they feel truly respected will they give the enterprise their all.

Positive anxiety provokes the desire to reach peak performance.

Fear chills minds, numbs souls, kills initiative and businesses. And yet, our arsenal can't be entirely devoid of fear. A certain amount of fear is necessary to improve performance—assuming that by fear one means positive anxiety, the edgy urge to do a great job and not let down the team.

Those incapable of instilling that feeling throughout a company may well invite disrespect for the common enterprise. They flirt with apathy and mediocrity. Leadership without a pinch of fear is like cooking without salt.

But the ambitious don't take advice easily—as Bill Gross's initial reaction to his board's advice suggests. Once they are in charge, they may feel their position threatened by other opinions, particularly those that differ from their own.

More likely, ambitious people just believe that they are right. In their minds, they suffer no fools. Time is too short for that.

Sometimes, they also select men and women for their boards who reflect their own opinions. That's a dangerous practice, especially if somewhere in the exercise of your ambition, you are wrong (it happens, you know). Someone needs to be present who dares to disagree with you.

Gross had chosen his board well, surrounding himself with people holding different outlooks who had the courage to express themselves. For all his dislike of being disagreed with, Gross was a good enough leader to tap the expertise of a broad range of people and then listen when they opposed his viewpoint.

Of course, much depends on the quality of the advice given. Alexander the Great's advisers were dead set against his territorial ambitions. Alexander ignored their counsel and went on to conquer lands that stretched from Egypt to India.

Obviously, advisers are human, too, and can be no more omnipotent than you are. But the importance of the interplay of ideas can't be denied. All too often, the ambitious are so confident of their inherent superiority that they totally ignore the advice of others, thinking it inevitably inferior to their own ideas.

Napoléon Bonaparte, for one, convinced himself that his refusal to accept anyone's advice confirmed his greatness as a leader. Writing in 1796, he boasted: "I have conducted the campaign without consulting anyone. I should have done no good if I had been under the necessity of conforming to the notions of another person."

It was just this modus operandi that led to the final and complete destruction of Napoléon's ambition. He lost his footing in his march toward ultimate victory in part because he ignored a key point on the arc of ambition: Sow and reap the product of the ambition of others.

Abraham Lincoln was, in many respects, a wiser man than Napoléon. In a contemporary memoir titled *The Inner Life of Abraham Lincoln,* Francis Carpenter, a painter who spent several months in the White House during the Civil War year of 1864, records Lincoln's way of responding to advice that countered his own plans.

In one segment, Carpenter quotes Lincoln on the genesis of the Emancipation Proclamation:

> It had got to be, midsummer, 1862. Things had gone from bad to worse, until I felt that we had reached the end of our rope on the plan of operations we had been pursuing; that we had about played our last card and must change our tactics, or lose the game! I now determined upon the adoption of the emancipation policy; and, without consultation with, or the knowledge of the Cabinet, I prepared the original draft of the proclamation, and, after much anxious thought, called a Cabinet meeting on the subject . . . I said to the Cabinet that I had resolved upon this step, and had not called them together to ask their advice, but to lay the subject-matter of a proclamation before them; suggestions as to which would be in order, after they had heard it read.

At that point, Carpenter wrote, various suggestions were heard, but none of them made much sense to Lincoln until Secretary of State William Seward spoke. Seward said he approved of the proclamation but questioned the timing, suggesting that its announcement be postponed until the country was buoyed by a military success, less it be viewed as "the last measure of an exhausted government, a cry for help."

Lincoln was impressed, telling Carpenter: "The wisdom of the view of the Secretary of State struck me with very great force. It was an aspect of the case that, in all my thought upon the subject, I had entirely overlooked. The result was that I put the draft of the proclamation aside . . . waiting for a victory."

Some ambitious people will allow no one to offer advice. Others encourage advice from any quarter. The subject is treated at some length in one of the most famous of all management treatises, *The Prince,* by Niccolo Machiavelli.

In a chapter titled "How Flatterers Must Be Shunned," Machiavelli writes that the only way to guard against flattery is to let it be known that speaking the truth will not offend you. But he immediately warns that "when everyone can tell you the truth, you lose their respect."

The prudent prince, he goes on, must choose only wise people for his council and then give them "full liberty to speak the truth to him, but only of those things that he asks and of nothing else." If that sounds too restrictive, be reassured: Machiavelli says the prince should also ask about everything and be a patient listener. In fact, he adds, if the prince "finds that anyone has scruples in telling him the truth, he should be angry."

It is as true today as it was in the sixteenth century of Niccolo Machiavelli: The effective "prince" is not so high and mighty, not so full of himself or herself, that he or she will not solicit helpful advice.

One of the most famous of all aphorisms was penned by John Emerich Edward Dalberg, the first Baron Acton: "Power tends to corrupt and absolute power corrupts absolutely." The words, appearing in a letter Lord Acton wrote to a bishop, imply that power is inherently evil, its holders not to be trusted.

Power is not inherently evil.

We beg to differ. In our view, power is value neutral and potentially just as benign as it is immoral. It simply bestows on its possessor the ability to make good (or bad) things happen.

Yes, many ambitious leaders become authoritarian. They micromanage and eventually become isolated. People come to fear giving them advice. Every meeting becomes a corporate show-and-tell. There is no real debate, no search for the truth. Blind to priorities, mired in details, they resemble Captain Queeg, the self-destructive skipper of Herman Wouk's 1952 Pulitzer Prize-winning novel *The Caine Mutiny,* whose runaway neuroses torpedoed his naval career.

In contrast, by challenging people with ever more responsibility and rewarding them with ever more praise, the ambitious leader can instill the kind of loyalty that empowers a workforce. In fact, at a certain level of intensity, sharing control can transform the way people perceive their jobs. Their fate, they sense, is synonymous with the company's fate, which itself is entwined with the arc of ambition of their leader.

Before Bill Gross ever got to create Knowledge Adventure in 1994, he had an experience that would later determine his relationship to his employees. In 1986, after he and his brother Larry produced an accounting template for Lotus 1-2-3, their company was bought out by giant Lotus Development Corporation. For the next seven years, they were employees of Lotus, developing new programs like Hal and Lotus Magellan. Unlike other employees, however, they earned a 5 percent royalty on the products they developed.

That meant they were unwilling to leave the marketing of their products like Magellan totally in Lotus's hands. One year, when the computer industry trade show, Comdex, was about to open in Chicago, Illinois, the brothers invested $1,500 of their own money to buy a used disk-duplicating machine, got hold of 15,000 disks that were about to be thrown out of the Lotus factory, and proceeded to copy the Magellan program on all of the disks using the duplicating machine, shrouded in black cloth, under Bill Gross's desk. At Comdex, they stood at the taxi line outside handing out disks. A coworker later commented that the brothers "looked more like two wild-eyed entrepreneurs than the corporate drones [they] were."

All that changed when the Grosses received an offer they could not refuse: Lotus paid a grand sum to take over Magellan totally and stop paying royalties to the brothers. Suddenly, they were compensated as regular company employees. Years later, Bill Gross remembered the effect that transformation had on him: "It was as if the new chemistry in my body could not have conceived of going to Comdex and hawking diskettes in line. It's not that I would have thought of it and decided not to do it. The idea just wouldn't have come up. I was conditionally incapable of such a notion. . . . I turned to my brother and gulped: 'Now I get it. This is what everyone else here must feel like.'"

Gross had lost not only his uniqueness but his power, his sense of control.

Years later, after he accepted his board's advice and gave the workers at Worlds, Inc., their head and 80 percent of the equity in their new operation, Bill Gross had occasion to remember his own experience at Lotus. He saw that by giving the workers a major stake in the enterprise, by yielding operational control, he had unleashed their creativity and inspired their commitment. No longer just bit players, the employees had taken center stage—and it showed up on the bottom line.

Bill Gross's idea of creating spinouts is not unique. The idea was first made popular by George Hatsopoulos, who built Thermo Electron Corporation.

A Greek immigrant, Hatsopoulos, came to the United States to pursue a Ph.D. He also arrived with another great ambition.

Hatsopoulos had been a high school student in Athens during the German occupation of Greece in the 1940s. The terror of that occupation—Hatsopoulos recounted to us that 50 Greek citizens were regularly shot in retribution for the death of a single German—constantly disrupted the high-school day.

So Hatsopoulos was able to spend time in the library reading about the accomplishments of others and deciding on the best country in which to pursue his dream.

His hero became Thomas Edison, and he wanted to build a company like General Electric. In his words, "I wanted to build a highly diversified technology company, ready and able to enter any business in any field where it could sell superior technological solutions."

Hatsopoulos also believed that he should be able to choose the country in which to pursue his ambition, and the United States was the place that had the right entrepreneurial environment.

Initially a research-and-development outfit for the space program, Thermo Electron became better known for its start-ups and spinouts, a fertile business that constantly generates other businesses.

"We have no inhibitions about new ventures, but we do have some rules," Hatsopoulos told us. "First and foremost, we do not enter any business until we're sure we have something unique to offer. That something is nearly always technological."

Hatsopolous takes great pride in the companies that he has created. One of them is the world's largest instrumentation company.

It grew out of a joint project between Thermo and the Ford Motor Company. Again in Hatsopoulos's words, "We were visiting with Ford on a joint project to develop a low emission engine. New federal laws required that we be able to test engine emission for nitrogen oxide to an accuracy of a few parts per million. Conventional testing techniques were taking too long. So we said to Ford, give us an order for a new testing instrument and a deadline of three months to build it. They laughed, but gave us the order. We did it, and in twelve months became the leader in this type of instrumentation. Today, we have the world's largest instrumentation company."

Hatsopoulos is also proud of Thermo Cardio Systems, a company that has an 80 percent share of the mechanical heart market. It was a venture that began in 1966, but its mechanical heart did not win FDA approval until 1992.

It's a great story of perseverance and chasing an ambition with a higher purpose. We'll talk about perseverance and higher purpose later in this book, but this company is about saving human lives. The challenge was to design a device and medical protocol that would prevent the blood clotting that other mechanical hearts had experienced.

After eight years of work, Thermo Cardio had solved the problem. Today, 2,000 people have mechanical hearts and new lives—thanks to the company Hatsopoulos had built.

"We don't have a specific group running around trying to find these things," Hatsopoulos reflected.

In recent years, Thermo Electron's strategy and performance has not always won the stock market's approval. Every business model has its risks. But we still believe in the soundness of the Hatsopoulos philosophy of sharing power.

But despite the strong advocacy of leaders like George Hatsopoulos, the resistance to sharing power is strong. Bill Gross thinks he knows why: "Executives are accustomed to spinning off their underperforming units, but letting go of their best people and ideas and technologies—well, that's something else entirely, something deeply discomforting, something that feels like corporate apostasy."

And he adds, "In a world where executive pay and prestige are still largely linked to the size of the assets under one's control, the idea of relinquishing control represents a direct threat to a CEO."

But the success of idealab! argues for another approach. If you want to inspire your current workforce to greater achievement, if you want to attract the able new people every organization needs, you must give them the freedom to develop their skills and ambitions. Simply put, everyone must be free to follow his or her own dreams.

Coming to grips with our own ambitions is ultimately a forewarning about the myth of omnipotence. No solo ruler of a complex company can ever have enough creativity, knowledge, and time to make the right decisions single-handedly. His or her survival depends on sowing and reaping the brilliant work of others. By sacrificing the appearance of power, we achieve the substance—the real reward—of power.

In the next chapter, we discuss something you already know: Nothing lasts forever. No matter how successful you've been in the past, things change. Your product becomes old hat, and no longer a very elegant one at that. Smart new competitors are eyeing your lunch.

What can you do?

One thing only: You, too, must change.

9

Reinvention Is the Key to Longevity

Change or Die

~

Knowing how and when to react to events is the secret of changing things for the better. Examples abound. Sometimes a person reinvents a business, and himself or herself with it. See Jim Rogers and Colin Powell. Sometimes a person transforms a country. See Peter the Great and Margaret Thatcher. And sometimes a person can go as far as to change his ideology. See Deng Xiaoping.

THE NOTION OF DOING business at your own pace is an oxymoron wrapped in a fantasy. Not that it is impossible.

For example, you could daydream yourself into a commercially pure life running the only general store serving a tiny village of one hundred souls in northernmost Vermont. But as soon as you got settled in this hamlet of harmony, some demonic developer would almost surely buy the whole county and turn it into New England's most lavish ski resort for thirty-something investment bankers.

Good-bye, harmony.

Perhaps you could save yourself by redefining your store as an up-market epicurean or antique emporium offering yuppie browsers authentic Vermont syrup cans for as little as $500 apiece, empty. Better yet, you could padlock the store and flee out of town. But one thing's for sure: You couldn't sit still and expect to survive.

> *Dynamic disharmony between a*
> *business and its market is the ideal in*
> *the face of constant change.*

If growth is the life force of business, then the commercial ideal is not stable equilibrium between a business and its market but a dynamic disharmony—one that keeps the business changing slightly faster than its market changes.

And the market will change. Tastes, incomes, fads, taxes, technologies, advertising, competition—everything imaginable conspires to change the customer's needs and perceptions at dizzying speeds.

New products constantly dislodge old ones. Even the personal computer may soon become antique, done in by your television set displaying the Internet menu as fast as you can say, "Mail, please."

At other times, you have to update your product to match changing tastes. In the 1960s, everyone predicted that television would kill off magazines. Wrong. But it did force magazines to seek niches for special interest audiences.

To keep ahead of the market, the mantra of ambition must be: Change or die.

Change or die is the imperative that has driven ambitious people throughout history. Era by era, innovators have tirelessly pursued and achieved countless transformations. Changes in how we live, work, play, and procreate. Changes in how we make money, peace, and war. Changes in how we communicate, run organizations, govern society, envision the universe, explain the meaning of life. Over and over, new generations mobilize new resources to invent industries, cure diseases, rebuild cities, remedy injustices, and make everything generally better.

Consider Peter the Great, the seventeenth-century Russian czar who grew up to be so farsighted—he was 6 feet, 7 inches tall—that he glimpsed even the future years way ahead of his subjects. He knew that their isolated country could not conceivably prosper in its self-wounding ignorance of Europe's cutting-edge countries to the west. Russia would have to go to school in Europe.

Peter was ten years old when he succeeded his father and became czar in 1682 (a seven-year regency followed). As a child, he was devoted to war games; as a czar's son, he had already been indulged to the point that he was allowed to stage mock battles between real soldiers armed with real weapons. He was equally entranced with sailing and at an early age spent months working with carpenters to build boats. Battles and boats became his lifelong passions.

Peter was alive with nervous energy, constantly on the move, curious about everything new, especially European science and technology. During his forty-three-year reign, the West was bubbling with fresh ideas. In 1687, for example, the seminal English mathematician, Isaac Newton, announced his theory of gravity and three laws of planetary motion. Peter was then fifteen and ruler of his own planet, a continent-sized intellectual desert parched for knowledge.

Prior to his reign, Russia had been a virtually closed society. Lying athwart Asia and Europe, the country was surrounded by hostile neighbors: Poland to the west, Sweden to the north, Tatars and Turks in the south, and unfriendly tribes roaming the east.

The Russian Orthodox Church scorned all other forms of Christianity in favor of its own primitive piety. The Russian elite ignored and learned nothing from the few foreigners who managed to visit Moscow, usually as representatives of European trading companies. Thus, Russia experienced neither the Renaissance nor the Reformation, two movements that brought western Europe out of the Middle Ages.

During the regency, Peter was less interested in governing than in sailing, soldiering, and boisterous drinking. But once the throne was his, the young czar blossomed as an extraordinary leader, pushing and pulling his reluctant country out of medievalism into the modern age.

Despite its vastness, Russia was then virtually landlocked. The nearest thing to a year-round seaport was Archangel, 130 miles from the Arctic Circle and frozen shut six months of the year. Peter decided to give Russia outlets to the sea, an agenda that required him to assemble a modern army to conquer a foreign port where the Russians could then build warships and create a modern navy. By forceful expansion, Peter aimed to vitalize Russia as northern Europe's leading military power.

In 1696, the czar's army defeated Turkish outposts on the Sea of Azov, and Russia acquired its first seaport. But Peter knew that to fulfill his ambition and acquire a sea route to western Europe, he needed to control Russia's Baltic coast, then in Swedish hands. So in 1700, he declared war on Sweden, but Peter was defeated in his first battle.

A defeat calls for reorganization,
not retirement.

With his customary energy, he reformed the Russian army, bringing in trained foreign officers and disciplining his troops. He finally won a series of small engagements, allowing him to control the Neva River and establish a port on the Baltic coast. He called it St. Petersburg. It eventually became his capital.

To Peter, Moscow symbolized the claustrophobic Russian past. He hated the town, especially the dark rooms and narrow passageways of the Kremlin, where, at the age of ten, he had seen family members murdered by rebellious soldiers. St. Petersburg, in contrast, was to be a city of light and openness.

At the pivotal battle of Poltava, in the Ukraine, Peter personally led his troops to their final victory over Sweden in 1709. Russia thereby replaced Sweden as the great Baltic power. After the battle, writing to one of his admirals, Peter declared, "Now, with God's help, the last stone has been laid to the foundation of St. Petersburg."

*A leader must be ever alert to
the world outside an organization's walls.*

One of the turning points in Russian history was Peter's eighteen-month journey to Holland and England in 1697. Traveling incognito to avoid official folderol, he studied shipbuilding, often working as a carpenter, while avidly observing European architecture, craftsmanship, medicine, and manners. What he learned on that journey became his checklist for westernizing Russia.

When he returned to Moscow, Peter was greeted by an assemblage of nobles and courtiers who were stunned, to put it mildly, when he proceeded to whip out a razor and cut off their beards. In those days, a Russian's beard affirmed his faith in God. Ivan the Terrible once said, "To shave the beard is a sin that the blood of all the martyrs cannot cleanse."

Peter had wasted no time in sending a message to his people: Russia was in for radical change.

And so it was. Peter changed the Russian calendar to conform to the Western one and established a coinage backed by the government. He began awarding decorations for loyal service, replacing the previous expensive custom of handing out huge estates. He even ordered nobles to wear Western clothes instead of their traditional caftans.

In 1712, St. Petersburg was officially declared the capital of Russia. It remained so for two centuries until the Bolshevik Revolution of 1917 reinstated Moscow as the seat of power. (Peter's city may never again be Russia's capital, but its Soviet name—Leningrad—has now disappeared, and St. Petersburg lives again.)

Besides inventing Russia as a military power, Peter shook up the country's archaic administrative systems, established merit as a basis for government promotion, opened schools for the upper classes, subsidized European-managed factories, and weakened the power of the Orthodox Church by abolishing the office of the patriarch and replacing it with a synod.

Peter is known as the Great Transformer. He did turn a medieval state into a likeness of an eighteenth-century European state, but he lacked a true understanding of the underlying forces that had created western Europe. Always a Russian despot in the czarist tradition, he never quite grasped that political freedom was essential to the growth of the strong merchant class that could bring Russia into the company of major trading nations. Peter died in 1725 at the age of fifty-three, insisting to the end that the necessities of change never lured him into tyranny.

More recently, and with somewhat different methods, Margaret Thatcher set out to remake Britain. "I am not a consensus politician," she announced in 1979 when she became the country's first woman prime minister. "I am a conviction politician."

Her convictions led her to lengthy and fierce battles with entrenched unions, which had dominated not only the Labour Party but the Conservatives as well. Refusing to give in to strikes, she broke the unions' hold on domestic economic policies. She introduced the word *privatize* into the English language when she "sold" state-owned enterprises such as British Airways.

The welfare state, which had its roots in the Great Depression of the 1930s and officially came into being after World War II, was wiped away. In 1982, Thatcher went to war with Argentina over the Falkland Islands—and won.

Maggie Thatcher, the Iron Lady as the Russians nicknamed her, succeeded in changing Britain. But the cost was great for some. For example, the ranks of the unemployed swelled to 3 million.

Still, Thatcher continued to gain popular support for her policies, within her party and out of it. With her practical idealism and singular persona—a Royal Marine drill sergeant inside a classic English matron—Thatcher exemplified an idea whose time had come.

Britain was fed up with its failed postwar ideology of half-hearted socialism. Thatcher, with her political skills and un-flinching faith in free enterprise, was exactly the right change agent, partly because she was so open and direct. Nobody had ever expected a woman to be quite so tough, hardheaded, ob-stinate, and uncompromising, yet sometimes charming. (François Mitterand, the French president, claimed she had "the eyes of Caligula and the mouth of Marilyn Monroe.")

Thatcher led her party for eleven years, until, as often happens to even the most popular leaders, her critics made head-way and she wore out her welcome. When she resigned in 1990, she had done more than reform her country. She had trans-formed it.

Knowing when and how to act are the tricky parts of any change effort.

The change-or-die mandate is, of course, one of those decep-tively simple laws that are more easily voiced than imple-mented. Knowing when to act is hard enough. Knowing how to act is much harder.

We are usually taught that moving incrementally is the safest course. Incremental change, the argument goes, avoids unnecessary risk. But if dramatic change is required, incremental moves are risky—not enough gets changed. But doing nothing may be the riskiest course of all.

Just as form follows function in architecture, so action must fit the occasion in business. It takes a cool mind and a brave heart to see what's fitting.

When the fabled John F. Welch, Jr., took over as chairman and chief executive officer of the General Electric Company in 1981, the far-flung company seemed to be in perfect working order and in need of only incremental changes to preserve the legacy of Welch's respected predecessor, Reginald Jones.

Yet, Welch undid much of what Jones had put in place. It is well known in business mythology that the many GE people whose cages Welch rattled and whose toes he crunched soon nicknamed him Neutron Jack. But as it turned out, his upheavals vastly upgraded General Electric to the benefit of all.

Welch clearly had the courage to risk major disapproval in order to achieve what he considered best for the company and, ultimately, best for himself as well. With time, Welch moderated his style and adjusted the pace and magnitude of the change at GE to fit the occasion. His change sensibilities made him one of the most admired managers of this century.

James Rogers is a notable example of someone who has the courage to change to fit the requirements of the challenge at hand. He seems to relish challenges partly because they provide opportunities to reinvent himself. It is almost as if Jim Rogers has made a career of personal transformations.

Rogers is the president and chief executive officer of Cinergy Corporation, one of the nation's leading electric utilities. Cinergy is in the vanguard of the deregulation that has lately shocked electric utilities, destroying the cozy local monopolies to which most companies in the industry had become accustomed.

Deregulation has transformed many another industry—from airlines to telecommunications—but few can match the profound upheaval electric utilities are undergoing. Their familiar world has all but vanished.

Unlike some of his peers, Rogers is not at all distraught. He is, in fact, exhilarated. He views change as a healthy catalyst that strengthens not only the industry and his company but Jim Rogers personally.

Indeed, he believes that the only way managers can respond to the changes around them is by reinventing themselves, probably at least once every decade. He reckons that, in his life, he has reinvented himself three times already and is on the cusp of a fourth.

Rogers became an entrepreneur at the age of eleven, when his father started a business at home. The business involved making a chemical that could be poured into car radiators to seal any leaks. Rogers helped his father mix the chemicals and package the final product.

"When I was sixteen, I became a salesman over the weekends and holidays," Rogers told us. "I would drive around to gas stations in our area carrying a quart can with leaks, demonstrating to skeptical gas station owners how the leaks could be fixed. It was a tough but wonderful learning experience."

Rogers says he still remembers what his father told him: "You learn this little business from the beginning to the end, and you'll learn to run any business in the world."

Transformations can take many forms, each a learning experience.

The college years were difficult for Jim Rogers. He started as a math and science major at Emory University in Atlanta, Georgia, but eventually transferred to business study at the University of Kentucky in Lexington. Early on, he got married and quickly had two children.

With a young family to support, he had to work full time. He found himself doing a variety of odd jobs, ultimately landing a full-time job as a night-beat reporter for the local paper. Rogers remembers the editor asking what newspaper experience he had, to which he quickly replied: "None, but the good news is that you won't have to un-train me. I'll learn the craft exactly as you would like." He got the job and quickly made himself into a skilled reporter.

Upon finishing college, Jim went to the University of Kentucky Law School. But after a stellar first semester that saw him reach the top of his class, he had to drop out to take a full-time job again. He needed to earn extra money because his wife was now pregnant with their third child.

This time, Rogers worked at selling veterinary drugs for Pfizer, Inc., another sea change, and then returned to school to complete his degree. What he describes as "my lawyer period" was about to begin.

"I clerked for the Kentucky Supreme Court," Rogers began. "I then became a state assistant attorney general, handling consumer advocacy cases. Next, I got a job offer from the Federal Power Commission (FPC) to work in Washington as a trial lawyer for cases that resulted from the deregulation of the natural gas industry."

With his marriage beginning to sour, Rogers saw the FPC job as an opportunity to make a break. "I got divorced and moved to Washington," he says. For the next two years, Rogers was a self-described "animal for work . . . willing to do almost anything."

In the process, he became a "pretty good trial lawyer." And the next thing he knew, he got a call from a private law firm, Akin,

Gump, Strauss, Hauer, and Feld. "I joined and became a billing machine," he says. But just when he was on the verge of becoming a partner, he went back to the FPC, which had by now become the Federal Energy Research Commission (FERC) as deputy general counsel.

"I had 120 lawyers working for me," Rogers remembers. "We settled 18 gas deregulation-related cases in the next 18 months. I was developing quite a reputation for resolving tough cases."

Then, in 1983, Rogers rejoined his former law firm as a partner and helped create the Natural Gas Clearinghouse, which attempted to facilitate market transactions in the now-deregulated natural gas industry.

"I met virtually every CEO in that industry," Rogers says. "One of them was Ken Lay, CEO of Enron [Corporation], who invited me to join his company. I figured he wanted me as his general counsel, but he wanted me to be an operating manager.

"Here I was, at the pinnacle of my law career, when I had to make the decision about whether I was ready to reinvent myself again to become an operating manager." Rogers didn't hesitate. He joined Enron as senior vice president for regulatory affairs, planning, and budgeting. In a year, he was president of the company's $2.6 billion gas pipeline business.

In 1988, Rogers was asked to become CEO of PSI Energy, Inc., a near bankrupt electric utility. Despite the company's bleak prospects, "I was drawn to the challenge," he remembers.

"Here was an opportunity to reinvent myself again," he says. "I was just over forty, and I had a chance to run the whole show. Even if I failed, I figured it would be a great learning opportunity. It would allow me to figure out what it meant to be a CEO."

Over the past decade, Jim Rogers has completely rebuilt the company he inherited, positioning it at the forefront of the transformation taking place in the industry. "Along the way," he says, "we have been among the first to introduce some of the changes that have come to redefine our industry."

Among those changes, PSI embraced consumer choice and allowed open access to its transmission system. It merged with another utility of similar size following passage of the Energy Policy Act of 1992, which marked the beginning of an accelerating wave of industry consolidation. The rush to consolidate was such that PSI had to fight off a hostile takeover bid following its merger announcement.

The new combined company Cinergy was among the first contingent of utility companies that went abroad, acquiring a 50 percent stake in MEB, an electric distribution company located in the United Kingdom. "We were the leaders in reorganizing our company into different divisions," Rogers says, "so that we could focus on separating the regulated and unregulated elements of our business."

While making these pioneering changes, Cinergy has achieved one of the industry's best total returns to shareholders over the past decade, Rogers notes with pride.

This Houdini will be the first to tell you that "the only thing that remains a constant is the need to keep on changing. I expect we will need to fundamentally transform ourselves again in the next decade," he says. "We will have to learn to operate in a globally competitive field against competitors we have not yet recognized." And managers, too, will have to don new hats.

"Two decades ago, all that mattered in our industry," Rogers goes on, "was our physical asset base, because we earned a guaranteed regulated rate of return on those assets. What now matters more and more are our intellectual assets. Learning to be a leader in this new world is the transformation I am looking forward to. I would be lying if I denied a twinge of fear, but the excitement is far more intense."

*"Sensing" is a valuable capability for leaders,
who must react to the force of events.*

The stories of Jack Welch and Jim Rogers both illustrate a key leadership challenge—how to react to the force of events. As different as these leaders are from one another, all share a gift for what we call "sensing," meaning that they are adept at spotting trends and seizing opportunities ahead of their competitors. Skilled at pacing their actions, they thus become neither the victims of change nor the victims of tradition.

Welch is acknowledged as one of the great industry trend spotters of our time. He has sensed fundamental shifts in one business after another, changing his management style accordingly. Still, he has remained true to his principles and values.

Rogers, too, exhibits a knack for spotting trends and acting on them. Rogers, finding himself in the midst of radical change affecting an entire industry, keeps reinventing himself to capitalize on those shifts.

Both of these managers act with a sense of mastery, appearing almost in control of the events that could overcome them. But sometimes dramatic action—charging forcefully ahead through apathy, inertia, mediocrity, red tape—may be the only way to save an enterprise.

Take the case of Sealed Air Corporation, the packaging-materials maker that held the original patents on Bubble Wrap®, the stuff your kids love to pop. Given Bubble Wrap®'s popularity, plus the company's patent protection, Sealed Air was free of competition and booming.

But Sealed Air's chief executive officer, Dermot Dunphy, sensed problems that were being masked by the company's success. Even as the company's cash built up, he saw few attractive acquisition possibilities that could utilize the cash. Moreover, patents expire. And Sealed Air's patents were due to expire in five years. Dunphy was concerned that the company's current success might make it complacent and slow to respond to the competition that was inevitable in the future.

*When things are going well,
sometimes what is needed is radical change.*

What to do? Rather than take incremental steps, Dunphy had a brainstorm. He created what he called a "controlled crisis." He borrowed a huge sum equivalent to the company's entire market capitalization and paid out all this money as a one-time dividend to shareholders. At the same time he significantly increased employee stock ownership. This radical carrot-and-stick strategy worked like a charm.

The employees responded with alacrity, cutting costs, implementing a world class manufacturing philosophy, staving off would-be competitors. The debt was paid down, business boomed again, and everybody lived happily ever after. Dunphy's dramatic action had saved the day.

But usually the challenge of change in business goes far beyond cutting costs. Sometimes a total reinvention is required, and that takes inordinate skill to pull off.

*Radical change leaves people
wondering if more foresight might have
prevented the upheaval.*

Radical change can be risky. It leaves people breathless and maybe a little worn down if you don't manage it well. It makes people wonder whether the necessity for fast action might have been prevented with some foresight.

Could the business have been changed in advance of its markets? they might well wonder. Could anticipation, preparation, and incremental action have prevented the disruptions?

In a democracy, change, which is dependent on the public's willingness to accept it, usually comes slowly. Henry Kissinger, Richard Nixon's national security adviser and secretary of state, was convinced that sooner or later the United States would have to stop pretending that China did not exist.

Nonrecognition had been the official policy of the United States toward China for many years. But all that changed with President Nixon's visit to China in 1972. It was Nixon's job to make this radical foreign policy change palatable to the electorate.

The first step was taken when Kissinger made a secret visit to Beijing in 1971. Not long after, Nixon announced that he would go to China himself. His spotless record of anticommunism deflected opposition to the move. Nevertheless, Nixon had the courage to change a dead-end American policy that was both controversial and emotional for some.

General Colin Powell, former chairman of the Joint Chiefs of Staff of the United States, honed a clear philosophy of military action during his two tours of duty in Vietnam as a young army infantry officer. As he later wrote, the experience taught him that "when we go to war, we should have a purpose that our people understand and support. . . . In Vietnam, we had entered a halfhearted half-war," Powell said, "with much of the nation opposed or indifferent, while a small fraction carried the burden."

At the same time, Powell also faulted the army high command for its willingness to go along with the false promises of imminent victory when officers in the field knew that the war was going badly. "Many of my generation," Powell says, "vowed that when our turn came to call the shots, we would not quietly acquiesce in halfhearted warfare for half-baked reasons."

In 1989, when the United States sent troops into Panama and Colin Powell was Army Chief of Staff, he articulated what a new military generation soon called the Powell Doctrine: "Have a clear political objective and stick to it. Use all the force necessary, and do not apologize for going in big."

That policy governed the Desert Storm victory against Iraq in 1991. Whether it will govern all future interventions by the United States abroad remains to be seen. It may be that change, even in a democracy, is accelerating.

> *Leaders who accumulate power and*
> *experience gradually tend to*
> *outlast the rapid risers.*

On the issue of incrementalism versus radicalism, history suggests that people who rise gradually tend to outlast those who soar out of nowhere. From Otto von Bismarck to Winston Churchill, from Richard Nixon to Bill Clinton, the road to the top is seldom short and easy. It may be that what you learn along the way is the real key to longevity.

But sometimes the force of events themselves can be so radical as to require a dramatic response. When a new technology like the Internet arrives on the scene, for example, it forces businesspeople to rethink how they go to market. It was, in fact, a combination of technology and open global markets that led China and its leaders to go so far as to rethink their ideology.

Few leaders have faced the kind of change-or-die challenge that confronted communist China's Deng Xiaoping when his vast country's two top rulers died in 1976. The rigidly Marxist society that Deng inherited from Mao Zedong and Zhou Enlai was clearly headed for economic irrelevance in a world of information technology and global markets.

Isolationism had proved fatal to China in the past. The trick now was to unleash China's never entirely repressed market instincts without relinquishing the Communist Party's monopoly of power. Deng's brilliance was to see that the two need not be in conflict at all—the function and image of the party had to be transformed.

Previously, the party derived its legitimacy from its struggle to seize and hold power. Now, it was to be seen as the guarantor of social stability and provider of the means for prosperity. Deng's strategy was to scrap an outmoded ideology by creating the slogan, "It doesn't matter if a cat is white or black as long as it catches mice." At the same time, he provided the party with a new ideology, another slogan to which the Chinese people could relate wholeheartedly: "To get rich is glorious."

Of course, the more frequent challenge for an ambitious person is coping with defeat. When that happens and you fall from grace, you shouldn't assume that you have to get back in the saddle immediately. Although that may be the popular macho approach, you may need time to weigh what happened and learn from what were, almost surely, your own mistakes. A measured approach is the best way to increase the chances that your next attempt will succeed.

The pause for reflection is especially important for one whose fall derives from some character flaw that isn't easily corrected. Just as power tends to exacerbate a person's character flaws, so loss of power tends to generate rationalizations aimed at papering over the flaws. But Band-Aids® won't cover a flawed character for long. Such deep-seated failings invariably resurface and will once again bring down the person exhibiting them.

Failure, if properly channeled, can be an inspiration to future success.

Failure need not be self-perpetuating, however. Niccolo Machiavelli was, paradoxically, inspired by a failure.

In 1498, he was elected secretary to the second chancery of the Republic of Florence in Italy, which was in charge of that city-state's foreign and military affairs. Influential and effective, he was sent on twenty-four missions, including four to the king of France and several to Rome.

But when the French took over Florence, they relieved Machiavelli of his office. He was essentially confined to his small estate and forbidden to set foot in Florence. It was during this time, when everyone else was counting him out, that he wrote *The Prince,* a book that would gain him fame in his own time and influence political leaders and thinkers for centuries to come.

Accept change and move ahead without regrets.

In today's corporate world, the change-or-die mandate is alive and flourishing. One of its most ardent advocates is Lee Iacocca, a man who before July 1973 had known little but success.

That was when, after working for the Ford Motor Company for thirty-two years, and serving as its president for eight, he lost his post and was exiled to an office in a warehouse that featured cracked linoleum and two plastic coffee cups. It was a perfect place for self-pity, but it was also a perfect place to take charge of oneself. Then and there, Iacocca chose to accept change and move ahead, without regrets.

"As you go through life," he later wrote, "there are thousands of little forks in the road, and there are a few really big forks—those moments of reckoning, moments of truth. This was mine as I wondered what to do. Should I pack it all in and retire? I was fifty-four years old. I had already accomplished a great deal. I was financially secure. I could afford to play golf for the rest of my life."

That was one reasonable option. "But that just didn't feel right," he said. "I knew I had to pick up the pieces and carry on."

Fashion something constructive out of adversity.

There are times in everyone's life when something constructive is born out of adversity, Iacocca believes—times when things seem so bad that you've got to grab your fate by the shoulders and shake it.

"I'm convinced," he says, "it was that morning at the warehouse that pushed me to take on the presidency of Chrysler [Corporation] only a couple of weeks later." Iacocca was still moving along his arc of ambition.

Many years later, after a storied stint as Chrysler's chief executive officer, Iacocca handed over the reins to Robert Eaton. But he says that he had a hard time letting go. He wanted to climb back on the horse, when it was clearly better for him to stay off.

In this chapter, we have examined the issue of just when ambitious people should embrace change. In the next, we will discuss when they should let go.

10

The Dead Can't Lead the Living

Leave Gracefully

~

A graceful exit is the peak of the arc, the ambitious person's finest hour. Only the wisest achieve it. Some ambitious people refuse to let go and their arcs turn south. Witness Sewell Avery and Herbert Haft. Others retreat with flags flying, gaining more mastery all the way. Witness Roberto Goizueta, Dean F. LeBaron, Peter Lynch, and Andrew Carnegie. And then there is the messy saga of Apple Computer, which gave four chief executives in a row no chance to leave gracefully.

IN 1944, *LIFE* MAGAZINE captured a classic moment in the annals of pigheaded behavior. It was a photograph laughed at round the world. In it, Montgomery Ward & Company's obstinate chief executive, Sewell Avery, was shown sitting grimly in his office chair, arms folded, while two military policemen hoisted both chair and occupant high in the air and lugged them off the corporation's premises.

Avery loathed the New Deal, in general, and Franklin Delano Roosevelt, in particular. In 1944, defying a wartime labor rule, he refused to sign a union contract with his employees—whereupon President Roosevelt ordered the United States Army to take over the company, minus Sewell Avery.

Avery's unyielding myopia hurt Montgomery Ward even more when he took back the company at war's end. Convinced that poverty was just around the corner, he predicted yet another Great Depression and girded his company for disaster by slashing maintenance costs and refusing to buy land for new outlets. He even ordered Montgomery Ward's stores to remain unpainted.

Meantime, Avery's chief competitor, Sears, Roebuck & Company, built ninety-two new stores and dominated the suburbs just as land prices soared. The move shut out Montgomery Ward even if Avery had been willing to expand.

He was not.

Avery remained as implacably self-righteous as if he were still nailed to that chair. The directors finally ousted him in 1955, when the company had become a virtual shadow of its once-thriving self.

They were too late.

The Avery effect was so damaging that Montgomery Ward never recovered. After finally going bankrupt in 1997, the corporation vanished.

Once an achiever tastes real power, with all its challenges and privileges, it becomes harder to go gently into the night. The illusion of indispensability dies hard. Some never lose it.

Peter Lynch is a recent example of a person who knew how to leave gracefully. After several years managing one of Fidelity's most successful mutual funds, Lynch decided it was someone else's turn. Besides, he wanted to spend more time with his family. So, in 1990, he stepped down from running the fund.

Initially, he was not publicly visible in Fidelity's business, though his personal writing and publishing activities increased. But in the last decade, he has emerged as a public figure in Fidelity's marketing campaigns and as a director of the company. Lynch is not making investment decisions, but he is leveraging his reputation for smart investing.

Some leaders exit gracefully but never really leave.

Sam Walton, whose ambition and achievements we have described elsewhere is this book, is another person who exited gracefully. In truth, Walton, like Lynch, never completely left. Walton found retirement wanting and soon gave it up in favor of cheerleading all those he had left in charge of his burgeoning Wal-Mart Stores, Inc., empire.

In 1992, the last year of his life, and despite suffering from bone cancer, Sam Walton relished traveling around his nationwide domain, dropping in unexpectedly on one Wal-Mart store, then flying off to the next.

He was a plain man, perhaps the world's most unpretentious billionaire. He always wore a Wal-Mart baseball cap and a name tag reading "Sam." No longer chief executive—he had wisely stepped down to free his successors—he piloted himself in his own secondhand plane, flying from small town to small town to visit Wal-Mart stores. He loved flying, he told a reporter. "I really like the independence of being able to go where I want to when I want—in a hurry."

Next to flying and quail hunting, Walton most loved visiting Wal-Mart employees, chatting with them, and making sure they both deserved and were given bonuses, profit sharing, and stock purchase plans. Speaking to large groups, he customarily sat them on the floor and squatted among them like a football coach bucking up his team between halves.

"Are you thinkin' of doing those extra little things?" he asked. "Are you lookin' the customer in the eye and offering help? If you don't care about your store and your customers, it won't work."

Wandering through his beloved stores until the last months of his life, Sam Walton remained true to his rural origins and never stopped inspiring people with his clear thinking and simple strategies. He was so good at his work that he never had to quit, retiring in name only.

In some ways, he achieved the dream that only those at the very top of the arc of ambition can hope for. He died with his boots on, still looked up to as the most competent person in the huge company he created.

> *Ambitious leaders often sabotage—*
> *unwittingly or not—a successful transition*
> *to the next generation.*

One excuse that achievers often use for hanging on is the lack of a competent successor. That lack is nearly always the fault of the ambitious leader. He or she has either failed to groom a first-rate successor or has selected an obedient courtier— somebody unlikely to surpass the leader's own sterling record. To feel threatened by one's successor is a futile but remarkably common reaction to inevitable departure. It is almost as though a former leader has to mourn the death of his or her previous self.

It seems to us that Lynch and Walton found a graceful—and useful—way to make the transition to a nonoperating role. The problem, however, is that most ambitious people don't know how to leave and still contribute to the enterprise they created.

The second-in-command can, of course, grow into a job or surprise everyone with hitherto unexpected leadership qualities. When Franklin Roosevelt died in 1945 of a cerebral hemorrhage, the country was still at war. Vice President Harry Truman moved into the White House.

Throughout the country, many were concerned. What were his qualifications for the job? After all, hadn't he been the protégé of Missouri's corrupt Democratic boss, Tom Pendergast? It was widely assumed that he was a political nonentity.

Instead, with little preparation for the job beyond having been an excellent United States Senator, Truman rose to great heights in his new position. Under his White House watch, he brought the war to a successful conclusion, he established the Truman Doctrine to keep in check the expansion of communism, and domestically he pushed for civil rights and abolished segregation in the armed forces.

Roosevelt's succession was forced by a tragic event. But those who don't choose to leave in time—or provide for succession in time—invariably harm themselves or their organizations or both. And, sooner or later, all achievers in all fields must confront their universal destiny—exit.

The question is when and how. Most avoid the answer. Like borrowers who evade repayment, they forget that procrastination always costs more.

In truth, it is wise to plan your endgame in advance, much as some undaunted people specify their funeral wishes. There is nothing macabre about ensuring a departure that heartens others, especially if you are captain of an organization with hundreds of de facto dependents.

Consider, for example, the remarkable foresight of Roberto C. Goizueta, a Cuban immigrant who arrived penniless in the United States in 1960. Goizueta found an entry-level job at the Coca-Cola Company's headquarters in Atlanta, Georgia. Ambitious, brilliant, and charismatic, Goizueta rose and rose. By 1981, he was Coke's chairman and chief executive officer, having turned the corporation into a highly admired multinational company with one of the world's strongest brands.

Goizueta considered himself indispensable, but he also was a consummate long-term strategist. He began training his successor, M. Douglas Ivester, the company's chief financial wizard, at least four years before the unexpected event that ended Goizueta's career.

That event was lung cancer.

When Coca-Cola disclosed the condition of its seemingly irreplaceable chief executive in late 1997—he died at sixty-five a few months later—Wall Street's reaction was strikingly calm. The price of Coke's shares fell less than a dollar apiece. Everyone knew that Goizueta had signaled Ivester as his heir apparent back in 1994. Accordingly, the Street reacted to Goizueta's cancer with a vote of extraordinary confidence in his legacy, the company he had built.

The courage to leave gracefully is always in short supply. The more a person lacks it, the more others are likely to suffer.

Napoléon Bonaparte was an egregious example. Had he been content to accept his enforced exile on the island of Elba, had he not escaped to France to restore his army and fight again, the lives of thousands of Frenchmen, Englishmen, and Germans would have been saved at the Battle of Waterloo.

Otto von Bismarck, the powerful chancellor of Germany, had this advice, "You can retire or you can be forced into retirement, which is humiliating and can end in depression." He, though, didn't follow his own good advice and was forced into retirement by Kaiser Wilhelm II.

Obstinacy can diminish an otherwise accomplished career.

Many an individual has tarnished his or her accomplishments by refusing to step aside. But knowing when to step aside doesn't just come at the end of a career. Impossible situations can arise that challenge even the most ambitious person. Quitting an impossible situation is not cowardice. It may be the intelligent and honorable thing to do.

Just ask Dean Francis LeBaron, a Boston financier. For him, sudden opportunity arrived in 1990 when Mikhail S. Gorbachev's government invited him to lead an economic rescue mission aimed at resuscitating the ailing economy of the then Soviet Union.

LeBaron had founded Batterymarch Financial Management, then a handler of nearly $10 billion in client money and a pioneer in creating index funds, quantitative investing, and Western investment in developing nations. He was a confirmed contrarian: Whatever the market trend of the day, he invested in the opposite direction.

In the summer of 1990, other institutional investors in the United States and Europe were distinctly allergic to the deteriorating Soviet Union. Their disinterest naturally whetted LeBaron's contrarian appetite.

It all started when LeBaron was invited to speak at a Harvard University conference in Cambridge, Massachusetts. Sponsored by a research organization in the United States and the Soviet Academy of Science, the meeting was titled "Swords into Plowshares." The topic: how to convert U.S. and Soviet military production into peacetime uses.

In his speech, LeBaron described the Soviet Union's enormous potential as a capitalist player in the global economy. Once rid of communist rigidities and military ambitions, he argued, the country would enjoy a free economy powered by skilled workers and vast natural resources. And once that happened, he surmised, the Soviet Union's 300 million citizens would eagerly buy the Western goods they coveted—a huge market for Western companies and a ripe opportunity for Western investors.

All of this would, in turn, benefit the global economy as a whole. "Capitalism," LeBaron noted, "thrives most vigorously when not constrained by political boundaries."

To speed the transformation, LeBaron urged the privatization of all state-run Soviet enterprises and the creation of a large investment fund to encourage Western companies to enter partnerships with newly privatized Soviet companies. He also observed that privatization would require great quantities of hard currency, which only foreign investors could supply. That meant the Soviets would have to revamp their legal system to protect those investors.

The Soviet government duly invited LeBaron to Moscow to elaborate on his ideas. He was struck by the abject mediocrity of Soviet consumer goods, badly produced by central planning, and the high-level talent of a workforce with skills and schooling that more than equaled those of workers in the West. This disparity, caused in large part by the Soviet stress on military production, had bequeathed the country both millions of frustrated consumers and a talent pool of 1.5 million defense scientists and engineers who could help reform the economy.

LeBaron's meetings with Soviet economic officials led him to believe that he was riding the wave of the transition from central planning to free-market trade. In October 1990, Batterymarch signed a joint-venture agreement setting up the Soviet Companies Fund, a $1-billion kitty aimed at investing in Soviet companies.

LeBaron had seized the opportunity thrust upon him at the Boston meeting to become a pioneer in establishing trust and promoting coventures between Western investors and Soviet partners. The fund, he says, was intended to "serve as a model for the future privatization of other state-owned enterprises."

Stay alert for signs that may indicate
it is time for you to go.

In the months that followed, dozens of leading companies in the United States began exploring joint-ventures with Soviet counterparts. But ominous straws were in the wind. The ruble began its downward spiral, to the point that LeBaron's drivers insisted on being paid in dollars. Then his telephone bills and domestic air travel required hard-currency payments. The Russian mafia was growing stronger, with the government seemingly unable to control these marauding, gun-toting groups. Russian society was unraveling before him.

It became evident that some Soviet officials and institutions were being less than helpful and even withholding promised support for the joint ventures. Agreements to help finance privatization were often breached.

In the middle of July 1991 came the annual G-7 (Group of Seven) meeting of the leaders of the United States, Japan, Germany, Great Britain, France, Canada, and Italy. LeBaron had high hopes that G-7 would endorse the Grand Bargain, a proposal backed by Mikhail Gorbachev to infuse the Soviet Union with up to $20 billion in aid over a three-year period. But the leaders, who had other concerns in mind, refused.

Gorbachev appeared at the sessions to press his cause. He left empty-handed. Back home, the fifteen Soviet republics stepped up pressure to win independence from Moscow.

A month after the summit meeting, the fate of the Soviet empire was sealed when Gorbachev signed the so-called Union Treaty, which stopped Moscow from taxing the republics without their permission. In effect, the Soviet Union was fragmented and therefore doomed.

After that, events moved quickly. In August, a cabal of communist hacks conspired to oust Gorbachev. Tension heightened as the Soviet president vanished from sight and huge tanks roared around Moscow, chewing up pavement.

In the end, the conspirators proved inept. Their coup fizzled. Gorbachev reappeared and consigned them all to cells. But his days were numbered. The balance of power was rapidly shifting toward Boris Yeltsin, then the president of Russia.

The isolation of the central government was bad news for LeBaron's plans, which assumed at least a functioning Soviet Union, if not a healthy one. But the game was not quite over. In October, the Overseas Private Investment Corporation (OPIC) agreed to insure investments in the Soviet Companies Fund up to $100 million.

Meanwhile, a steady stream of corporate economists and technical experts was still pouring into Moscow. Corporations like Fabbrica Italiana di Automobili di Torino (Fiat), Standard Oil Company, and Xerox Corporation had entered into joint ventures with former state enterprises.

As LeBaron recalls, his contrarian gauge was flashing a warning: He was moving with the investment flow instead of, as was his custom, against it.

Some of the companies, worried about the obvious risks of investing in Russia, insisted that LeBaron personally supervise the Soviet Companies Fund. He agreed. It was dispiriting work.

In one case, LeBaron discovered a superb Russian optical manufacturer called Lomo and labored to find a foreign partner that would enable Lomo to sell its endoscopes and other excellent products abroad. He finally lined up Switzerland's Leica, only to learn that, behind his back, Lomo had signed up with a Japanese company to handle its exports. The end of the Lomo deal marked the beginning of LeBaron's postgraduate education in the reality of doing business in Russia.

On Christmas Day of 1991, President Gorbachev, the Soviet architect of the privatization policy, resigned. Any semblance of the Union of Soviet Socialist Republics departed with him.

All through Batterymarch's months in Moscow, LeBaron's staff had worked out of a handsome estate in Lenin Hills on the city's outskirts, where U.S. President Ronald Reagan once stayed. The central government provided the dacha for free.

Now that it was the property of the new Russian government, LeBaron was informed he would have to pay. The price tag:

some $100,000 a month. But as was true in so many of his deal-
ings, he had trouble finding out which of the government's al-
leged representatives was in charge.

In February 1992, still hoping to salvage something from the
rapidly deteriorating situation, LeBaron received a phone call
from an aide who reported that the staff was locked out of the
dacha. The news "somehow sparked a kind of mental video of
the whole experience" in the Soviet Union, he recalls.

"Of course, dollars could have opened the padlock, but my
mouth was bitter with the taste of betrayal and defeat." He told
his staff: "Get on a plane and leave this country . . . now."

LeBaron's great experiment was over. "Nothing," he concluded, "is ever quite as contrary as reality."

Like many before him, Dean LeBaron had had a great opportunity thrust upon him and he seized it—in spite of its risks and
uncertainties. Like many before him, he had applied every
ounce of energy and skill to the task.

But the gods of politics, economics, and history withheld their
blessing. In the end, LeBaron lost the game. He knew it and
walked away.

Knowing when to go
ultimately puts you in control.

In addition to protecting yourself and colleagues from harm, a
clear sense of when to walk puts you in control. You are not just
a pawn of other people's ambitions.

The key is to be in a position to take the step. That is, you
must be both independent enough and secure enough to be able
to make an exit. And walking away may be your only defense
against being victimized by the actions corporations sometimes
take in hard times.

Paranoia is not a requirement of business success, but more than a little helps, especially in a troubled company when fault-finders take to conspiring against one another. This was the kind of corrosive atmosphere that enveloped Apple Computer, Inc., in the 1980s, when its board forced out four chief executives in succession.

Apple's disarray was totally unexpected. Steven P. Jobs, the company's presiding genius and cofounder (with Stephen Wozniak), had taken the company through dizzying growth. During the first five years of Macintosh computer sales under Jobs's freewheeling leadership, the company's annual gross reached $2 billion.

But even the golden Apple was not immune to fate's bite and the consumer's whim. Apple sales began a downward spiral in 1985. The directors and top managers agreed that Steve Jobs had to go.

Losing Jobs, clearly one of the industry's creative giants, was bad enough news for Apple. (The competition, led by a temporarily rejuvenated IBM, was slicing off bigger and bigger chunks of Apple's market share.) But the atmosphere at Apple was further poisoned by the way the company carried out the changing of the guard.

When the board kicked Jobs upstairs, they already had a successor in mind, John Sculley. Sculley had come to work for Apple in 1983 after a successful career at PepsiCo, Inc. And it was Sculley who broke the news to Jobs. Furious, Jobs responded, "If you do that, you're going to destroy this company."

Sculley's first order of business was to reorganize the company and introduce new efficiencies. It took him two years to remake Apple and put it back on what he thought was the right road.

His rescue operation started with great promise. In 1986, when a new Mac was marketed, Apple regained its prominent spot in the computer limelight. Profits soared, shareholders smiled. But trouble was just around the corner.

Insiders claimed that Sculley did not communicate well with his senior managers, which meant that a strategic unity of purpose was lacking. And the communication gap was supposedly widening as time passed.

Big mistakes began to surface. During one Christmas season, for example, Apple hiked the price of its computers 29 percent. Not surprisingly, other companies' cheaper IBM clones flew off store shelves, leaving Macs gathering dust. Apple fell short of projected sales by about 50 percent.

By 1993, the company was in such dire trouble that death appeared imminent. Fighting a two-front war was draining precious resources. On the one hand, costly research was needed to keep Apple's software hot, while the company was also struggling to maintain its edge in hardware. Profits were taking a drubbing as a result.

Sculley tried to negotiate a merger with IBM. He failed. His next solution was to break up the company into two separate entities, software and hardware. The in-house outcry among executives put an end to that idea.

Sculley's days were numbered. Though he had previously talked of resigning, when the ouster came, he was taken by surprise. It was abrupt and crude, forcing an undignified departure upon a leader once hailed as a savior.

Sculley's successor as chief executive was an insider, Michael Spindler, formerly the senior manager in charge of day-to-day operations. Spindler cut back on everything: Employees were let go, raises and bonuses were canceled. Among the least well received of Spindler's unpopular moves were the petty economies he introduced, like charging for use of the company gym and raising prices at the cafeteria.

No matter how close the corner-cutting, it wasn't enough to solve Apple's problems. Despite some success with a new and faster microprocessor, the company's share of worldwide computer sales had fallen to 8.3 percent by 1995.

Apple took the unprecedented step of deciding to license Apple clones, but, alas, none of the big players like Compaq Computer Corporation or Dell Computer Corporation were interested. Instead, Apple made a deal with the Korean conglomerate, Daewoo Corporation.

The arrangement worked well for Daewoo, but not for Apple, which, as it turned out, had simply created its own direct competition. By the end of 1995, the company was in such turmoil that it twice again tried to merge, first with Royal Philips Electronics, then with Sun Microsystems, Inc. Both attempts failed.

Although Apple had some 22 million loyal customers around the world, the company's market share was stagnant, profits were declining, and the research-and-development department had apparently run out of fresh ideas. Christmas sales, typically Apple's best season, were so low in 1995 that the corporation posted a loss.

If you are a source of pessimism within your organization, recognize that your days may be numbered.

Management itself reflected the epidemic of pessimism spreading throughout the company. Morale plunged. Many believed that the only hope for Apple was to sell the business before it became worthless. Shareholders demanded Michael Spindler's resignation.

On January 31, 1996, the directors fired Spindler much as they had Sculley, with no hint of their intentions beforehand

and without the courtesy of a resignation offer. Spindler left the Apple campus without any personal good-byes. Whereas Jobs had left in a rage, Sculley and Spindler had gone with resentment and disappointment.

Five days later, Gilbert Amelio took over as Apple's fourth chief executive officer since the company was incorporated in 1977— and its third since Jobs was sent packing in 1985. Each tenure had been successively shorter, indicating a business in serious trouble. Amelio, a native of New York City and an established technocrat, was also a two-year member of the Apple board.

Prior to assuming the helm at Apple, Amelio had worked for five years at National Semiconductor Corporation. There, he managed a successful turnaround. But fixing Apple would prove to be more difficult.

It wasn't until June that Amelio began to grapple with Apple's crucial problem, software. That is where Microsoft was trouncing the company. But there was a disturbing sense of déjà vu about Amelio's efforts: Once again, Apple's research-and-development people failed to produce a marketable operating system. And once again, the new chief executive reorganized the company without improving performance.

Knowing when to enter can be just as important as knowing when to exit.

Ironically, Gil Amelio's most significant achievement at Apple turned out to be his hiring of a most unexpected white knight: Steve Jobs riding a horse named NeXT. NeXT Software, Inc., the company Jobs founded after leaving Apple, had developed an operating system with a proven track record, just what Apple needed.

First, Amelio bought NeXT for more than $400 million, and then Jobs returned to Apple as Amelio's special adviser. Amelio's move came just in time: Apple's losses for 1996 totaled a whopping $816 million.

However, finances did not improve at first as losses climbed still higher, to $1.6 billion by March of 1997. And many of the company's best-trained and loyal staff made the decision to walk rather than wait for what they believed would be the ultimate disaster. In the summer of 1997, the board removed the chief executive officer himself. Amelio had lasted almost seventeen months.

Although he officially declined the title of chief executive, Steve Jobs was already Apple's de facto leader. From the moment Amelio departed, Jobs stepped in to run his old company with skill and assurance. Like a much-divorced man who eventually goes back to his first wife, Jobs had returned home to his first and greatest love.

In January 1998, Apple announced fiscal first quarter profits of $47 million, a New Year's present for Apple's beleaguered workers—to say nothing of its long-suffering shareholders. Apple topped that performance the next quarter, when profit increased by another $10 million. If the recovery keeps rolling along, Jobs will have pulled off a classic comeback worthy of inclusion in business history books, while vindicating himself in the process.

Dedicated leaders deserve the chance to leave gracefully.

But the real lesson in Apple's saga lies in the inability of three capable and ambitious men—Sculley, Spindler, and Amelio—to turn around a tough situation, or to leave gracefully when it became apparent that they could not succeed.

The board must accept its share of the blame, to be sure. It was unable to see what was going on within the enterprise or to find a leader with the skills and savvy to fit the conditions at Apple. More to our point, the board's ham-handed approach denied the ousted executives even the appearance of a graceful exit.

Like many technology companies, Apple had grown out of a unique mix of its founders' audacity, ambition, and greater purpose. Technology for Jobs and Wozniak was a way of empowering humans. They built a company focused on developing exciting products. They didn't build the perfect corporate machine. In that sense, they were Creators, dedicated to pioneering new technologies that would make old ones obsolete.

Those who followed were Capitalizers. Sculley and Amelio knew how to build infrastructures but couldn't make them work in a quirky company like Apple.

Now Jobs is being challenged to build the infrastructure Apple has always needed. If he fails, the company probably will fall to Consolidators. And, eventually, Consolidators would smother Apple's extraordinary creativity. Should this scenario come to pass, Jobs would be seen as having overstayed his welcome.

Perhaps there is something peculiarly American in the notion that people in power should eventually go quietly, making way for the next generation of leaders. To most of the world, this notion verges on the miraculous.

Americans were the first people to proclaim a bedrock faith in limited government, which ensures peaceful succession, a principle still nonexistent in scores of other countries. Indeed, one can read political history as a relentless round of coups, regicides, and revolutions sparked by pent-up rage against rulers who refuse to be succeeded.

By contrast, Americans can take great pride in having created a succession system far more effective than even the best royal dynasty. It is a system that has thus far enabled the governed to change their president forty-two times.

Surely, this record provides organizations with a best-practice standard of governance. That it is sometimes ignored does not contradict the fact that nothing is more common in healthy companies than a chief executive carefully grooming the top candidates for his or her job so that there will be a smooth shift of power when the time comes.

To appreciate the singularity of this achievement, one need only cite a rogue's gallery of intractable rulers. What was ugly in Rome in 44 B.C. when Brutus assassinated Julius Caesar was ugly in Moscow almost 2,000 years later when Vladimir Lenin, incapacitated by a series of strokes (there was no talk of resignation) realized that his death would trigger a power struggle between his henchmen Leon Trotsky and Joseph Stalin.

Lenin's testament criticized both men but clearly favored Trotsky as the lesser of two evils. With customary cunning, Stalin quickly admitted his faults and vowed to change. He knew full well that Trotsky's ego would prevent him from following suit. Stalin's phony humility sealed Trotsky's doom.

*An inability to relinquish control
virtually assures a damaging struggle
among would-be successors.*

Exiled from the Soviet Union, Trotsky was assassinated in Mexico City in 1940. When his own death loomed, Stalin named no successor and stubbornly rode his power to the grave. A triumvirate formed to assume control, but it was quickly dominated by Nikita Khruschev and the succession issue was never resolved.

Mikhail Gorbachev almost broke the mold. Named general secretary of the Communist Party in 1985, he vainly tried to save the crippled Soviet Union from self-destruction. His actions basically ended the Soviet Union's seventy-year stultification, freeing the revolutionary forces led by Boris Yeltsin and forcing out Gorbachev in the process.

As Dean LeBaron discovered, however, Yeltsin & Company soon destroyed the promise of Russia's post-Soviet future as a free-market democracy. And what is most striking amid Russia's current chaos is the familiar nightmare of a leader (Yeltsin) totally ineffective and totally unwilling to arrange a peaceful succession.

Succession issues roil family businesses, too, and often spark bitter battles.

Although some might expect succession in a family business to run smoothly, the opposite is often true. The children of Barry Bingham, owner of the *Louisville Courier-Journal,* tore his media empire apart, largely out of sibling spite. Nor is this tale of family feuding over a succession an isolated incident.

In Washington, D.C., Herbert Haft built up a chain of drugstores that came to be known as the Dart Group. When his son Robert, a graduate of the Harvard Business School, came into the company, he acquired Crown Books and Trak Auto. All might have run smoothly had Robert not decided that it was time for his father to retire. His father disagreed. The struggle between father and son ended in a bitter court fight, which Herbert lost.

The Dart Group was sold off as were other interests. The family shared the spoils, but any semblance of family fellowship virtually ceased to exist—all over the issue of retirement.

A happier tale is the story of John H. Johnson, the entrepreneur who in 1945 founded *Negro Digest,* which later became the immensely successful and pioneering *Ebony* magazine. Johnson's beginnings were modest. Born in Arkansas in 1918, his mother brought him to Chicago when she found out that there was no school for black children in their hometown.

Johnson did well in high school and won a scholarship to the University of Chicago. After graduation, he decided that the United States was ready for a first-rate magazine about the lives and times of black people. To raise seed money, Johnson used his mother's furniture as collateral for a $500 loan. *Negro Digest* was such a hit that in 1945 Johnson launched *Ebony,* which was an immediate success.

Johnson designated his daughter Linda as his successor while she was still attending college. After business school, Linda began her career in the family-owned cosmetics company before moving to the parent company to become its president.

"He welcomed me with open arms," Linda has said, describing the transition. "He's very respectful of me and my decisions. That has laid the groundwork for me doing a good job."

Transitions are never easy, of course, but difficulties are foreordained in a family business where old resentments and sibling rivalries get in the way of common sense and plain self-interest. Unlike the Johnsons, the Binghams, the Hafts, and similar riven families seem incapable of doing themselves the favor of compromise.

A *timely exit can produce unexpected dividends for others—and sometimes for the world at large.*

On the whole, business has a relatively good record of timely exits. One of the most spectacular was that of Andrew Carnegie.

The mercurial Scotsman conquered American capitalism with Napoléonic skill and then stepped aside in a coup that gave his adopted country the world's biggest steel empire—not to mention enormous philanthropic benefits.

Born in 1835, the son of an idealistic, impecunious weaver, Carnegie grew up with conflicting values. His father was a radical Chartist, a political movement in Scotland that demanded a wider suffrage from the British authorities. Although Carnegie admired his father's humanism, his pragmatic mother, impatient with pie-in-the-sky hopes, set the boy's priorities by bundling her family off to Pennsylvania when Andrew was only twelve but already a breadwinner.

In the United States, Andrew made up his mind to achieve two goals: to become very rich and to be very good, in that order. How he achieved both objectives is legend.

At eighteen, having spent his adolescence as a bobbin boy, engine tender, messenger, and telegraph operator, Carnegie found a mentor in Thomas Scott, future president of the Pennsylvania Railroad. Scott hired the young man as his personal secretary, gave him invaluable experience as a military transport manager during the Civil War, and best of all, lent him money to buy his first ten shares of stock.

That was the beginning of a portfolio that would mushroom in the postwar economic boom so that, by 1868, when Carnegie was all of thirty-three years old, he had investment income alone of nearly $50,000 a year. It was a huge sum at the time.

Taking a hard look at his achievement, which reflected his mother's ambitions for him, Carnegie recalled his father's values and duly wrote himself a powerful memo pledging to stop chasing money in two years. "The amassing of wealth is one of the worst species of idolitary [sic]. No idol is more debasing than the worship of money," he wrote.

Despite his good intentions, the memo wound up in Carnegie's desk drawer, forgotten amid the irresistible opportunities he spotted and seized during the depression of 1873. Buying all sorts of Pittsburgh steelmaking businesses for a pittance, he created the Carnegie Steel Corporation and acquired the latest Bessemer furnaces to make high-quality steel and sell it for low prices.

A demon cost-cutter, Carnegie kept improving productivity by turning his business into a vertically integrated operation controlling raw materials, transportation, manufacturing, distribution, and finance, an expansionist policy very much in tune with the one followed by John D. Rockefeller in the oil business. Heavy tariffs on foreign steel gave Carnegie an advantage, and eventually he was making steel rails for $12 a ton and selling them for double that amount.

In 1889, more than twenty years after Carnegie had penned his high-minded memo, the ideals it expressed apparently began to nag at Carnegie's conscience. In a self-assessment titled, "The Gospel of Wealth," published by the prestigious *North American Review*, Carnegie came down on both sides of his moral sense. Building capital was essential to human progress, he wrote, but the rich were also morally obliged to share their wealth and "produce the most beneficial results for the community."

The depression of 1893 to 1897 put Carnegie's sharing plans on hold. Once again spotting bargains for anybody with cash and courage, he acquired massive iron deposits in Minnesota's Mesabi Range and bought a railroad to transport cheap ore supplies for his Pittsburgh steel mills. He also supported his associate Henry Clay Frick's union busting during the bloody Homestead strike of 1892. (Curiously, Carnegie's lovely vision of shared wealth apparently didn't extend to those who worked to turn out his products.) He wound up with virtual control of the steel industry in the United States.

According to Carnegie's 1889 treatise, "A man who dies rich dies disgraced." So he now set about practicing what he had preached. His preliminary steps in that direction involved one of the greatest bluffs in business history.

In the year 1900, Carnegie Steel netted $40 million, of which Carnegie himself pocketed $25 million. That same year, he reached the then-venerable age of sixty-five, and it was widely assumed that he would retire to the castle he owned in Scotland.

At this point, the few big companies that controlled the manufacture of finished steel envisioned Carnegie and his crude-steel monopoly fading away. Thus, they announced plans to launch their own operations. It was, in effect, a bald threat to begin a price war aimed at pushing a supposedly tired Carnegie into selling out and disappearing from the scene.

Instead, Carnegie declared war. He suddenly announced plans to build scores of new specialty plants all over the country for the manufacture of finished steel, including tubes, rods, wires, and tin plate. He also disclosed that he would build a railroad from Pittsburgh to the Atlantic Ocean, which would deprive the two existing railroads of their steel traffic.

Aghast at the potential damage to their own investments, the other steel companies took their fears to the House of Morgan, realm of J. Pierpont Morgan, the nation's shrewdest investment banker. Morgan put together a deal that envisioned using Carnegie's holdings as the core of an even bigger steel colossus.

*Leaving while still in control gives
an ambitious achiever the power and
the flexibility to set a direction for
the next stage of life.*

In December of 1900, Morgan ordered one of his men to go and find out Carnegie's price. Carnegie responded by pricing Carnegie Steel at $480 million. Of that immodest sum, Carnegie's cut was $350 million in stocks and bonds.

Barely batting an eye, Morgan agreed to the sum without demur, merely commenting later that it "made Carnegie the richest man in the world."

A year or so later, Carnegie encountered Morgan on a transatlantic steamer. "I made one mistake, Pierpont," he said, "I should have asked $100 million more than I did." Legend has it that Morgan responded with his usual glower: "If you had, I should have paid it, if only to be rid of you."

Andrew Carnegie, now retired from the steel business, went off in a new direction. He took his millions and spent them, of course, but not on a summer mansion in Newport, Rhode Island, a luxurious yacht, or a profligate social life as was the custom of the wealthy at the time. Instead, Carnegie lavished his wealth on plans and projects for the common good.

In a previously unmatched pursuit of philanthropy, he gave millions to every imaginable aspect of human betterment. An avid reader as a boy, he decided to dedicate $56 million for building more than 2,500 library buildings in the United States and Great Britain. (His love for books also made him proud to claim warm friendship with writers like Mark Twain, Matthew Arnold, and Herbert Spencer, while disparaging most new tycoons of the Gilded Age as never having "read any book except a ledger.")

The autodidactical Carnegie had a special passion for education and scientific research. Hence, $30 million went to various universities, $29 million to endow pensions for underpaid college professors, $44 million to establish two new Carnegie Institutes in Pittsburgh and Washington, D.C., and $125 million to launch the pioneering Carnegie Foundation, which became a fount of new ideas for improving education in the United States.

Another of Carnegie's favorite causes reflected his abhorrence for war. Although his company thrived on selling steel for arms, he preferred to put his faith in human reason. So, in 1910, he gave $10 million to launch the Carnegie Endowment for International Peace, aimed at promoting ways to abolish war.

Carnegie despaired when four years later, in August 1914, the nations he had thought too advanced to slaughter each other plunged into the worst of all wars. He vanished from public view and even brought his memoirs to a halt as of 1914. He died in 1919, after a brief illness. "His heart was broken," his wife said.

The story of Andrew Carnegie provides a fitting conclusion to our discussion of ambition. With aspiration to spare, Carnegie elegantly traced his own achievements along the stages that define what we call the arc of ambition.

He brought his dream of great wealth to life by dint of hard work and the foresight to see the advantages to be gained from investing in new technology—the Bessemer process—which allowed him to produce better and cheaper steel at a time of great postwar growth. Known during his career as "the Happy Millionaire," his unbounded optimism helped sustain his faith that the world moves "ever onward and upward," and he wasn't afraid to move with it.

On the arc of ambition, he conceived and carried out his extraordinary achievements—to first get rich, then do good. To that end, Carnegie seized the moment when opportunity presented itself in the form of a buyout offer from J. P. Morgan. He knew precisely when to fold his cards and pocket his winnings.

Equally impressive, he fulfilled his ambition to disperse his wealth so that he might die in a state of grace: Of the $350 million in United States Steel first mortgage bonds Carnegie acquired from J. P. Morgan, not a single bond remained at Carnegie's death eighteen years later. Every dollar had gone to fulfill his ambition to help others.

Carnegie's graceful retirement from the world of business was merely the prelude to a new life that solidified his reputation as a man of generosity and probity. He proved that an ambitious person with a transcendent purpose can vastly multiply his life's worth, while at the same time, winning some small measure of immortality.

To be sure, few will reach the extraordinary heights of an Andrew Carnegie. But by following the principles we have outlined in this book, everyone can increase his or her chances of ascending to the peak of the arc of ambition.

Epilogue

What good is ambition? In this book, we have tried to answer that question in multiple ways. But if you rephrase the question—what good does ambition do?—you begin swimming in deeper water, surrounded by a fast-moving school of prickly philosophers. And swim you must.

Ambition is powerful stuff, capable of propelling a fast rise or a calamitous fall, and those propelled by it are wise to examine their ends as thoroughly as they make use of their means. Just where do you think you're headed, and will the course you set get you there? And can you do good along the way?

After all, this is a time when enterprises are being formed in new ways—with what are sometimes short-term objectives. But this is also a time when technology might enable the democratization of ambition. The historical barriers of capital, time, and geography have become easier to surmount.

Not that we have any wish to subject you to heavy moral lifting that might dilute your ambition. As our book makes clear, we believe the world needs more ambition, not less. It's our desire to inoculate as many people as possible with confidence to use their talents.

Given the high price of overweening ambition, though, we would also add a dose of humility to make our confidence vaccine—a recognition that excess is self-defeating, moderation is smart, and neither power nor wealth are passkeys to heaven.

All of this adds up to the necessity of balance, a theme constantly repeated in these pages as we scaled the arc of ambition from its beginning, when ambition may be nothing more than a dream or a glint in the eye, to the end, when the challenge is to leave gracefully and allow the next generation of achievers to realize their own ambitions. Along the way, we observed the ascent of Creators as they turn dreams into real achievements by persevering until they find an opportunity to seize upon. We observed how Capitalizers ensure that initial achievements become long-lived institutions through the disciplined pursuit of a greater purpose and an uncompromising adherence to a set of values. In this stage of the arc, we discovered that bringing others into your ambition by sharing your dreams and your power is the true basis for sustained achievement. As the arc reaches its peak, we observe how it runs the risk of turning south in the hands of Consolidators who don't respond in a timely and proactive manner to the changes and challenges that the environment continuously presents. We also confronted the inevitable mortality of all human phenomena—even the most ambitious person must know when to call it a day. A balanced ambition comprises a strong purpose governed by strong values, preferably values that keep you brave, honest, persevering, and more than a little stubborn.

To be sure, the perfect formula eludes us. Perhaps you can know true balance only when you see it, as in those rare, wonderfully buoyant achievers who always seem to know when to act and how fast or slow; when to fight and when to cut their losses or simply quit to fight another day. An arc of ambition so perfectly balanced cannot be easily replicated.

One can also infer from the morning newspaper that most aspiring achievers who crash and burn are, to be charitable, imbalanced in some egregious way that should have warned them not to fly so high. You can't take off with an overload of purpose on your starboard side and expect to fly safely with a deficit of values on your port side. Which is to say that a good ambition not only has to work but has to be balanced to work.

If your ambition is to build a great company, for example, getting the right balance in purpose and values from the outset will very likely establish the company's entire context from birth to eventual success or failure. We were reminded of this when we recently encountered two ambitious companies with totally opposite contexts, neither of them promising in the long term.

One was a fine old New England textile mill, now defunct for the painful reason that its owners were too honorable, too overweighted with humanistic values. Its owners had pledged to manage the size of their workforce so that nobody would ever have to be laid off. This commitment to full employment made them community heroes, but only for a time, since it eventually killed the company and all its jobs.

Equally imbalanced, this time with nonhumanistic values, was a startup Internet company being launched by a band of digital wunderkind armed with inordinate cash and chutzpah. In devising a hiring standard for potential colleagues, the young founders invented a new-low criterion—the greater the candidate's family and outside interests, the less he or she was deemed suitable. Relentless business ambition must come before anything else. We may be wrong, but it seemed to us that a context of emotional frigidity is no help in building a great company.

Balance also applies to matching the scope and pace of what you do to the resources and capabilities you can muster. We believe in setting the proverbial "stretch goals"—but we also don't believe in the impossible. People who let hubris triumph over reality do so for only a limited period. At the same time, focusing only on the barriers to achieving your dreams can transform you into a pessimist, depriving you of the oxygen of optimism so necessary for great achievement.

And what good does ambition do? As we end this tour of the arc of ambition, we find ourselves reiterating the common-sense notion that ambition must be measured by what and whom it benefits. A good ambition is holistic. It's not simply adding more chips to a stack of successes. Ambitious people benefit themselves to the degree that in pursuing their dreams, they also respect their own lives and loved ones. Ambitious people benefit society to the degree that their achievements enrich others as well as themselves. Accepting these rules seems to be the final stop on the arc of ambition.

As we finished this book, we were encouraged to learn that the world's wealthiest man had apparently reached the same conclusion. Bill Gates and his wife Melinda have lately created the world's second largest foundation. Like Andrew Carnegie's vast benefactions, the Gates Foundation is dedicated to improving education and public health. It reminds us of Carnegie's (and Adam Smith's) belief in the duty and the power of wealth-builders to achieve that Everest of high ambition—giving back to the broad public much of the treasure they earned but can't take with them. That, we submit, is more than good ambition in action. It is the best.

Sources and
Recommended Reading

Alexander the Great: A. B. B. Bosworth, *The Myth of the Magus: The Ruin of Alexander the Great* (Cambridge University Press, 1988); Donald W. Engels, *Alexander the Great and the Logistics of the Macedonian Army* (University of California Press, 1980); Robin Lane Fox, *Alexander the Great* (Viking Penguin, 1994); John F. C. Fuller, *The Generalship of Alexander the Great* (Da Capo Press, 1989); N. G. L. Hammond, *Alexander, The Genius of Alexander the Great* (University of North Carolina Press, 1998); Richard Stoneman (Editor), *Legends of Alexander the Great* (Tuttle, 1994); Ulrich Wilcken, *Alexander the Great* (Norton, 1977).

Ambania, Dhirubhai H.: Sumatra Ghoshal, "Reliance Industries," London Business School Case Series (1995) Gita Piramal, *Business Maharajas* (South Asia Books, 1996); Hamish McDonald, *The Polyester Prince: The Rise of Dhirubhai Ambani* (Allen & Unwin, 1999).

Amelio, Gilbert: Gilbert Amelio and William L. Simon, *On the Firing Line* (HarperBusiness, 1999); Gil Amelio andWilliam L. Simon, *Profit from Experience: The National Semiconductor Story of Transformation Management* (Wiley, 1995).

Aristotle: John L. Ackrill, *Aristotle the Philosopher* (Oxford University Press, 1994); John L. Ackrill (Introduction), *Aristotle* (Routledge, 1995); Jonathan Lear; *Aristotle: The Desire to Understand* (University of Cambridge, 1988); G. E. R. Lloyd;Moses I. Finley (Editor), *Early Greek Science: Thales to Aristotle* (Norton, 1990).

Avery, Sewell: John Brooks, "Sixty Years of American Business," *Forbes*, September 15, 1977; Stephen Goode, "Big Labor Matured with World War II Generation" *Insight on the News*, May 6, 1996.

Bannister, Roger: Roger Bannister, *The Four-Minute Mile* (Dodd, Mead, 1957).

Begin, Menachem: Robert C. Rowland, *The Rhetoric of Menachem Begin: The Myth of Redemption through Return* (University Press of America,

1985); Hillel Seidman andMordecai Schreiber, *Menachem Begin: His Life and Legacy* (Shengold, 1990).

Bingham, Barry: William E. Ellis, *Robert Worth Bingham and the Southern Mystique: From the Old South to the New South and Beyond* (Kent State University Press, 1997); John M. McGuire, Richard Schickel, "The Bingham Saga," *Fortune*, April 11, 1988; Barry Bingham; Samuel W. Thomas (Editor), *Barry Bingham: A Man of His Word* (University Press of Kentucky, 1993); Susan E. Tifft andAlex S. Jones, *The Patriarch: The Rise and Fall of the Bingham Dynasty* (Summit Books, 1991) "Another Episode of Louisville Soap Opera," *St. Louis Post-Dispatch*, August 18, 1991.

Bismarck, Otto Von: George O. Kent, *Bismarck and His Times* (Southern Illinois University Press, 1978); Otto Pflanze, *Bismarck and the Development of Germany: The Period of Fortification, 1880–1898* (Princeton University Press, 1990); Otto Pflanze, *Bismarck and the Development of Germany: The Period of Unification, 1815–1871* (Princeton University Press, 1990); Alan John Percivale Taylor, *Bismark—the Man and the Statesman* (Random House, 1975).

Bonaparte, Napoléon: David G. Chandler;Designed by Abe Lerner, *The Campaigns of Napoleon: The Mind and Method of History's Greatest Soldier, Vol. 1* (Simon & Schuster, 1977); Henry Lachouque; Anne S.K. Brown; and John R. Elting, *The Anatomy of Glory* (Stackpole Books, 1997); Felix M. Markham, *Napoleon* (New American Library, 1988); Claude-Francois Meneval, *Napoleon* (Random House, 1992); Alan Schom, *Napoleon Bonaparte: A Life* (HarperCollins Publishers, 1997); David Hamilton-Williams, *The Fall of Napoleon: The Final Betrayal* (Wiley, 1996).

Brando, Marlon: Truman Capote; Lothar Schirmer (Editor), *Marlon Brando: Portraits and Film Stills, 1946–1995* (Stewart, Tabori & Chang, 1996); Gary Carey, *Marlon Brando* (Salvat America, 1987); Tony Thomas, *The Films of Marlon Brando* (Carol Publishing, 1975).

Bronfman, Samuel: Kathryn Harris, "Bronfman Underwhelms Hollywood," *Bloomberg News*, November 27, 1998; Michael Robert Marrus, *Samuel Bronfman: The Life and Times of Seagram's Mr. Sam* (University Press of New England, 1992).

Buffett, Warren: Robert G. Hagstrom, *The Warren Buffett Portfolio: Mastering the Power of the Focus Investment Strategy* (Wiley, 1999); Robert G. Hagstrom, *The Warren Buffett Way: Investment Strategies of the World's Greatest Investor* (Wiley, 1995); Janet C. Lowe with Warren Buffett, *Warren Buffett Speaks: Wit and Wisdom from the World's Greatest Investor* (Wiley, 1997).

Caesar, Julius: Theodore A. Dodge, *Caesar: A History of the Art of War Among the Romans Down to the End of the Roman Empire,* (Greenhill Press, 1995); J. F. C. Fuller, *Julius Caesar: Man, Soldier, and Tyrant,* (Da Capo Press, May 1991); Matthias Gelzer, Peter Needham, *Caesar: Politician and Statesman* (Harvard University Press, 1985).

Canute, King: Laurence Marcellus Larson, *Canute the Great, 995,* (AMS Press, 1970); M.K. Lawson, *Cnut: The Danes in England in the Early Eleventh Century,* (Addison-Wesley, 1993).

Carlyle, Thomas: James Anthony Froude, *Thomas Carlyle: A History of His Life in London, 1834–1881* (Scholarly Press, 1970); Richard Garnett, *Life of Thomas Carlyle* (AMS Press, 1987); Simon Heffer, *Moral Desperado: A Life of Thomas Carlyle* (Trafalgar Square, 1996); Fred Kaplan andThomas Carlyle, *Thomas Carlyle: A Biography* (University of California Press, 1993).

Carnegie, Andrew: Andrew Carnegie; Foreword by Cecelia Tichi, *The Autobiography of Andrew Carnegie* (Northeastern University Press, 1990); Harold C. Livesay; Oscar Handlin (Editor), *Andrew Carnegie and the Rise of Big Business* (HarperCollins, 1991); James Mackay, *Andrew Carnegie* (Wiley, 1998); Milton Meltzer, *The Many Lives of Andrew Carnegie* (Watts Franklin, 1997); Joseph Frazier Wall, *The Andrew Carnegie Reader* (University of Pittsburgh Press, 1992); Joseph Frazier Wall, *Andrew Carnegie* (Oxford University Press, 1970); Joseph Frazier Wall, *Andrew Carnegie* (University of Pittsburgh Press, 1989).

Carrier, Willis H.: Scot M. Stevens, "In the Midst of Transition—Carrier Corporation," *Appliance,* October 1989. www.carrier.com.

Chanakya: Krishna N. Jha andLalit K. Jha, *Chanakya: The Pioneer Economist* (Nataraj Books, 1997); V. K. Subramanian, Maxims of Chanakya Kautilya (South Asia Books, 1980). Chandragupta Maurya: Purushottam L. Bhargava, *Chandragupta Maurya: A Gem of Indian History* (South Asia Books, 1996); Radha Kumud Mookerji, *Chandragupta Maurya and His Times: Madras University, Sir William Meyer Lectures, 1940–41* (South Asia Books, 1988).

Chappell, Tom: Tom Chappell, *The Soul of a Business* (Bantam, 1994); Tom Richman, "Identity in Crisis," *Inc.,* October 1989; "The Consumer's Guide to Planet Earth," *Business Wire,* April 10, 1990.

Chavez, Cesar: Susan Ferriss and Ricardo Sandoval, *The Fight in the Fields— Cesar Chavez and the Farmworkers Movement* (Harcourt Brace, 1997); Ruperto Garcia andConsuelo Rodriguez, *Cesar Chavez* (Chelsea House Publishers, 1991); Richard Griswold; Del Castillo andRichard A. Garcia, *Cesar Chavez: A Triumph Spirit* (University of Oklahoma Press, 1997);

John C. Hammerback andRichard J. Jensen, *The Rhetorical Career of Cesar Chavez* (Texas A&M Press, 1998); Consuelo Rodriguez, *Cesar Chavez* (Chelsea House, 1994).

Child, Julia: Noel Riley Fitch, *Appetite for Life* (Random House, 1999).

Churchill, Winston: James C. Humes;Foreword by Richard M. Nixon, *The Wit and Wisdom of Winston Churchill: A Treasury of More Than 1,000 Quotations and Anecdotes* (HarperCollins, 1994); R. Crosby Kemper (Editor), *Winston Churchill: Resolution, Defiance, Magnanimity, Good Will* (University of Missouri Press, 1995); William Raymond Manchester, *The Last Lion, Winston Spencer Churchill: Vol. I, Visions of Glory 1874–1932* (Dell, 1984); Stephen Mansfield;George E. Grant (Editor), *Never Give in: The Extrordinary Character of Winston Churchill* (Cumberland House, 1996).

Cohen, Bennett: Ben Cohen andJerry Greenfield, *Ben and Jerry's Double-Dip: How to Run a Values-Led Business and Make Money, Too* (Simon & Schuster, 1998); Ben CohenWith Jerry Greenfield; Meredith Maran, *Ben & Jerry's Double-Dip: Lead with Your Values and Make Money Too* (Simon & Schuster, 1997); Ben Cohen, *Ben and Jerry's Homemade Capitalism: Ingredients for Running a Socially Responsible Business* (Random House, 1989); Fred Chico Loger, *Ben and Jerry's: The Inside Scoop* (Random House, 1995); Mary Louise Schumacher, "Ben & Jerry's Brings Sweet Deal to Pr. George's," *The Washington Post*, July 21, 1999; Andrew Serwer, "Ben & Jerry's Is Back," *Fortune*, August 2, 1999; www.benjerry.com.

Columbus, Christopher: Fernando Colon andBenjamin Keen, *The Life of the Admiral Christopher Columbus by His Son Ferdinand* (Rutgers University Press, 1992); John Edens (Illustrator), *Meet Christopher Columbus* (Random House, 1989); Samuel Eliot Morison; Erwin Raisz (Illustrator), Bertram Greene (Illustrator), *Admiral of the Ocean Sea: A Life of Christopher Columbus* (Fine Communications, 1997); Samuel Eliot Morison, *Christopher Columbus, Mariner* (NAL/Dutton, 1990).

Confucius: Confucius; Tsai Chih Chung (Editor), *Confucius Speaks: Words to Live By* (Doubleday, 1996); Confucius andD. C. Lau *The Analects of Confucius* (Penguin Group, 1979); Confucius;James Legge (Translator), *Confucius: Confucian Analects, the Great Learning and the Doctrine of the Mean* (Dover, 1989); Herbert Fingarette, *Confucius: The Secular as Sacred* (Waveland Press, 1998).

Cooke, Jay: John Lewis Harnsberger;Stuart Bruchey (Editor) *Jay Cooke and Minnesota: The Formative Years of the Northern Pacific Railroad, 1868–1873* (Ayer, 1981); Ellis P. Oberholtzer, *Jay Cooke, Financier of the Civil War* (Reprint Services, 1993).

Copernicus, Nicolaus: Nicholas Copernicus;Jerzy Dobrzycki (Editor), Edward Rosen (Translator) *On the Revolutions: Nicholas Copernicus' Complete Works* (Johns Hopkins Press, 1992); Owen Gingerich, *The Great Copernicus Chase: And Other Adventures in Astronomical History* (Cambridge University Press, 1992); Alexandre Koyre, *The Astronomical Revolution: Copernicus, Kepler, Borelli* (Dover Publications, Incorporated, 1992); Edward Rosen, *Copernicus and His Successors* (Hambledon, 1995); Edward Rosen, *Copernicus and the Scientific Revolution* (Krieger, 1984).

Curie, Madame: Laura Conway, *Cities of Madame Curie* (Zeitgeist, 1990); Eve Curie; Vincent Sheean (Translator) *Madame Curie: A Biography* (Da Capo Press, 1990); Robert Woznicki, *Madame Curie Daughter of Poland* (American Institute of Polish Culture, 1984).

da Gama, Vasco: Rebecca Stefoff and William H. Goetzmann (Editor) Michael Collins, *Vasco Da Gama and the Portuguese Explorers* (Chelsea House, 1993); Sanjay Subrahmanyam and Vasco da Gama, *The Career and Legend of Vasco Da Gama* (Cambridge University Press, 1998).

da Vinci, Leonardo: David Alan Brown, *Leonardo Da Vinci: Origins of a Genius* (Yale University Press, 1998); Kenneth Lord Clark; Martin Kemp (Illustrator), *Leonardo Da Vinci* (Penguin Putman, 1988); Bruno Santi and Leonardo da Vinci, *Leonardo Da Vinci* (Riverside, 1990); Jack Wasserman and Leonardo Da Vinci (Artist), *Leonardo Da Vinci* (Abrams, 1984).

Darwin, Charles R.: Peter J. Bowler, *Charles Darwin: The Man and his Influence* (Cambridge University Press, 1996); E. J. Browne, *Charles Darwin* (Knopf, 1995; Janet J. Browne, *Charles Darwin: Voyaging* (Princeton University Press, 1996); Frederick H. Burkhardt; Sydney Smith (Editor), *Correspondence of Charles Darwin, Vol. 1* (Cambridge University Press, 1985); Charles Darwin, *The Origin of Species* (Grammercy, 1998; Charles Darwin; John Clare; and J.W. Tibble, *Voyage of the Beagle* (Wordsworth, 1998); Charles Darwin, *Autobiography of Charles Darwin and Selected Letters* (Dover, 1992); Ernst W. Mayr, *One Long Argument: Charles Darwin and the Genesis of Modern Evolutionary Thought* (Harvard University Press, 1993).

Dayan, Moshe: Moshe Dayan, *Moshe Dayan: Story of My Life* (Da Capo Press, 1992); Moshe Dayan, *Breakthrough* (Knopf, 1981); Yael Dayan, *My Father, His Daughter* (Farrar, Straus & Giroux, 1985); Robert Slater, *Warrior Statesman* (St. Martin's Press, 1991).

Dell, Michael: Rebecca Saunders, *Business the Dell Way: 10 Secrets of the World's Best Computer Business* (Login, 1999); Andrew E. Serwer, "Michael Dell Turns the PC World Inside Out," *Fortune*, September 8,

1997; Florence M. Stone, *Business the Dell Way: 100 Secrets of the World's Best Computer Business* (Capstone, 1999); www.dell.com.

Disney, Walt: Christopher S. Finch,Walt Disney (Artist), *The Art of Walt Disney: From Mickey Mouse to the Magic Kingdoms* (Abrams, 1995); Amy Boothe Green; Howard E. Green;Foreword by Ray Bradbury, *Remembering Walt: Favorite Memories of Walt Disney* (Disney Press, 1999); Katherine Greene;Richard Greene andKatherine Barrett, *The Man Behind the Magic: The Story of Walt Disney* (Viking Penguin, 1998); Kathy Merlock Jackson, *Walt Disney: A Bio-Bibliography* (Greenwood, 1993); Bob Thomas, *Walt Disney: An American Original* (Hyperion, 1994).

Disraili, Benjamin: Robert Blake, *Disraeli* (Trafalgar Square, 1998); Benjamin Disraeli;J. A. Gunn andM. G. Wiebe, *Benjamin Disraeli Letters: Early Letters, 1815–1834, Vol. 1* (University of Toronto Press, 1981); Robert W. Seton-Watson, *Disraeli, Gladstone, and the Eastern Question: A Study in Diplomacy and Party Politics, Vol. 594* (Norton, 1972); Paul Smith, *Disraeli: A Brief Life* (Cambridge University Press, 1999).

Drucker, Peter: Jack Beatty, *The World According to Peter Drucker* (Broadway, 1998); Peter F. Drucker With Isao Nakauchi, *Drucker on Asia: A Dialogue Between Peter Drucker and Isao Nakauchi* (Butterworth-Heinemann, 1997); John E. Flaherty, *Peter Drucker—Shaping the Managerial Mind: How the World's Foremost Management Thinker Crafted the Essentials of Business Success* (The New Lexington Press, 1999); Nan Stone (Editor), *Peter Drucker on the Profession of Management* (Harvard Business School, 1999).

Du Pont, Pierre: Du Pont De Nemours Pierre S.; Edmond E. Lincoln (Translator), *Du Pont de Nemours on the Dangers of Inflation: An Address by Pierre Sanvel DuPont, 1790* (Kelley, 1949); Thomas Jefferson; Dumas Malone (Editor),Linwood Lehmann (Translator), *Correspondence between Thomas Jefferson & Pierre Samuel Du Pont de Nemours, 1798–1817* (Da Capo Press, 1970); Robert J. Taggart, *Private Philanthropy and Public Policy: Pierre S. Du Pont and the Delaware Schools, 1890–1940* (University of Delaware Press, 1988); James P. Womack; Daniel T. Jones and Daniel Roos, *The Machine That Changed the World* (Rawson Associates, 1990).

Duncan, Isadora: Ann Daly; Isadora Duncan, *Done into Dance: Isadora Duncan in America* (Indiana University Press, 1995); Arnold Genthe, *Isadora Duncan* (Ayer, 1980); Ruth Lurie Kozodoy; Designed by Matina S. Horner *Isadora Duncan* (Chelsea House, 1991); Lillian Loewenthal, *The Search for Isadora: The Legend and Legacy of Isadora Duncan* (Princeton, 1992); Carol Pratl; Doree Duncan Seligmann (Editor); Cynthia Splatt (Editor);

Foreword by Agnes de Mille, *Life into Art: Isadora Duncan and Her World* (Norton, 1993).

Dunlap, Albert J.: John A. Byrne, *Chainsaw* (HarperCollins, 1999); John A. Byrne, "The Inside Story of What Drove Sunbeam's Board to Act," *Business Week*, July 6, 1998; Albert J. Dunlap, *Mean Business* (Simon & Schuster, 1997); Davan Maharaj, "Al Doesn't Work Here Anymore," *The Los Angeles Times*, June 19, 1998; "Sunbeam Girds for Fight With Ousted Chief," *Bloomberg News*, June 17, 1998.

Dunphy, Dermot: Michael Sivy, "How this bubble-wrap maker boomed by popping its own bubble," *Money*, March 1994; "Sealed Air; By the Throat," *The Economist*, September 14, 1991.

Durant, William C.: Axel Madsen, *The Deal Maker: How William C. Durant Made General Motors* (Wiley, 1999); James P. Womack; Daniel T. Jones and Daniel Roos, *The Machine That Changed the World* (Rawson Associates, 1990).

Edison, Thomas Alva: Paul Israel, *Edison: A Life of Invention* (Wiley, 1998); Robert Conot, *Thomas A. Edison: A Streak of Luck* (Da Capo Press, 1986); Lawrence A. Frost, *Thomas A. Edison Album* (Amereon, 1996); Martin V. Melosi andOscar Handlin, *Thomas A. Edison and the Modernization of America* (Addison Wesley, 1990).

Einstein, Albert: Denis Brian, *Einstein: A Life* (Wiley, 1997); Ronald William Clark, *Einstein: The Life and Times* (Avon, 1972); Stephen F. Pollard and Nigel Calder, *Einstein Universe* (Viking Penguin, 1980); Michael White andJohn Gribbin, *Einstein: A Life in Science* (Penguin USA, 1995).

Ellison, Lawrence J.: Mike Wilson, *The Difference Between God and Larry Ellison—Inside Oracle Corporation* (Quill, 1998); "Oracle—Surviving the Crash," case study, Harvard Business School; www.oracle.com.

Enlai, Zhou: David W. Chang, *Zhou Enlai and Deng Xiaping in the Chinese Leadership Succession Crisis* (University Press, 1984); Chae-Jin Lee, *Zhou Enlai: The Early Years* (Stanford University Press, 1996); Harrison E. Salisbury, *The New Emperors* (Little Brown, 1992); Kuo-Kang Kang Shao, *Zhou Enlai and the Foundations of Chinese Foreign Policy* (St. Martin's Press, 1996); Han Suyin;Paul De Angelis (Editor), *Eldest Son: Zhou Enlai and the Making of Modern China, 1898–1976* (Kodansha America, 1995).

Enrico, Roger A.: Roger A. Enrico, "Letter to Shareholders," PepsiCo, Inc., 1997 *Annual Report*.

Fisk, Jim: R. W. McAlpine; Steve Bedney (Editor),

Life and Times of Col. James Fisk, Jr. (Ayer, 1981); Marshall P. Stafford; Stuart Bruchey (Editor), *Life of James Fisk, JR.: A Full and Accurate Narrative of All the Enterprises in Which He Was Engaged* (Ayer, 1981).

Flaubert, Gustave: William J. Berg andLaurey K. Martin, *Gustave Flaubert* (Macmillan, 1997); Philippe Desan andMark Wolff, *Literary Objects: Flaubert* (University of Chicago, 1997); Gustave Flaubert; Francis Steegmuller (Editor), *Flaubert in Egypt* (Penguin USA, 1996); Francis Steegmuller (Editor), *The Letters of Gustave Flaubert, 1857–1880, Vol. 2* (Belknap Press of Harvard University Press, 1982); Francis Steegmuller (Editor), *The Letters of Gustave Flaubert, 1857–1880* (Belknap Press of Harvard University Press, 1984).

Forbes, B. C.: Marshall Loeb, "Words to Profit by," *Time*, December 7, 1998.

Ford, Henry: Ray Batchelor, *Henry Ford, Mass Production and Design* (St. Martin's Press, 1995); Ford R. Bryan, *Beyond the Model T: The Other Ventures of Henry Ford* (Wayne State University Press, 1997); David L. Lewis, *The Public Image of Henry Ford: An American Folk Hero and His Company* (Wayne State University Press, 1988); Sidney Olson; Foreword by David L. Lewis, *Young Henry Ford: A Picture History of the First Forty Years* (Wayne State University Press, 1997); Reynold M. Wik, *Henry Ford and Grass-Roots America* (University of Michigan Press, 1972).

Freud, Sigmund: Sigmund Freud and A. A. Brill, *The Basic Writings of Sigmund Freud (Modern Library Series)*(Random House, 1995); Peter Gay, *Freud: A Life for Our Time* (Norton, 1998); Philip Rieff, *Freud, the Mind of the Moralist: The Mind of the Moralist* (University of Chicago Press, 1990); Michael S. Roth,Library of Congress, *Freud Conflict and Culture: Essays on his Life, Work, and Legacy* (Knopf, 1998).

Frick, Henry Clay: Martha Frick Sanger, *Henry Clay Frick: An Intimate Portrait* (Abbeville Press, 1998); Kenneth Warren, *Triumphant Capitalism: Henry Clay Frick and the Industrial Transformation of America* (University of Pittsburgh Press, 1995).

Frobisher, Martin: William W. Fitzhugh (Editor);Jacqueline S. Olin (Editor), *Archeology of the Frobisher Voyages* (Smithsonian Institution Press, 1993) Thomas H. Symons, *Meta Incognito: A Discourse of Discovery Martin Frobisher's Arctic Expeditions, 1576–1578* (Canadian Museum of Civilization, 1999).

Galilei, Galileo: Mario Biagioli and Galileo Galilei,

Galileo Courtier: The Practice of Science in the Culture of Absolutism (University of Chicago Press, 1994); Stillman Drake, *Galileo: Pioneer Scientist* (University of Toronto Press, 1994); Maurice A. Finocchiaro (Editor);J. L. Heilbron (Editor), *The Galileo Affair: A Documentary His-*

tory, Vol. 1 (University of California Press, 1990); Jerome J. Langford and Stillman Drake, *Galileo, Science, and the Church* (Saint Augustine's Press, 1998) Michael Sharratt, *Galileo: Decisive Innovator* (Cambridge University Press, 1996).

Gandhi, Mohandas K.: A. L. Basham and Arun Bhattacharjee. *The Father of the Nation—Life and Message of Mahatma Gandhi* (Ashish, 1988); Yogesh Chadha, *Gandhi—A Life* (Wiley, 1998); Eknath Easwaran and Michael N. Nagler, *Gandhi the Man—The Story of His Transformation* (Nilgiri Press, 1997); Mohandas K. Gandhi, *Autobiography—The Story of My Experiments with Truth* (Dover, 1983); Mohandas K. Gandhi, *Gandhi on Non-Violence* (Norton, 1965); Mahatma Gandhi and Louis Fischer, *Essential Gandhi: An Anthology of His Writings on His Life, Work and Ideas* (Random House, 1983); B.R. Nanda and Mohandas K. Gandhi, *Mahatma Gandhi: A Biography: Complete* (Oxford University Press, 1996).

Garibaldi, Giuseppe: Giuseppe Garibaldi, *Garibaldi's Memoirs—From His Manuscript, Personal Notes and Authentic Sources* (International Institute of Garibaldian Studies, 1981); Benedict S. Lipira, *Giuseppe Garibaldi—A Biography of the Father of Modern Italy* (Noble House, 1998); John Parris, *The Lion of Caprera—A Biography of Giuseppe Garibaldi* (D. McKay Co., 1962); Jasper Godwin Ridley, *Garibaldi* (Viking, 1974); Herman J. Viola and Susan Viola, *Giuseppe Garibaldi* (Chelsea House, 1987).

Gates, William H. III: Joan D. Dickinson, *Bill Gates: Billionaire Computer Genius* (Enslow, 1997); Bill Gates With Collins Hemingway, *Business at the Speed of Thought: Using a Digital Nervous System* (Time Warner, 1999); Bill Gates With Nathan Myhrvold, *The Road Ahead* (Penguin USA, 1996) Janet C. Lowe With Bill Gates, *Bill Gates Speaks: Wisdom from the World's Greatest Entrepreneur* (Wiley, 1998); Stephen Manes and Paul Andrews, *Gates: How Microsoft's Mogul Reinvented an Industry-and Made Himself the Richest Man in America* (Simon & Schuster, 1993); Wendy Goldman Rohm, *The Microsoft File: The Secret Case Against Bill Gates* (Random House, 1998); James Wallace and Jim Erickson, *Hard Drive: Bill Gates and the Making of the Microsoft Empire* (Wiley, 1992).

Geneen, Harold S.: John A. Byrne, "Egotism Can Breed Corporate Disaster—and the Malady Is Spreading," *Business Week*, April 1, 1991; Harold S. Geneen with Brent Bowers, *Synergy and Other Lies* (St. Martin's Press, 1998).

George, Judy: Interview with the authors.; Judy George with Todd Lyon, *The Domain Book of Intuitive Home Design* (Crown, 1998); Margo Miller,

"Selling style for the way we live now," *Boston Globe,* August 5, 1995; Stacy Neale, "Judy George in her own Domain," *Boston Business Journal,* June 3, 1994; Chris Reidy, "In her Eminent Domain," *Boston Globe,* June 22, 1994; Charlyne V. Schaub, "Who are you?", *Sun-Sentinel,* February 12, 1999; Louise Witt, "Judy George—The Passion and Profits," *Boston Business Journal,* August 6, 1990.

Gilbert, Walter H.: Barnaby J. Feder, "Biogen Seeks Profits to Call Its Own," *The New York Times,* August 15, 1992; www.nobel.se.

Gingrich, Newton L.: Elizabeth Drew, *Showdown: The Struggle between the Gingrich Congress and the Clinton White House* (Simon & Schuster Trade, 1997); Newt Gingrich, *Lessons Learned the Hard Way: A Personal Report* (HarperCollins, 1998); Joe Sciacca, "Clinton Didn't Do In Gingrich— Newt Fell On His Own Sword," *The Boston Herald,* November 9, 1998; "After the Impeachment," *The Press,* February 15, 1999; Mel Steely, *The Gentleman from Georgia: The Biography of Newt Gingrich* (Mercer University Press, 1999); John K. Wilson, *Newt Gingrich: Capitol Crimes and Misdemeanors* (Common Courage Press, 1996).

Goizueta, Roberto C.: David Greising, *I'd Like the World to Buy a Coke: The Life and Leadership of Roberto Goizueta* (Wiley, 1998).

Gorbachev, Mikhail S.: Archie Brown, *The Gorbachev Factor* (Oxford University Press, 1997); Alexander Dallin (Editor), *The Gorbachev Era* (Garland, 1992); Mark Galeotti, *Gorbachev and His Revolution* (St. Martin's Press, 1997); Mikhail Gorbachev, *Oh My Country and the World* (Columbia University Press, 1999); Mikhail Gorbachev, *Memoirs* (Doubleday, 1996); Mikhail Gorbachev, *Perestroika* (Spokesman, 1990) Zhores A. Medvedev, *Gorbachev* (Norton, 1987); Richard Sakwa, *Gorbachev and His Reforms, 1985–1990* (Prentice Hall, 1991).

Gould, Jay: Julius Grodinsky, *Jay Gould, His Business Career, 1867–1892* (Ayer, 1981); Maury Klein, *The Life and Legend of Jay Gould* (Johns Hopkins University Press, 1997).

Graham, Martha: Merle Armitage and Martha Graham, *Martha Graham: The Early Years* (Da Capo Press, 1995).

Grant, Ulysses S.: Ulysses S. Grant, *Memoirs and Selected Letters—Personal Memoirs of U.S. Grant, Selected Letters 1839–1865* (Library of America, 1990); Ulysses S. Grant; Caleb Carr (Editor); Geoffrey Perret (Introduction), *Personal Memoirs: Ulysses S. Grant* (Random House, 1998); Al Kaltman, *Cigars, Whiskey, and Winning—Leadership Lessons from General Ulysses S. Grant* (Prentice Hall, 1998); William S. McFeely, *Grant—A Biography* (American Political Biography Press, 1996); Geoffrey Perret, *Ulysses S. Grant—Soldier and President* (Random House, 1997); Frank J.

Scaturro, *President Grant Reconsidered* (Madison Books, 1999); Brooks D. Simpson, *Ulysses S. Grant: Triumph Over Adversity–1822–1865* (Houghton Mifflin, 1999).

Greenfield, Jerry: Ben Cohen and Jerry Greenfield, *Ben & Jerry's Double Dip* (Simon & Schuster, 1997); Ben Cohen, *Ben & Jerry's Homemade Capitalism* (Random House, 1989); Mary Louise Schumacher, "Ben & Jerry's Brings Sweet Deal to Pr. George's," *The Washington Post*, July 21, 1999; Andrew Serwer, "Ben & Jerry's Is Back," *Fortune*, August 2, 1999; www.benjerry.com.

Gretzky, Wayne: Steve Dryden, *Total Gretzky: The Magic, the Legend, the Numbers* (McClelland & Stewart/Tundra, 1999); Scott Morrison, *Wayne Gretzky: The Great Goodbye* (Key Porter, 1999); Andrew Podnieks, *The Great One: The Life and Times of Wayne Gretzky* (Triumph, 1999); Thomas R. Raber, *Wayne Gretzky: Hockey Great* (Lerner, 1999); Gerry Redmond, *Wayne Gretzky: The Great One* (ECW Press, 1993).

Gross, William: Bill Gross, "The New Math of Ownership," *Harvard Business Review*, November 1998; Alex Gove, "Idea Factory," *Red Herring*, July 1997; Larry Kanter, "Deep-Thinker Gross Built Incubator for Internet Ideas," *Los Angeles Business Journal*, August 21, 1997; Michael Krantz, "Billion Dollar Brain Drain," *Time Digital*, September 23, 1996; Ann Marsh, "Promiscuous Breeding," *Forbes*, April 1997; Eric Matson, "He Turns Ideas Into Companies—At Net Speed," *Fast Company*, December 1996; Jerry Useem, "Startup Factory," *Inc.*, February 1997; Jerry Useem, "Unfocused and Still Successful," *Inc. Extra*, February 27, 1997; www.idealab.com.

Grove, Andrew S.: Jeremy Byman, *Andrew Grove and the Intel Corporation*, (Morgan Reynolds, 1999); Andrew S. Grove, *Only the Paranoid Survive* (Bantam Doubleday Dell, 1996); Tim Jackson, *Inside Intel: Andrew Grove and the Rise of the World's Most Powerful Chip Company* (Viking Penguin, 1997).

Haas, Robert: Interview with Professor Richard Tedlow, Harvard Business School; www.levistrauss.com.

Haft, Robert: David J. Morrow, "Private Sector," *The New York Times*, June 20, 1999.

Hatsopoulos, George: Interview with the authors.

Hewlett, William: David Packard; David Kirby (Editor);Karen Lewis (Editor), *The HP Way: How Bill Hewlett and I Built Our Company* (Harper Business, 1996); Wet Feet Press Staff, *Hewlett-Packard Company: Bill and Dave's Excellent Adventure* (Wet Feet, 1996).

Hill, James: Craig Johnson, *James J. Hill House* (Minnesota Historical Society Press, 1993); Michael P. Malone, *James J. Hill: Empire Builder of the Northwest, Vol. 12* (University of Oklahoma Press, 1997); Albro Martin;W. Thomas White (Introduction), *James J. Hill and the Opening of the Northwest* (Minnesota Historical Society Press, 1991); Joseph G. Pyle, *Life of James J Hill* (Smith Peter, 1990).

Hitler, Adolf: Joachim C. Fest; Richard Winston (Translator); Clara Winston (Translator), *Hitler* (Harcourt Brace 1992); Peter N. Hoffman, *German Resistance to Hitler* (Harvard University Press, 1988); John Lukacs and Shelby Hearon, *The Hitler of History* (Knopf, 1997); Hugh Trevor-Roper, *The Last Days of Hitler* (University of Chicago Press, 1992); John Toland, *Adolf Hitler* (Doubleday, 1991).

Huizenga, H. Wayne: Jill Dutt, "Wizard Without a Wand?", *The Washington Post*, September 21, 1977; Gail DeGeorge, *The Making of a Blockbuster—How Wayne Huizenga Built a Sports and Entertainment Empire from Trash, Grit, and Videotape* (Wiley, 1995); Barry Horn, "Man for All Seasons," *The Dallas Morning News*, January 26, 1995; Kathleen Kerwin and Gail DeGeorge, "Hurricane Huizenga," *Business Week*, February 24, 1997; www.republicindustries.com.

Hussein, Saddam: Andrew Cockburn and Patrick Cockburn, *Out of the Ashes: The Resurrection Of Saddam Hussein* (HarperCollins, 1999); Efaim Karsh and Inari Rautsi, *Saddam Hussein: A Political Biography* (Macmillan, 1991); Rebecca Stefoff, *Saddam Hussein: Absolute Ruler of Iraq* (Millbrook Press, 1995); David Wurmser, *Tyranny's Ally: America's Failure to Defeat Saddam Hussein* (American Entrepreneurs Association, 1999).

Huxley, Thomas H.: Edward Clodd, *Thomas Henry Huxley* (AMS Press, 1977); J. R. Ainsworth Davis, *Thomas H. Huxley* (AMS Press, 1973); Thomas Henry Huxley and Leonard Huxley, *Life and Letters of Thomas Henry Huxley (by His Son, Leonard Huxley)* (AMS Press, 1979); J. Vernon Jensen, *Thomas Henry Huxley: Communicating for Science* (University of Delaware Press, 1991); Sherrie L. Lyons, *Thomas Henry Huxley: The Evolution of a Scientist* (Prometheus Books, 1999).

Iacocca, Lee: David Abodaher, *Iacocca* (MacMillan, 1982); Lee Iacocca, *I Gotta Tell You—Speeches of Lee Iacocca* (Wayne State University Press, 1994); Lee Iacocca and William Novak, *Iacocca—An Autobiography* (Bantam, 1986); Doron P. Levin, *Behind the Wheel at Chrysler: The Iacocca Legacy* (Harcourt Brace, 1996).

Jefferson, Thomas: Fawn M. Brodie, *Thomas Jefferson: An Intimate History* (Bantam Doubleday Dell, 1975); Noble E. Cunningham, *In Pursuit of Reason—The Life of Thomas Jefferson* (Ballantine, 1988); Joseph Ellis,

American Sphinx—The Character of Thomas Jefferson (Vintage Books, 1998); Thomas Jefferson; Lawrence S. Kaplan *Thomas Jefferson—Westward the Course of Empire* (Scholarly Resources, 1998) Merrill D. Peterson (Editor), *The Portable Thomas Jefferson* (Viking Penguin, 1977); Thomas Jefferson, *The Life and Selected Writings of Thomas Jefferson* (Modern Library, 1998).

Jobs, Steven P.: Lee Butcher, *Accidental Millionaire—The Rise and Fall of Steven Jobs at Apple Computer* (Paragon, 1988); Randall E. Stross, *Steve Jobs and the Next Big Thing* (Maxwell Macmillan, 1993); Jeffrey S. Young, *Steve Jobs* (Scott, Foresman, 1988).

Johnson, John H.: John H. Johnson and Lerone Bennett, *Succeeding Against the Odds* (Amistad, 1993); Saunja Johnson, "The Man who Created a Publishing Empire," *The Philadelphia Tribune,* February 11, 1997; Patricia Smith, "The Ebony Empire," *The Boston Globe,* January 13, 1993.

Kautilya: V. K. Subramanian, *Maxims of Chanakya Kautilya* (South Asia Books, 1980).

Keats, John: John Barnard, *John Keats* (Cambridge University Press, 1987); Walter Jackson Bate, *John Keats* (Harvard University Press, 1979); John Keats, *The Complete Poems of John Keats* (Modern Library, 1994); Andrew Motion, *Keats* (University of Chicago Press, 1999); Robert Woof and Stephen Hebron, *John Keats* (Rutgers University Press, 1997).

Khayyám, Omar: Tony Briggs, *The Omar Khayyam,* (Tuttle, 1998); Omar Khayyaam; Edward Fitzgerald (Translator), *The Rubaiyat of Omar Khayyam* (St. Martin's Press, 1983); Omar Khayysam; Daoud S. Kasir (Editor), *The Algebra of Omar Khayyam* (AMS Press, 1972).

King, Martin Luther, Jr.: David J. Garrow, *Bearing the Cross—Martin Luther King, Jr., and the Southern Christian Leadership Conference* (William Morrow, 1986); Martin Luther King, Jr., *The Autobiography of Martin Luther King, Jr.* (Warner, 1998); Mark Lane and Dick Gregory, *Murder in Memphis: The FBI and the Assassination of Martin Luther King* (Thunder's Mouth Press, 1993); Stephen B. Oates, *Let the Trumpet Sound: A Life of Martin Luther King, Jr.* (HarperCollins, 1993); Gerald L. Posner, *Killing the Dream: James Earl Ray and the Assassination of Martin Luther King, Jr.* (Macmilla, 1998).

Kirstein, Lincoln: Lincoln Kirstein; Nicholas Jenkins (Editor), *By with to and from: A Lincoln Kirstein Reader* (Farrar, Straus & Giroux, 1990).

Kissinger, Henry: William P. Bundy, *A Tangled Web: The Making of Foreign Policy in the Nixon Presidency* (Farrar, Straus & Giroux, 1998); Gregory D. Cleva, *Henry Kissinger and the American Approach to Foreign Policy* (Bucknell University Press, 1989); Walter Isaacson and Henry Kissinger,

Kissinger: A Biography (Simon & Schuster, 1993); Robert D. Schulzinger, *Henry Kissinger: Doctor of Diplomacy* (Columbia University Press, 1991).

Kroc, Ray: Ray Kroc with John Anderson, *Grinding It Out* (St. Martins, 1990); John F. Love, *McDonald's Behind the Arches* (Bantam, 1995.)

LeBaron, Dean F.: Interview with authors; www.deanlebaron.com.

Lenin, Vladimir: Stuart A. Kallen, *The Lenin Era 1900–1924* (ABDO, 1992); Richard Pipes (Editor); David Brandenberger (Editor); I. A. Buranov (Editor); Catherine A. Fitzpatrick (Translator), *The Unknown Lenin: From the Secret Archives* (Yale University Press, 1996); Robert C. Tucker (Editor), *The Lenin Anthology* (Norton, 1990); Nina Tumarkin, *Lenin Lives!: The Lenin Cult in Soviet Russia,* (Harvard University Press, 1996); Dmitri Volkogonov; Harold Shukman (Translator), *Lenin: A New Biography* (Free Press, 1994).

Lincoln, Abraham: Jim Bishop, *The Day Lincoln Was Shot* (Random House, 1997); Robert V. Bruce; Designed by Benjamin P. Thomas, *Lincoln and the Tools of War* (University of Illinois Press, 1989); William Henry Herndon; Jesse William Weik (Photographer); Designed by Henry S. Commager, *Herndon's Life of Lincoln: The History and Personal Recollections of Abraham Lincoln* (Da Capo Press, 1983); Abraham Lincoln, *Abraham Lincoln—Speeches and Writings 1832–1858* (Library of America, 1989; Abraham Lincoln, *Abraham Lincoln—Speeches and Writings 1859–1865* (Library of America, 1989; Abraham Lincoln and Allan Nevins, *The Life and Writings of Abraham Lincoln* (Modern Library, 1999); Stephen B. Oates, *With Malice Toward None—A Life of Abraham Lincoln* (HarperPerennial, 1994); Douglas L. Wilson, *Honor's Voice: The Transformation of Abraham Lincoln* (Knopf, 1998).

Lindbergh, Charles: A. Scott Berg, *Lindbergh* (Putnam, 1998); Jim Fisher, *The Lindbergh Case* (Rutgers University Press, 1994); Susan M. Gray, *Charles A. Lindbergh and the American Dilemma: The Conflict of Technology and Human Values* (Bowling Green University Press, 1988); T. Willard Hunter, *The Spirit of Charles Lindbergh: Another Dimension* (Madison, 1993) Reeve Lindbergh, *Under a Wing: A Memoir* (Simon & Schuster, 1998).

Lopez, Antonio: Steven O'Brien;James D. Cockcroft andRodolfo Cardona, *Antonio Lopez de Santa Anna* (Chelsea House, 1992).

Lucas, George: Charles Champlin; Foreword by Steven Spielberg; Foreword by Francis Coppola, *George Lucas: The Creative Impulse* (Abrams, 1997); George Lucas and Sally Kline, *George Lucas: Interviews* (University Press of Mississippi, 1999); Dale Pollock, *Skywalking: The Life and Films of George Lucas* (Da Capo Press, 1999); Dana Meachen Rau and Christopher Rau, *George Lucas: Creator of Star Wars* (Grolier, 1999); Chris Salewicz, *George Lucas Close up: The Making of His Movies* (Thunder's Mouth Press, 1999); Curt Schleier, "Filmmaker George Lucas," *Investor's Business Daily*, May 19, 1999; Dana White, *George Lucas* (Lerner, 1999).

Machiavelli, Niccolo: Michael A. Ledeen, *Machiavelli on Modern Leadership* (St. Martin's Press, 1999); Niccolo Machiavelli; Peter Bondanella (Editor); Mark Musa (Editor), *The Portable Machiavelli* (Penguin USA, 1979); Harvey C. Mansfield, *Machiavelli's Virtue* (University of Chicago Press, 1996); Niccolo Machiavelli, *The Prince* (Oxford University Press, 1998); Niccolo Machiavelli, *Discourses* (Viking, 1985); Leo Strauss, *Thoughts on Machiavelli* (University of Chicago Press, 1995).

Mackey, John P.: Interview with the authors.

Magellan, Ferdinand: Jim Gallagher, *Ferdinand Magellan* (Chelsea House, 1999); Francis Henry Hill Guillemard, *The Life of Ferdinand Magellan and the First Circumnavigation of the Globe, 1480–1521* (AMS Press, 1971); B. Marvis, *Ferdinand Magellan* (Chelsea House, 1996); Charles McKew Parr, *So Noble a Captain : The Life and Times of Ferdinand Magellan* (Greenwood, 1976).

Mandela, Nelson: Mary Benson; Foreword by Desmond M. Tutu, *Nelson Mandela: The Man and the Movement* (Norton, 1994); Nelson Mandela, *The Struggle Is My Life* (Pathfinder, 1990); Andre Brink, "Nelson Mandela," *Time*, April 13, 1998; Bill Hewitt, "Nelson Mandela," *People*, February 26, 1990; Nelson Mandela, *Long Walk to Freedom* (Little, Brown, 1994); Nelson Mandela, speech, Nobel Peace Prize Award Ceremony, Oslo, Norway, December 10, 1993; Martin Meredith, *Nelson Mandela: A Biography* (St. Martin's Press, 1998); Anthony Sampson, *Nelson Mandela—The Authorized Biography* (Knopf, 1999); Richard Stengel, "The Making of a Leader," *Time*, May 9, 1994; www.anc.org.za.

Marconi, Guglielmo: Orrin Elmer Dunlap, *Marconi the Man and His Wireless* (Ayer, 1971); G. R. Garratt, *Early History of Radio: From Faraday to Marconi* (INSPEC, 1994); Degna Marconi, *My Father, Marconi* (Guernica, 1996); Giancarlo Masini; Foreword by Frank D. Stella; Preface by Emilio Segre, *Marconi* (Marsilio, 1998); www.nobel.se.

Mayer, Lous B.: Diana Altman, *Hollywood East: Louis B. Mayer and the Origins of the Studio System* (Carol, 1992); Samuel Marx, *Mayer and Thalberg: The Make-Believe Saints* (Sam French, 1989).

McClellan, George: Stephen W. Sears, *George B. McClellan: The Young Napoleon* (Da Capo Press, 1999).

McGovern, Patrick J.: Keith J. Kelly, "Media Midas Goes Public," *Daily News*, February 16, 1998; Chana R. Schoenberger, "Relying on Self-Reliance," *Boston Globe*, September 6, 1998; Todd Wallack, "IDG Gets Set for a Wave of IPOs," *The Boston Herald*, April 16, 1999.

Milosevic, Slobodan: Dusko Doder and Louise Branson, *Milosevic: Portrait of a Tyrant* (Free Press, 1999).

Monroe, James: Harry Ammon, *James Monroe—The Quest for National Identity* (American Political Biography, 1998); Noble E. Cunningham, *The Presidency of James Monroe* (University Press of Kansas, 1996); Ernest R. May, *The Making of the Monroe Doctorine* (Belknap, 1992); James Monroe, *The Autobiography of James Monroe* (Syracuse University Press, 1959); Anne Welsbacher, *James Monroe* (ABDO, 1998); Charles Wetzel, *James Monroe* (Chelsea House, 1989).

Morgan, J. Pierpont: Louis Auchincloss, *J.P. Morgan: The Financier as Collector* (Abrams, 1990); Ron Chernow, *The House of Morgan: An American Banking Dynasty and the Rise of Modern Finance* (Simon & Schuster, 1991); Carl Hovey, *The Life of J. Pierpont Morgan* (Ayer, 1977); Jeffrey M. Jones, *J. P. Morgan Saves the Nation* (Sun & Moon, 1996).

Motsohi, Thabang J.: Interview with the authors.

Mozer, Paul W.: Kurt Eichenwald, "Two Sued by SEC in Bidding Scandal at Salomon Brothers," *The New York Times*, December 3, 1992.

Nixon, Richard: Monica Crowley, *Nixon off the Record* (Random House, 1996); Stanley I. Kutler (Editor), Designed by Carla Bolte, *Abuse of Power: The New Nixon Tapes* (Simon & Schuster, 1997); Christopher Matthews, *Kennedy and Nixon: The Rivalry That Shaped Postwar America* (Simon & Schuster, 1997); Roger Morris; Designed by Claire M. Naylon, *Richard Milhous Nixon: The Rise of an American Politician* (Holt, 1989) Garry Wills, *Nixon Agonistes: The Crisis of the Self-Made Man* (Berg, 1978).

Norris, Chuck: Melanie Cole, *Chuck Norris* (Mitchell Lane, 1999); Reinhardt Krause, "IXC Left Out of Merger Party—For Now," *Investor's Business Daily*, May 6, 1999.

Packard, David: David Packard, David Kirby (Editor);Karen Lewis (Editor), *The HP Way: How Bill Hewlett and I Built Our Company* (Harper Business, 1996); Wet Feet Press Staff, *Hewlett-Packard Company: Bill and Dave's Excellent Adventure* (Wet Feet, 1996).

Parks, Rosa: Anne Benjamin, *Young Rosa Parks: A Civil Rights Heroine* (Demco, 1996); Kai Jabir Friese, *Rosa Parks: The Movement Organizes* (Silver Burdett, 1990); Rosa Parks and Jim Haskins, *The Rosa Parks: My Story* (Puffin, 1999).

Pasteur, Louis: Patrice Debre, Elborg Forster (Translator), *Louis Pasteur* (Johns Hopkins University Press, 1998); Rene Jules Dubos, *Louis Pasteur, Free Lance of Science* (Da Capo Press, 1986); Rene Dubos, *Pasteur and*

Modern Science (ASM Press, 1988); Gerald L. Geison, *The Private Science of Louis Pasteur* (Princeton University Press, 1995); Donald E. Stokes, Foreword by Michael H. Armacost, *Pasteur's Quadrant: Basic Science and Technological Innovation* (Brookings Institution, 1996).

Peter the Great: Evgenii Viktorovich Anisimov, John T. Alexander (Translator), *The Reforms of Peter the Great: Progress through Coercion in Russia* (Sharpe, 1993); Basil Dmytryshyn, *Modernization of Russia Under Peter I and Catherine II* (Wiley, 1974); Lindsey Hughes, *Russia in the Age of Peter the Great* (Yale University Press, 1998); V. O. Kliuchevskii, *Peter the Great* (Beacon, 1984); Robert K. Massie, *Peter the Great—His Life and World* (Ballantine, 1992); Thomas C. Owen, *Russian Corporate Capitalism: Peter the Great–Perestroika* (Oxford University Press, 1995).

Picasso, Pablo: Francoise Gilot and Carlton Lake, *Life with Picasso* (Doubleday, 1989); John Richardson and Marilyn McCully, *A Life of Picasso 1881–1906, Vol. 1* (Random House, 1995); John Richardson and Marilyn McCully, *A Life of Picasso: 1907–1917, Vol. 2* (Random House, 1996); Roland Penrose, *Picasso, His Life and Work* (University of California Press, 1980).

Powell, Colin: Lawrence Benenson, *Colin Powell Story* (Random House, 1996); Warren Brown; Nathan I. Huggins (Editor), *Colin Powell* (Chelsea House, 1992); Howard Means, *Colin Powell: A Biography* (Ballantine, 1993); Robert Parry and Norman Solomon, *Colin Powell: The Record Revealed* (Common Courage Press, 1996); Colin L. Powell, Lisa Shaw (Editor), *In His Own Words: Colin Powell* (Berkley, 1995).

Premji, Azim: Interview with the authors.

Price, Sol: Sam Walton with John Huey, *Sam Walton—Made in America* (Bantam Doubleday Dell, 1992).

Redstone, Sumner M.: Sumner M. Redstone, speech, NCCJ Humanitarian of the Year Award Dinner, April 23, 1998; www.viacom.com.

Rivera, Diego: Ernest Goldstein; Diego Rivera (Artist) *The Journey of Diego Rivera* (Lerner, 1996); Pete Hamill and Diego Rivera, *Diego Rivera* (Abrams, 1999); Cynthia Newman Helms (Editor); Linda Downs (Introduction), *Diego Rivera: A Retrospective* (Norton, 1998); Andrea Kettenmann, *Diego Rivera 1886–1957 : A Revolutionary Spirit in Modern Art* (TASCHEN, 1997); Patrick Marnham and Diego Rivera, *Dreaming With His Eyes Open: The Life of Diego Rivera* (Knopf, 1998); Diego Rivera and Gladys March, *My Art, My Life* (Dover, 1992).

Rockefeller, John D.: John D. Rockefeller; Joseph W. Ernst (Editor), *Dear Father/Dear Son: Correspondence of John D. Rockefeller and John D. Rocke-*

feller, JR. (Fordham University Press, 1994); Ron Chernow, *Titan: The Life of John D. Rockefeller, Sr.* (Random House, 1998).

Roddick, Anita: Laura Board, "Stiff Competition Batters Body Shop," *National Post*, May 7, 1999; Eileen Gillibrand andJenny Mosley;Foreword by Anita Roddick, *She Who Dares Wins: A Woman's Guide to Professional and Personal Success* (Thorsons, 1998); Jules Older, Lisa Kopper (Illustrator), *Anita!: The Woman Behind the Body Shop* (Charlesbridge, 1998); Anita Roddick, *Body and Soul* (Crown, 1991); www.the-body-shop.com.

Rogers, James: Interview with the authors.

Roosevelt, Franklin D.: Robert Dallek, *Franklin D. Roosevelt and American Foreign Policy, 1932–1945* (Oxford University Press, 1995); Frank Freidel, *Franklin D. Roosevelt: A Rendezvous with Destiny* (Little, Brown, 1991) Waldo Heinrichs, *Threshold of War: Franklin D. Roosevelt and American Entry into World War II* (Oxford University Press, 1989); Irwin F. Gellman, *Secret Affairs: Franklin Roosevelt, Cordell Hull, and Sumner Welles* (Johns Hopkins University Press, 1995); William E. Leuchtenburg, *Franklin D. Roosevelt and the New Deal: 1932 1940* (HarperCollins, 1989).

Sadat, Anwar: Joseph Finklestone; *Anwar Sadat: Visionary Who Dared* (International Specialized Book Services, 1996); Eliahu Ben Elissar (Editor); Jon B. Alterman (Editor), *Sadat and His Legacy: Egypt and the World, 1977–1997* (Washington Institute for Near East Policy, 1998).

Salk, Jonas: Victoria Sherrow, *Jonas Salk* (Facts on File, 1993); Michael Tomlinson, *Jonas Salk* (Rourke, 1993).

Schopenhauer, Arthur: William Wallace, *Life of Arthur Schopenhauer* (Scholarly Press, 1970) .

Schultz, Howard: Howard Schultz, *Pour Your Heart Into It* (Hyperion, 1997).

Sculley, John: John Sculley and John A. Byrne, *Odyssey* (Harper & Row, 1987).

Seligman, Martin E. P.: Jane E. Gillham (Editor), *The Science of Optimism and Hope: Research Essays in Honor of Martin E. P. Seligman, Vol. 2* (Templeton Foundation Press, 1999); Martin E. P. Seligman, *Learned Optimism* (Simon & Schuster, 1998).

Shakespeare, William: David Waldo Clarke, *William Shakespeare* (AMS Press, 1976); Frederick Julius Pohl; Stephen Butterfield (Editor); Bruce A. Burton (Editor), *William Shakespeare: A Biography* (Security Dupont Press, 1983); A. L. Rowse, *William Shakespeare: A Biography* (Barnes & Noble Books, 1995); Barrett Wendell, *William Shakespeare: A Study in Elizabethan Literature* (MSG Hask, 1971).

Shapiro, Robert B.: Joan Magretta, "Growth Through Global Sustainability—An Interview with Monsanto's CEO Robert Shapiro," *Harvard Business Review,* Jaunuary/February 1997; Jeremy Rifkin, "The Biotech Century," *The Nation,* April 13, 1998; Robert B. Shapiro, speech, State of World Forum, San Francisco, California, October 27, 1998; Robert B. Shapiro, speech, Tidewater Development Conference, Washington, D.C., June 29, 1998; Robert B. Shapiro, speech, Biotechnology Industry Organization, New York, New York, June 17, 1998; "Are GM Foods Safe for Consumption?" *Sunday Mirror,* March 7, 1999; Robert Steyer, "It's Official—Monsanto to Divide into Two Firms," *St. Louis Post-Dispatch,* December 10, 1996; www.monsanto.com.

Sloan, Alfred P., Jr.: Alfred P. Sloan, Jr., *My Years With General Motors* (Doubleday, 1996); James P. Womack, Daniel T. Jones, and Daniel Roos, *The Machine That Changed the World* (Rawson, 1990).

Snead, Sam: Sam Snead andDon Wade, *Better Golf the Sam Snead Way: The Lessons I've Learned* (NTC Publishing, 1996).

Spielberg, Steven: Douglas Brode, *The Films of Steven Spielberg* (Carol Publishing, 1994); Elizabeth Ferber, *Steven Spielberg* (Chelsea House, 1995) Joseph McBride, *Steven Spielberg: A Biography* (Da Capo Press, 1999); George C. Perry, *Steven Spielberg* (Thunder's Mouth Press, 1998); Philip M. Taylor, *Steven Spielberg: The Man, His Movies, and Their Meaning* (Continuum International, 1992).

Spindler, Michael: Jim Carlton, *Apple* (NY Times Business, 1997).

Stalin, Joseph: Alan L. Bullock, *Hitler and Stalin: Parallel Lives* (Vintage Books, 1992); Robert Conquest, *Stalin: Breaker of Nations* (Viking Penguin, 1992); Milovan Djilas; Michael B. Petrovich (Translator), *Conversations with Stalin* (Harcourt Brace 1990); Cynthia Ann Ruder, *Making History for Stalin : The Story of the Belomor Canal* (University Press of Florida, 1999); Robert C. Tucker, *Stalin in Power: The Revolution from above, 1928–1941* (Norton, 1990); Adam Bruno Ulam, *Stalin: The Man and His Era* (Beacon Press, 1989).

Stein, Gertrude: Janet Hobhouse, *Everybody who was Anybody: A Biography of Gertrude Stein* (Doubleday Dell, 1989); Gertrude Stein; Edward M. Burns (Editor); With Thornton Wilder, *Mirrors of Friendship: The Letters of Gertrude Stein and Thornton Wilder* (Yale University Press, 1996); Linda Wagner-Martin and Gertrude Stein, *"Favored Strangers": Gertrude Stein and Her Family* (Rutgers University Press, 1995); Brenda Wineapple,*Sister Brother: Gertrude and Leo Stein* (Johns Hopkins, 1997).

Suetonius: Suetonius; J. C. Rolfe (Translator), *Suetonius: Lives of the Caesars, Volume 1* (Harvard University Press, 1988); J. C. Rolfe (Translator) *Suetonius: Lives of the Caesars, Volume 2* (Harvard University Press, 1988).

Thatcher, Margaret: Iain Dale (Editor); Margaret Thatcher, *As I Said to Dennis: The Margaret Thatcher Book of Quotations* (Parkwest Publications, Incorporated, 1997); James P. Gannon, "1990's Winners and Losers," *The Detroit News*, December 30, 1990; E. Bruce Geelhoed and James F. Hobbs, *Margaret Thatcher: In Victory and Downfall, 1987 and 1990* (Greenwood, 1992); Libby Hughes, *Madam Prime Minister: A Biography of Margaret Thatcher* (Silver Burdett, 1989); William Pfaff, "She Is Real, and She Is Serious," *The New York Times*, November 12, 1989; Margaret Thatcher, *The Collected Speeches of Margaret Thatcher* (HarperCollins, 1998); Margaret Thatcher, *The Downing Street Years* (HarperCollins, 1993); David Whetsone, "Bringing Discord to Downing Street," *The Journal*, May 4, 1999.

Trotsky, Leon: Philip Pomper, *Lenin, Trotsky and Stalin* (Columbia University Press, 1991); Leon Trotsky; Designed by J. Hansen, *My Life* (Pathfinder Press, 1972); Leon Trotsky; Sarah Lovell (Editor), *Leon Trotsky Speaks* (Pathfinder Press, 1993); Leon Trotsky; G. R. Fidler (Translator), *Problems of Everyday Life: Creating the Foundations for a New Society in Revolutionary Russia* (Pathfinder Press, 1993); Dmitri Volkogonov; Harold Shukman (Translator) *Trotsky: The Eternal Revolutionary* (Free Press, 1996).

Walton, Samuel Moore: John Huey, "America's Most Successful Merchant," *Fortune*, September 23, 1991; Bob Ortega, *In Sam We Trust: The Untold Story of Sam Walton and How Wal-Mart is Devouring America* (Random House, 1998); Sam Walton with John Huey, *Sam Walton—Made in America* (Bantam Doubleday Dell, 1992).

Welch, John F., Jr.: John A. Byrne, "Jack," *Business Week*, June 8, 1998; Stuart Crainer, *Business the Jack Welch Way: 10 Secrets of the World's Greatest Turnaround King* (AMACOM, 1999); Martha Groves, "The Bratty Bunch," *Los Angeles Times*, May 10, 1999; Janet C. Lowe, *Jack Welch Speaks* (Wiley, 1998); Thomas F. O'Boyle, *At Any Cost: Jack Welch, General Electric, and the Pursuit of Profit* (Knopf, 1998); Robert Slater, *Get Better or Get Beaten!: 31 Leadership Secrets from Ge's Jack Welch* (McGraw-Hill, 1996); Robert Slater, *The New GE: How Jack Welch Revived an American Institution;* (McGraw-Hill, 1992); Robert Slater, *Jack Welch and the GE Way* (McGraw-Hill, 1998); www.ge.com.

Wellesley, Arthur: Anthony S. Bennell, *The Making of Arthur Wellesley* (Mumbai, 1997); Leonard Cooper, *The Age of Wellington* (Dodd, Mead, 1963); Christopher Hibbert, *Wellington* (HarperCollins, 1997); Lawrence

James, *The Iron Duke* (Weidenfeld and Nicolson, 1992); Jac Weller and Andrew Uffindell, *On Wellington* (Stackpole Books, 1998).

Wendt, Gary C.: Interview with the authors.

Whitman, Margaret C.: Laura M. Holson, "Defining the Online Chief," *The New York Times*, May 10, 1999; Martha Mendoza, "EBay CEO Able to Cruise Over the Speed Bumps," *The Atlanta Journal and Constitution*, June 6, 1999; www.ebay.com.

Wilbeforce, Samuel: Standish Meachem, *Lord Bishop: The Life of Samuel Wilberforce, 1805–1873* (Harvard University Press, 1970).

Woods, Tiger: Bill Gutman, *Tiger Woods a Biography: A Biography* (Pocket Books, 1997); Sydelle A. Kramer, *Tiger Woods: Golfing to Greatness* (Random House, 1997); Tim Rosaforte, *Tiger Woods, Vol. 1* (St. Martin's Press, 1997); John Strege, *Tiger: A Biography of Tiger Woods* (Broadway Books, 1998).

Wozniak, Stephen: Rebecca Gold, *Steve Wozniak: A Wizard Called Woz* (Lerner, 1994).

Wright Brothers: Harry Combs; Wendell Minor (Illustrator), *Kill Devil Hill: Discovering the Secret of the Wright Brothers* (TernStyle Press, 1989); Deborah Hedstrom; *From Ground to Air with the Wright Brothers* (Multnomah, 1998); Fred Howard, *Wilbur and Orville* (Dover, 1998); Peter L. Jakab and Tom D. Crouch, *Visions of a Flying Machine* (Smithsonian Institution Press, 1997); Fred C. Kelly, *The Wright Brothers: A Biography* (Dover, 1989); Stephen Kirk, *First in Flight* (Blair, 1995).

Xiaoping, Deng: Richard Baum, *Burying Mao: Chinese Politics in the Age of Deng Xiaoping* (Princeton University Press, 1996); Richard Evans, *Deng Xiaoping and the Making of Modern China* (Viking Penguin, 1994); Merle Goldman, *Sowing the Seeds of Democracy in China: Political Reform in the Deng Xiaoping Era* (Harvard University Press, 1995); Maurice J. Meisner, *The Deng Xiaoping Era: An Inquiry Into the Fate of Chinese Socialism, 1978–1994* (Farrar, Straus & Giroux, 1996); Ruan Ming; Lawrence R. Sullivan (Editor); Peter Rand (Editor); Nancy Liu (Editor), *Deng Xiaoping: Chronicle of an Empire* (Westview Press, 1994); Bruce W. Nelan, "Watch Out for China," *Time*, November 29, 1993; Harrison E. Salisbury, *The New Emperors* (Little Brown, 1992).

Zedong, Mao: Delia Davin, *Mao Zedong* (Sutton, 1998); Arif Dirlik; Nick Knight and Paul Michael Healy, *Critical Perspectives on Mao Zedong's Thought* (Humanities Press, 1997); Harrison E. Salisbury, *The New Emperors (Little Brown, 1992).*

Index

achievement, 1, 26–27, 29–31
achievers, 29–31, 62, 65–68, 83
  opportunity and, 84–87
action, 84–85, 144–46
Acton, Lord, 177
Advanced Visual Systems, Inc., 93
advertising, 88–89
advisors, 175
African National Congress (ANC),
  56–60
African Queen, The, 156
Akin, Gump, Strauss, Hauer, and
  Field, 196–97
Alamo, 100
alchemists, 54
Alexander the Great, 105, 175
Allen, Paul, 171
Amazon.com, 95
Ambani, Dhirubhai Hirachand, 23,
  37–39, 41, 50, 148
ambition, ix, 1
  arc of, 3–5, 17–21
  components, 13
  good *vs.* bad, 14–16
ambitionem, 6
Amelio, Gilberto, 221–22, 223
American Baptist College,
  143–44
Americans, 223–24
America's Cup, 90
Amoco Corporation, 105

ANC. *See* African National
  Congress
anxiety, positive, 174–77
apartheid, 55–60
Apollo Computer, Inc., 93
Apple Computer, Inc., 134, 205,
  218–23
archetypal figures, 9–10
arc of ambition, 3–5, 17–21
Argentina, 190
Aristotle, 42
Arjuna, 141, 157–58
Army Intelligence Corps, 66
arrogance, 113, 163, 172, 207–8
arts, 44–46
athletes, 15
Atlanta Braves, 89, 90
Atlanta Hawks, 89
audacity, 35–38
authoritarians, 16
autocracy, 173–74
automobile industry, 10–11, 13, 29,
  99, 172–73, 202–3
automobile leasing, 112
AutoNation, 100
Avery, Sewall, 205, 207

Bain & Company, 94
balance, sense of, 113–14, 166–68,
  234–35
Bannister, Roger, 104

261

Barbee, William, 143–44
Barr, Albert H., 9
Batterymarch Financial
    Management, 212–16
Begin, Menachim, 159
Ben and Jerry's Homemade, Inc.,
    137
Ben Franklin franchise, 66–68
Bessemer process, 231
BET. *See* Black Entertainment
    Television, Inc.
Bhagavad-Gita, 157–58
Bingham, Barry, 225
Biogen N. V., 137
biotechnology, 119–22, 137
Bismarck, Otto von, 212
Black Entertainment Television,
    Inc. (BET), 27, 83–84
Blockbuster, 100
Body Shop International PLC,
    137
Boston Latin School, 180
BP-Amoco, PLC, 105
brand building, 94
Brando, Marlon, 80
bribery, 150–51
Britain, 75–79, 190–91
British Empire, 128–29
British Petroleum Company, PLC.,
    105
Bronfman, Samuel, 172
Brutus, 224
Bubble Wrap®, 199–200
Buddha, 109
Buffet, Warren E., 108
Burma Shell PLC, 37
Business 2.0, 16

cable TV, 27, 83–84, 89–92
Caine Mutiny, The (Wouk), 178

California Institute of Technology,
    167
Cambridge University, 43
Campaign for the Defiance of
    Unjust Laws, 56
Canute, King, 54
Capitalizers, 9, 66, 68, 87, 94, 136,
    194, 223, 234
Carlyle, Thomas, 5, 53
Carnegie, Andrew, 10, 15, 205,
    226–32, 236–37
Carnegie Endowment for
    International Peace, 231
Carnegie Foundation, 231
Carnegie Institutes, 231
Carnegie Steel Corporation, 228,
    229
Carpenter, Francis, 176–77
Carrier, Willis H., 136
Carrier Corporation, 136
Carrier Engineering Company, 136
CarTemps USA, 100
caste system, 128, 130
certainty, 79–80
challenges, context, 3
Chandragupta Maurya, 109
change, 20–21, 183
    adversity and, 203
    dynamic disharmony and, 185–88
    incremental steps, 191–92,
        200–202
    leadership and, 194–95
    outer world and, 189–91
    radical change, 200–200
    regrets and, 202–3
    reorganization and, 188
    sensing ability and, 199–200
    timing of, 191–92
Chanute, Octave, 34
Chappell, Tom, 138

charisma, 118–19

Chartists, 227

Chavez, Cesar, 115, 130–31

Child, Julia, 53

child labor, 161

China, 201

choices, 82–84, 155–56

Christianity, 109

Chrysler Corporation, 203

Churchill, Winston, 173

Cinergy Corporation, 194–95, 198

CitiCorp, Inc., 105

Citigroup, Inc., 12, 105

CitySearch, 170

Civil Aviation Department (South Africa), 63

civil rights movement, 56, 81–83, 95–96, 143–45

Civil War, 30–31

Clinton, William Jefferson (Bill), 97, 106

CNN, 91–92

Coca Cola Company, 111, 211

Cohen, Bennett, 137

Columbus, Christopher, 12

Comdex, 178–79

communication, 219, 223

Communist Party (China), 201

competition, 44

compromise, 20

computer industry, 4, 16, 46–49, 93, 134, 205, 218–23

software industry, 102–3

Computers and Automation, 49

Computerworld, 49

Confucius, 109

Congress, 73

Congress of Vienna, 78

Conn, Charles, 170

Consolidators, 9–10, 11, 29, 61, 99, 132, 223, 234

control, 20. *See also* letting go

Copernicus, 42–43

corporate culture, 13–14

corporations, life cycle, 11

costs
of immorality, 148–49
mistakes and, 155–56

courage, 35–38, 48–50, 80, 92

Creators, 9, 49, 54–55, 132, 134, 136, 223, 234

Crown Books, 225

Cunningham, Henry, 69

Curie, Marie, 5

cynicism, 138

Daedalus, 25, 32

Daewoo Corporation, 220

Dairy Queen, 86

Dalberg, John Emerich Edward, 177

Daly, James, 16

Dart Group, 225

Darwin, Charles Robert, 43–44

Dayan, Moshe, 159

debt, 88

DEC. *See* Digital Equipment Corporation

Dell, Michael S., 4, 23, 46–48, 50

Dell Computer Corporation, 4, 16, 46–48

Demoiselles d'Avignon, Les (Picasso), 45

Deng Xiaoping, 183, 200–201

deregulation, 194–95, 197

Desert Storm, 200

Digital Equipment Corporation (DEC), 126

direct-model sales idea, 47

discounting idea, 68–69, 81
Disney, Walt, 135
Disney Company, 135
Disraeli, Benjamin, 53
Dolan, Chuck, 27
Domain, Inc., 40–41
Drucker, Peter, 87, 125
Duncan, Isadora, 9
Dunlap, Alfred J. "Chainsaw," 97,
    107–8, 173
Dunphy, Dermot, 200
Du Pont, Pierre, 172
Durant, William Crapo, 99, 172–73
dynamic disharmony, 185–88

Eaton, Robert, 203
eBay, Inc., 94–95
Ebony, 83, 226
Edison, Thomas Alva, 136–37
egotism, 108–10
Egypt, 159
Einstein, Albert, 9, 26–27, 53
electric utilities, 194–98
Ellison, Lawrence J. (Larry), 97,
    102–3
e-mail, 121–22
Emancipation Proclamation, 176
empowerment, 163. *See also* power
    balance of freedom and control,
        166–68
    micromanagement *vs.,* 173–74
    partnerships, 171–73
    performance level and, 168–71
    positive anxiety and, 174–77
    power as neutral, 178–82
    purpose and, 133–34, 166
    treating others as equals, 165–66
Energy Policy Act of 1992, 198
Enrico, Roger A., 6
Enron Corporation, 197

environment, 138–39
equity investing, 39–40
equity ownership, 168, 169, 170,
    178–80, 200
ethical conflicts, 147–48
eToys,com, 170
excellence, 132–33
excuses, 80, 93
existentialism, 32
experience, 83, 92
Exxon Corporation, 12, 105
Exxon Mobil Corporation, 105

failure, change and, 202
Falkland Islands, 190
family businesses, 225–26
farmworkers, 130–31
fast food business, 85–87
fear, 13, 20, 173–74
Federal Energy Research
    Commission (FERC), 197
Federal Power Commission (FPC),
    196–97
Fidelity, 208
financing, 39–40
first step, 37–38
Flaubert, Gustave, 53
flight, history of, 25–26, 32–35
floating point unit (FPU), 153
Florence, 202
Forbes, 69
Forbes, B. C., 131–32
Ford, Henry, 8, 10–11
Ford Motor Company, 202–3
Four S's, 85
France, 73–74, 77–79
franchises, 66–67, 85–87
Freedom Riders, 143–45
Freud, Sigmund, 8
Frick, Henry Clay, 228

Frito Lay, 132
Frobisher, Martin, 12
fun and pleasure, 135–36
future, inventing, 136–37

G-7. *See* Group of Seven
Galilei, Galileo, 26, 43
Gama, Vasco da, 12
Gandhi, Mohandas K., 37, 81, 115, 126–30, 144
Garibaldi, Giuseppe, 115, 122–25, 130
Gates, Melinda, 236
Gates, William P. (Bill), 5, 12, 102, 171, 236–37
Gates Foundation, 236–37
GE Capital, 110–12
GE Capital Services, 85, 110
Geneen, Harold S., 108–9
General Electric Company, 110, 136, 192
General Motors Corporation, 13, 29, 99, 172–73
genius, 53, 103–5
Genome Project, 104, 106
George, Judy, 23, 40–41, 50
Gerstner, Louis V., Jr., 28–29, 50, 183, 199
Gilbert, Walter H., 136
Gingrich, Newton Leroy, 106
Gleanings in Bee Culture, 35
GNP, Inc., 167
goals, 4, 7–8, 58–60, 236
Goizueta, Roberto, 205, 211
Gorbachev, Mikhail S., 212, 215, 216, 225
"Gospel of Wealth" (Carnegie), 228, 229
GoTo.com, 170
Graham, Martha, 9

Grand Bargain, 215
Grant, Ulysses S., 30–31
grape boycott, 131
greed, 106
Greek mythology, 25, 32, 109
Greeks, 113–14
Greenfield, Jerry, 137
Gross, Larry, 178
Gross, William (Bill), 163, 167–71, 174, 175, 178–80, 181
Grove, Andrew S., 141, 153–55
growth, laws of, 104–5
Guernica (Picasso), 45

Haas, Robert, 156
Haft, Herbert, 205, 225–26
Haft, Robert, 225
Hamlet (Shakespeare), 101, 117, 145
Hammer, Michael, x
Hasbro, Inc., 94
Hatsopoulos, George, 163, 180–81
Hemingway, Ernest, 9
Hepburn, Katherine, 156
heroes, 5
Hewlett, Bill, 171
Hewlett-Packard Company, 103, 171
Hitler, Adolf, 109
HMS Beagle, 43, 44
Home Box Office (HBO), 27
Home Depot, Inc., 133
Homestead strike, 228
Huizenga, H. Wayne, 99–100, 106
human condition, 134–35
human dignity, 127–32
humility, 233–34
Huxley, Thomas Henry, 44

Iacocca, Lee, 202–3
IBM. *See* International Business
    Machines
Icarus, 25
idealab!, Inc., 167, 169–71, 181
ideas, 66, 69, 85, 180–81
imagination, 31–32, 41
Imbler, Stephen, 103
improvement, 42–48
incrementalism, 191–92, 200–202
India, 38–39, 76, 126–30, 148–49
Indian National Congress, 129
industrialism, 129
inertia, 107–8
information economy, 11–12, 48
information technology, 121,
    201–2
Inner Life of Abraham Lincoln, The
    (Carpenter), 176–77
insight, 17–18
inspiration, 19. *See also* purpose
integrity, 149–51
Intel Corporation, 16, 152–56
internalizing, 59, 60
International Business Machines
    (IBM), 28–29, 154–55, 218
International Data Group (IDG),
    48–49
International Olympic Committee
    (IOC), 161
Internet, 153, 156, 200
Internet businesses, 167, 169–71
Internet entrepreneurs, 16, 93–94,
    235–36
investing, 39–40
Ireland, 77
Israel, 159
Italy, 123–25, 202
ITT, Inc., 108–9
Ivan the Terrible, 189

Ivester, M. Douglas, 211

J.C. Penney Company, Inc., 66
Jefferson, Thomas, 31–32, 71,
    73–75, 95
Jobs, Steven P., 25, 134, 218,
    221–22
Johnson, John H., 83, 226
Johnson, Linda, 226
Johnson, Robert, 27, 83–84
Jones, Reginald, 192
Julius Caesar, 6, 224

Kautilya (Chanakya), 109
Keats, John, 6
Kennedy, Robert F., 131
Khrushchev, Nikita, 225
Kill Devil Hill, 34
King, Martin Luther, Jr., 56, 71,
    81–83, 95–96, 130
Kirstein, Lincoln, 9
Kissinger, Henry, 201
Kitty Hawk, North Carolina, 34
Kmart Corporation, 69
Knowledge Adventure, 167, 178
Krishna, 157–58
Kroc, Ray, 71, 85–87, 91, 94

Lay, Ken, 197
leadership
    change and, 194–95
    incrementalism and, 200–202
    sensing ability, 199–200
Learned Optimism (Seligman), 60,
    61
learning, 65
LeBaron, Dean Francis, 205,
    212–17, 225
Leica, 216
Lenin, Vladimir, 224

Leonardo da Vinci, 6–7, 26
Lesotho, 62, 63
letting go, 21, 205
  chance to leave gracefully,
    222–24
  dividends, 226–29
  family businesses, 225–26
  inability to relinquish control,
    224–25
  next stage of life and, 230–32
  nonoperating role, 208–9
  obstinacy and, 212–14
  pessimism and, 220–21
  sabotage of next generation,
    209–12
  signs, 214–17
  timing, 217–20
Levin, Jerry, 27
Levi Strauss & Company, 156, 161
Lewinsky, Monica, 106
Lewis, John R., 141, 143–45,
    161–62
Liberty Media Group, 83–84
Life, 207
life cycle of corporations, 11
Lilienthal, Otto, 33
Lily Cup Company, 85–86
Lincoln, Abraham, 5, 30, 163,
    176–77
Lindbergh, Charles, 8
Livingston, Robert R., 73, 74
Liz Claiborne, Inc., 161
Lomo, 216
Lotus 1–2–3, 178
Lotus Development Corporation,
    178
Louisiana Territory, 73–75
Louisville Courier-Journal, 225
Lucas, George, 51, 53, 135
luck, 61, 80

Lynch, Peter, 205, 208, 210

Machiavelli, Niccolo, 166, 177, 202
Macintosh computers, 218–20
Mackey, John P., 36, 41, 50, 71,
    84–85
Madame Bovary (Flaubert), 53
Magellan, 178–79
Magellan, Ferdinand, 31
Mahabharata, 157
Malone, John, 83–84
management control, 13
Mandela, Nelson, 51, 54–60, 61,
    64
Mann, Floyd, 143, 144, 145,
    161–62
Mao Zedong, 201
Marconi, Guglielmo, 136
Mastering the Art of French Cooking
    (Child), 53
Mayer, Louis B., 135, 172
McClellan, George B., 30
McDonald, Maurice (Mac), 86
McDonald, Richard (Dick), 86
McDonald's Corporation, 85–87, 94
McGovern, Patrick J., 23, 48–49,
    50
Mean Business (Dunlap), 107
meaning, 117–19
MEB, 198
medicine, 11–12
megalomaniacs, 107
mergers, 105
Mesabi Range, 228
MGM/UA Entertainment
    Company, 91
micromanagement, 173–74, 221
Microsoft Corporation, 5, 12, 16,
    102, 104, 171
miniaturization, 121

Minotaur, 25
mistakes, values and, 153–56
Mitterand, François, 191
Mobil Corporation, 12
momentum, 111–12
Monroe, James, 73, 74
Monsanto Company, 119–23, 135,
    138–39
Montgomery Improvement
    Association, 82
Montgomery Ward & Company,
    207–8
Morgan, J. Pierpont, 229, 230, 232
Morita, Akio, 5
Moscow, 188
Mother Teresa, 134
Motsohi, Thabang J., 51, 61–65
Mozer, Paul W., 108
My Art, My Life (Rivera), 157–58

nanotechnology, 121
Napoléon Bonaparte, 6, 73–74, 75,
    77–78, 92, 109–10, 175, 212
Napoléonic Wars, 109
Natal Indian Congress, 128
National Car Rental, 100
National Venture Capital
    Association, 170
Natural Gas Clearinghouse, 197
natural selection, 44
Negro Digest, 226
New Deal, 207
news programs, 90–92
Newton, Isaac, 187
NeXT Software, Inc., 221–22
Nike, Inc., 161
Nissan dealerships, 100
Nixon, Richard, 201
nonviolence, 120, 131, 144
Norris, Chuck, 84

North American Review, 228

obstinacy, 212–14
Olympic Committee, 161
Omar Khayyám, 80
*On the Origin of Species by Means
    of Natural Selection, or the
    Preservation of Favored Races in
    the Struggle for Life* (Darwin),
    44
On the Waterfront, 80
OPIC. *See* Overseas Private
    Investment Corporation
opportunity, 18–19, 71, 73–75
    achievers and, 84–87
    choices and, 82–84
    forms of, 79–80
    optimism and, 60–65, 91–92
    preparedness and, 75–79
    readiness and, 92–96
    timing and, 80–82, 83, 87, 92
    trend spotting, 87–92
optimism, 18, 60–65, 91–92,
    231–32
Oracle Corporation, 102–3
overreaching. *See* tempering
    ambition
Overseas Private Investment
    Corporation (OPIC), 215–16

Packard, David, 171
Pakistan, 129
paranoia, 218
Parks Rosa, 82
partnerships, 171–73
Pasteur, Louis, 75
Pendergast, Tom, 210
Peninsula War, 77
Pennsylvania Railroad, 227
Pentium processor, 153

PepsiCo, Inc., 6, 132, 218
performance level, 168–71
Peripatetics, 42
perseverance, 13, 18, 41, 51, 53–55
    building on success, 68–70
    determination, 55–58
    optimism and, 60–65
    steps toward goals, 58–60
pessimism, 60, 220–21, 236
Peter the Great, 183, 186–90
Pfizer, Inc., 196
philanthropists, 15–16. *See also*
        Carnegie, Andrew; Gates,
        William P. (Bill)
Picasso, Pablo, 45–46
Poduska, William, 71, 93
positive thinking. *See* optimism
Powell, Colin, 183, 201–0
Powell Doctrine, 200
power, 16, 163. *See also*
        empowerment
    as neutral, 178–82
pragmatism, 103–5
Premji, Azim, 141, 148–52
preparedness, 75–79
Price, Sol, 69
Price Club, 69
Prince, The (Machiavelli), 177, 202
privatization, 213
procrastination, 211
Procter and Gamble Company, 94
profits, public good and, 137–38,
        230–31, 236–37
projections, 39
Prometheus, 109
PSI Energy, Inc., 197–98
public good, 137–38, 230–31,
        236–37
purpose, 115, 223. *See also*
    inspiration

communication and, 219
environment and, 138–39
excellence and, 132–33
fun and pleasure, 135–36
hardship and, 123–24
heightening, 118
human condition and, 134–35
human dignity and, 127–32
individual empowerment and,
        133–34, 166
inventing the future, 136–37
life's turning points and, 124–27
meaning, 117–19
methods for heightening, 132–39
public good, 137–38
quality and, 132, 133
selflessness and, 118, 125–26
types, 119–23
value and, 133
values and, 146–47
PX, 64

quality, 132, 133

racism, 55–60, 81–83, 128
readiness, 92–96
reality, 32, 110–13
Redstone, Sumner M., 156
Reengineering Management
        (Champy, with Hammer), x
Reengineering the Corporation
        (Champy, with Hammer), x
regrets, 202–3
Reineman, Steve, 132
reinvention. *See* change
relational databases, 102
relativity, theory of, 26–27
Reliance Industries Limited, 37–38
reorganization, 188
risk, 81, 83, 112–13

Rivera, Diego, 141, 157–58
Rockefeller, John D., 15, 99, 228
Roddick, Anita, 137
Rogers, James (Jim), 183, 194–99
Roman Catholic Church, 42–43
Roosevelt, Franklin Delano, 207, 210
Rothko, Mark, 104
Rubaiyat, The (Omar Khayyám), 80
Russia, 186–90
Russian Orthodox Church, 187, 190

Sadat, Anwar, 159
St. Petersburg, 188, 189
sales, 47, 66–67, 85–86
Salk, Jonas, 9
Salomon Brothers, 108
Sam's Club, 69
Satcom I, 89
Scandinavian Design, 40
Schopenhauer, Arthur, 31, 32
Schultz, Howard, 6, 14, 27, 119
science, 42–44, 104
Science Adventure, 167
Scott, Thomas, 227
Scott Paper Company, 107
Sculley, John, 218–21, 223
Seagram Company Ltd., 172
Sealed Air Corporation, 199–200
Sears, Roebuck & Company, 207
seeing what others don't. *See* vision
self-delusion, 100
selflessness, 118, 125–26
Seligman, Martin E.P., 60, 61
sellouts, 16
sensing, 87–92, 199–200
setbacks, 59, 60
Seward, William, 176

Shakespeare, William, 27, 70, 101, 117, 145
Shapiro, Robert B., 115, 119–22, 135, 138–39
shared ambition, 19
shareholders, 137–38, 200
Sharpeville incident, 56
short-term thinking, 16
Silicon Valley, 49
Sloan, Alfred P., Jr., 13, 29, 172–73
Smith, Adam, 237
Snead, Sam, 15
Solar Devices, Inc., 167
Sony Corporation, 5
South Africa, 55–60, 61, 64
Southern Poverty Law Center, 144
Soviet Companies Fund, 216
Soviet Union, 212–17, 224–25
Spain, 77
Spielberg, Steven, 135
Spindler, Michael, 219–21
spinouts, 167–71, 180
Stalin, Joseph, 173, 224–25
Standard Oil, 99
Stanford, Leland, 15–16
Staples, Inc., 133
Starbucks Corporation, 6, 14, 19, 27, 119
start-up companies, 11, 180
steel industry, 231
Stein, Gertrude, 46
Stellar Computer, Inc., 93
stretch goals, 236
success
    building on, 68–70
    experience and, 83
    optimism and, 61
    timing and, 80–82
    values and, 149–51
succession system, 223–24

Suetonius, 6
Sunbeam Corporation, 107–8, 173
suppliers, 47–48, 67
sustainable development, 122
Sweden, 188

talent, 111
Tastee Freeze, 86
Tata Steel, Limited, 37
technological context, 8–12
Tembu tribe, 54–55
tempering ambition, 19, 27, 29, 97,
    99–101
  balance, sense of, 113–14
  checklist of realities, 110–13
  egotism and, 108–10
  genius and, 103–5
  greed and, 106
  imprudence and, 101–3
  inertia and, 107–8
  pragmatism and, 103–5
Teresa, Mother, 134
Thatcher, Margaret, 183, 190–91
Thermo Electron, 180–81
Thermo-Lase, 180–81
3-D technology, 167–68
time limitations, 110–11
Time Warner, Inc., 91
timing, 99, 191–92
  letting go and, 217–20
  opportunity and, 80–82, 83, 87,
    92
TNT. *See* Turner Network
    Television
Tolstoy, Leo, 5
Tom's of Maine, 138
Trak Auto, 225
Trans-Net, 61, 64
Travelers Group, 105
Treasury Department, 108

trend spotting, 87–92
Trotsky, Leon, 224
Truman, Harry, 210
Truman Doctrine, 210
truth, 177
Turner, Ed, 88
Turner, Robert Edwards (Ted) III,
    27, 87–91
Turner Network Television (TNT),
    91
turning points, 124–27

UFWU. *See* United Farm Workers
    Union
Union Treaty, 215
United Farm Workers Union
    (UFWU), 131
United States, 73–75
United Technologies, Inc., 136
universalizing, 60
Untouchables, 128, 130

value, 132
values, 19–20, 141, 235
  business purpose and, 146–47
  costs of immorality, 148–49
  ethical conflicts and, 147–48
  integrity and, 149–51
  mistakes and, 153–55
  rationalizing lapses, 160–62
  reversing wrong choices, 155–56
  right actions and, 144–46
  solutions, 157–60
  success and, 149–51
venture industry, 170
vertical integration, 13, 228
Viacom, Inc., 156
Vietnam War, 201–0
vision, 12, 23, 31, 35–38, 49
  aring, 35–38

change and, 42–48
clear, 29–31
conventions and, 26–27
courage, 35–38, 48–50
disbelief and, 32–35
imagination, 31–32, 41
improvement, 42–48
past achievement and, 28–29
pursuit of, 35–38
steps, 38–41
Vitoria, Battle of, 77–78
volume sales, 67
Von Hoffman, Nicholas, 172–73

Walgreen Company, 86
Wall Street, 211
Wal-Mart Stores, Inc., 3, 27,
    65–66, 68–70, 81, 133, 208–9
Walton, Ben, 67
Walton, Bud, 81
Walton, Helen, 81
Walton, Samuel Moore, 3, 27, 51,
    65–68, 81, 91, 133, 208–9,
    210
Waste Management, Inc., 100
Waterloo, Battle of, 78
Welch, John F., Jr., 192, 200
Wellesley, Arthur, 71, 75–80
Wellington, Duke of. *See* Wellesley,
    Arthur

Wendt, Gary C., 85, 97, 110–12
Whitaker, Don, 81
Whitman, Margaret C., 71,
    94–95
Whole Foods Market, Inc., 36,
    84–85
Wiener, Norbert, 9
Wilberforce, Samuel, 44
Wilhelm II, 212
Wipro, 148–52
Woolf, Virginia, 104
Worlds, Inc., 168–69, 179–80
World War II, 210
Wouk, Herman, 178
Wozniak, Stephen, 218, 223
Wright, Orville, 23, 32–35, 41
Wright, Wilbur, 23, 32–35, 41
WTCG (Watch This Channel Go"),
    89

Xerox Corporation, 132

Yahoo, 95
Yeltsin, Boris, 215, 225
Yom Kippur War, 159
Youth League (ANC), 56

Zhou Enlai, 201